ENERGY, SECURITY AND ECONOMIC DEVELOPMENT IN EAST ASIA

ENERGY, SECURITY AND ECONOMIC DEVELOPMENT IN EAST ASIA

Japan, South Korea and Taiwan, the strong capitalist economies of East Asia, are all hopelessly energy deficient, importing over 80% of their energy resources. Moreover their industries are mostly energy intensive. This vulnerability has long been perceived by the countries in question and much of their foreign policy is directed towards safeguarding their energy supplies. At the same time the three major communist countries in the region – the Soviet Union, mainland China and Vietnam – have considerable energy reserves which they have so far not managed to exploit to any great degree, partly because they lack the necessary technical and capital inputs. This book examines the energy politics of the east Asian countries. It looks at the energy situation in each country, surveys the sources of supply and shows how foreign policy has been directed towards safeguarding supply. It explores how the situation has changed over time, concentrating on the period from the late 1960s, including the two oil price shocks and coming right up to the present. Much of the international politics of the region is bound up with energy supply and many unusual foreign policy positions are explained by energy politics, notably Sino-Japanese petroleum joint ventures, moves towards Soviet-Japanese co-operation in developing the Sakhalin oilfields, Japan's continuing links with both moderate and radical Islamic countries and Japan's reluctance to go along with American policy on many major international issues.

Ronald C. Keith is Associate Professor in the Department of Political Science, University of Calgary, Alberta, Canada.

ENERGY, SECURITY AND ECONOMIC DEVELOPMENT IN EAST ASIA

Edited by Ronald C. Keith

ST. MARTIN'S PRESS
New York

 For information, write:
Scholarly & Reference Division,
St. Martin's Press, Inc., 175 Fifth Avenue, New York, NY 10010
First published in the United States of America in 1986
Printed in Great Britain

Library of Congress Cataloging-in-Publication Data

Energy, security, and economic development in East
Asia.

Bibliography: p.
Includes index.
1. Energy policy — Asia. 2. Asia — National
security. 3. Asia — Economic policy. I. Keith,
Ronald C.
HD9502.A782E54 1986 333.79'095 86-13102
ISBN 0-312-25208-0

CONTENTS

TABLES AND FIGURES

Tables

Figures

Acknowledgements

This edited volume was made possible by a very generous grant from the Strategic Studies Programme at the University of Calgary. The editor would especially like to thank the Director of the Programme, Dr. Harriet Critchley for her long-term support and encouragement of the project. Also, the editor is indebted to the Canadian Social Sciences and Humanities Research Council for a grant covering the travel costs of a series of energy-related interviews in Beijing and Shanghai.

Dr. Thomas Huang provided very helpful assistance in setting up the final text which was prepared by Sue Humphrys. Finally, the editor would like to thank his wife, Rita Dickson, for moral support and editorial assistance in the last stages of the project.

INTRODUCTION

Energy is critical to national economic development; therefore, it is critical to national security. The study of the evolving global politics of energy supply and demand encompasses a tortuous correlation of domestic and international economic and strategic variables. These politics cannot be understood in the exclusive terms of the geopolitics of oil; however, the two major oil crises of the 1970s did spawn the development of resource diplomacy. The latter often became the conscious extension of policies correlating domestic economic priorities and the totality of national energy development with national interest and geopolitical necessity. The present edited volume primarily focuses on the correlation of factors relating to energy, security and economic development in the East Asian context.

A comparison of the several national energy structures of surplus and deficiency in East Asia suggests a significant asymmetry of strategic and economic opportunities and liabilities. Vietnam in energy terms is dependent upon a Soviet life-support system. Despite rational and strenuous efforts, Japan, the Republic of Korea, (ROK), and Taiwan all still appear as hopelessly dependent upon external sources of energy supply, which for the most part originate in the Middle East. Even energy-surplus states such as the Soviet Union and the People's Republic of China, (PRC), are not fully independent actors within this regional framework of strategic and economic relations.

The USSR and PRC are at different stages of economic development, but they have both attempted to facilitate the priorities of domestic economic development through the international exchange of natural resources for foreign technology and capital investment. In both cases oil exports have played a particularly significant role in the generation of the all important foreign currency reserves which pay for high priority technological imports. In 1980, the PRC's petroleum exports rose to 23 per cent of total export volume as compared to 12 and 17 per cent between 1975 and 1979.(1) With the steady increase of oil exports the PRC was less constrained by an unfavourable balance of payments in developing trade relations with the Western industrial countries. As of the same year, the Soviet Union derived approximately half of its hard currency earnings from the exports of oil and natural gas.(2)

Both the geopolitical and economic dimensions of this exchange of vital natural resources for Western technology were seriously debated within the Soviet and Chinese leaderships. Brezhnev, for example, had argued that Western technological imports could be applied as a salve to soothe the ailments of dated and inefficient industry, but the requisite outflow of natural resources became the subject of disagreement between Brezhnev and Kosygin. The implications of energy exports for the future pattern of internal energy consumption were especially contentious.(3) Also, Brezhnev apparently supported the rapid development of Siberian oil and gas, while Kosygin argued for a more balanced approach which gave greater emphasis to coal and nuclear power.(4)

Similarly, the senior leaders of the PRC in the late 1970s had to face up to the question as to whether their ambitious programmes for technological importation and industrial renovation could proceed on the basis of expansion of resource exports and even foreign investment in internal resource development. The earlier accusations of the 'Gang of Four' to the effect that Deng Xiaoping would turn the PRC into a 'raw materials base' for 'Western Imperialism' were, repudiated(5), but the Chinese remain very committed to comprehensive industrialisation and are still quite wary of any vertical terms of trade which might cast the PRC in the exclusive role of exporter of raw materials.

The ability of either the USSR or the PRC to influence regional patterns of energy consumption has thus far appeared to be quite uneven and patchy. The Soviet Union has, as is pointed out by Professor Justus van der Kroef, attained an economic dominance over the Socialist Republic of Vietnam (SRV), and the latter is unquestionably energy dependent upon the Soviet Union. However, as Professor Allen Rodgers points out, the Soviet Union is facing its own internal energy dilemma, which may only be saved by the increased production of natural gas, and

Professor Rodgers argues that it is very unlikely that the Soviet Union will be able to develop significant new reserves in Eastern Siberia.

For both strategic and economic reasons, Japanese interest in Siberian resource development has declined considerably. However, the larger Sino-Japanese economic relationship has grown despite the years of domestic 'readjustment' in China, and energy is a critical component in this relationship. The extent to which the PRC is able to generate a significant and real exportable surplus of energy in the context of rapid domestic modernisation is, nevertheless, very controversial.

Japan acquires 82 per cent of its total energy requirements from abroad. Energy is obviously the Achilles heel of 'Japan Inc.' In Chapter Five, Professor Quo notes that from within the traditional security arrangement with the US Japan's resource diplomacy has sought a greater degree of strategic and economic independence, and he argues that in response to the recent history of international energy crisis Japan consciously developed an integrated strategy of domestic energy switching, research and development into new energy sources and technology, and international investment; however, while these programmes may have produced moderately successful results, they do not in sum constitute a comprehensive solution to qualitative dependence on outside energy sources.

At one time in the mid-1970s Japan may have aspired to a more balanced network of economic relations with Beijing and Moscow; however, the Japanese eventually opted for a larger economic relationship with the Chinese. The choice has not by any means been mutually exclusive, but there has been an obvious preference given to the Sino-Japanese exchange of Chinese energy for Japanese capital and technology.

However, the Japanese have pointed to the asymmetries of comparative energy dependence between the various Western economies to stress Japan's qualitatively greater dependence. Japanese reaction to energy dependence has tested the underlying assumptions of the Japanese-American security relationship. There has not been a comprehensive and systematic challenge to the latter, but Japanese foreign policy has in an incremental way attempted to deal with what it regards as a more complex international environment. Japan's foreign policy still assigns a great deal of emphasis to the Soviet threat to regional stability, but this has not been translated into automatic compliance with all US strategic priorities. Japan has, for example, favoured closer economic ties with both 'radical' and 'moderate' OPEC states. Japanese resource diplomacy remains acutely aware of the signficance of traditional Middle Eastern oil supplies.

China's energy strategy and resource strategy must be placed in the context of the PRC as a developing country, and the Chinese reaction to the spectre of 'imperialism'. While the 1973-4 crisis traumatised Japan, the rise in global demand and the sudden price increases provided the Chinese with new economic and strategic opportunities. The two countries viewed the crisis from different starting points. In 1963 Japan's oil imports already accounted for 50 per cent of that country's total energy needs and Japan made a rapid transition over the next several years from coal to inexpensive oil consumption. Whereas, the PRC was still very much in the coal age as of 1963 and in the same year the PRC achieved basic self-sufficiency in oil production and for the first time exported 90,000 tons of crude oil.(6) Coal was more important in domestic terms of consumption, but self-sufficiency in oil had extremely important political implications in relation to the Sino-Soviet split and the PRC's historical dependence on Soviet and Romanian oil imports. In the context of the 1973-4 crisis, the PRC as an oil exporter could afford to take a positive view of the rise of OPEC. Also, the 'oil weapon' was then construed in terms of the developing states of the South striking back against the economic dominance of the North, hence Deng Xiaoping insisted during the Sixth Special Session of the UN General Assembly: 'The oil battle has broadened people's vision.'(7)

As an important industrialised state with historical ties to the United States, Japan reacted quite differently. The origins of contemporary Japanese resource diplomacy, however, lie in the Japanese response to Middle East crisis and Arab boycott. The minister responsible for the MITI, Yasuhiro Nakasone then insisted that energy is as important as defence.(8) More than 90 per cent of Japan's oil had to be imported, and this percentage accounted for 75 per cent of total national energy consumption. Seventy per cent of Japan's imports originated in the Middle East and had to pass through the stratetically vulnerable Straits of Hormuz and the Straits of Malacca. Such double jeopardy was in itself a persuasive argument for the diversification of the sources of supply, but the extent of Japanese dependence also called for defensive diplomacy in the Middle East. The 'resource faction' within the Japanese goverment realised the need for an integrated, multidimensional response which would include larger economic relations with producer states.(9) Nakasone toured the Middle East reassuring traditional suppliers that Japan would not join Kissinger's 'consumer alliance', and the Japanese declaration of 22 November 1972 supporting Palestinian self-determination demonstrated a lack of faith in the future effectiveness of a consumer alliance of Western industrial states.

Geopolitically, the Japanese found themselves at a crossroads of shifting regional political alignments. A diversification in economic and energy relationships with both the USSR and PRC might have appealed to the heightened Japanese awareness as to the need for greater independence, but the international environment was characterised by declining detente, increasing Sino-Soviet hostility and the potential of Sino-American normalisation. It was no longer easy for the Japanese to make such neat distinctions between 'economics and politics'. The larger geopolitical dynamic tended to force a choice between Brezhnev's scheme for regional collective security and a treaty relationship with the PRC. The latter posed a diplomatic dilemma in that it called for a compromising statement concerning Soviet 'hegemonism'. In terms of energy options, the Japanese had to choose between the Soviet resources of Tyumen and the Chinese resources of Daqing and the Bohai Gulf. Apparently, successive Japanese formulations of 'equidistant diplomacy' and 'omnidirectional diplomacy' could not offset the practical thrusts of international and regional geopolitical dynamics and the attractiveness of new economic opportunities in nearby China.

The explicit extent of Japanese energy vulnerability and the changing geopolitical picture might also help to explain the exaggerated claims of the mid-1970s concerning Chinese resource potential.(10) With hindsight the claims that China's offshore development would rapidly turn the PRC into a 'Second Saudi Arabia' now appear as irresponsible, if not absurd. The head of the Japan-China Oil Import Council, Ryotaro Hasegawa then suggested that with timely Japanese technical assistance Chinese oil production could reach 400 million tons by 1980 and that 25 per cent of this production could be exported to Japan.(11) One could surmise that members of the so-called 'petroleum faction' within the Chinese government had their own domestic political reasons for encouraging such speculation. Certainly the precipitous climb in oil prices appeared to offer a quick financial solution to the need for the extensive and costly acquisition of technologies in the context of a growing emphasis on rapid modernisation. Also, for strategic reasons, it was very clear that the Chinese government preferred that the Japanese focus on participation in the development of Chinese as opposed to Siberian energy resources.

During the 1973-4 crisis the Soviets saw oil not only in terms of its importance to the acquisition of Western technologies, but also as an important geopolitical resource. Apparently, Soviet diplomats had combed the Middle East urging a more strict embargo of the West so as to push the international price of oil even higher.(12) The Chinese vociferously accused Soviet 'revisionist social imperialism' of having 'long thirsted for Middle Eastern petroleum'(13) and for having engaged in an illicit 'trading of arms for petroleum'. Chinese analysis speculated as to the positive strategic benefits to be derived from East and West Europen attempts to negotiate direct deals with OPEC producing states.(14) Any sign of European independence was taken as beneficial to the reduction of both Soviet and American 'hegemonisms' although the Chinese made it clear that they believed the USSR was the 'more hungry' and, therefore, the more dangerous superpower.

The Soviets for their part were uncomfortably saddled with soft-currency sales of precious oil to Eastern Europe and Cuba at a time when greater and more lucrative sales to the West promised potentially much greater gain in terms of foreign currency and technological imports. Strategists in the West grappled with the economic and trading implications of detente, but it become less obvious in the mid-1970s that the commerical opportunities of detente would actually modify expansionist Soviet behaviour. While US strategists argued as to whether it would be strategically constructive to help the Soviets to upgrade their industrial infrastructure, the Soviet leaders argued among themselves as to whether the exchange of natural resources for technology would seriously affect their future margin of energy surplus for expanded domestic energy consumption.

Historically, rigid industrial centralisation in the USSR had created the need for greater efficiency through the massive injection of imports. It would also appear that centralised planning has not necessarily proven to be an advantage in Soviet attempts to modify the structure of domestic energy consumption. High energy consumers such as iron and steel have continued successfully to mobilise bureaucratic interests to protect their privileged status within the economy. While the Soviets have had some success in developing new Siberian oil and gas resources in order to compensate for the depletion of established western reserves, they have not been as effective as the Chinese in sustaining a credible programme of domestic energy conservation.

The events of the late 1970s seemed to drive home the implications of the first energy crisis. In frustration Henry Kissinger had once remarked: 'One embargo--and one economic crisis-- should be enough to underline the implications of dependency'.(15) The fall of the Shah of Iran, the subsequent volatility of Middle Eastern politics, the hostage-taking in Iran and the Soviet invasion of Afghanistan all tended to confirm the CIA's faith in the 'worse-case' scenario. It was not clear as to whether either the US or the USSR could over the long-term guarantee their allies' energy requirements. The prospect of internal Soviet production declines and rising energy consumption of energy dependent allies in Eastern Europe certainly coloured Western interpretations of Soviet motivation in the invasion of Afghanistan. The energy demands of Poland and East Germany especially taxed Soviet resources, and it was often assumed that as Eastern Europe was 85 per cent dependent upon imported oil that the Soviets would soon need Middle Eastern oil to meet its rising domestic and international commitments. Also, it was often assumed that the USSR wished to manipulate vital Middle Eastern suplies upon which Western allies in Europe depended and that the invasion of Afghanistan was the first step in a grand and malevolent strategic design.(16)

There was a surprising convergence of American and Chinese strategic speculation on this very point. The second energy crisis set off 'the alarm bells ringing in the night' with Senator Henry Jackson warning of a 'major oil supply disruption in the 1980s'.(17) Senator Jackson's famous US Congressional committee on the 'geopolitics of oil' focused on the fact that NATO countries were importing 75 per cent of their oil from the Persian Gulf. The Committee was informed of a Stanford projection which suggested that in the event of a cutoff of Persian Gulf oil for one year the losses in annual GNP would run from 18 per cent for the US to 23 per cent for the Western European allies to an ultimately debilitating 27 per cent for Japan.(18) A US congressional subcommittee investigating Soviet energy concluded that Soviet energy policies should be seen as 'a major factor in their overall domestic and foreign policies' and that Soviet 'energy diplomacy' is 'an effective tool to spread Soviet influence and to stymie Western initiatives'.(19) While the projected declines in Soviet domestic energy production were correlated with a new Soviet focus on Middle Eastern resources, the possibility of any increases in Soviet domestic energy development were sometimes alternatively interpreted in terms of their projected use to manipulate the energy deficient economies of Western Europe.(20)

Admiral Stansfeild Turner in his 22 April 1980 testimony to the Jackson Committee hearings asserted that the CIA's 1977 projections of Soviet energy production declines were 'not pessimistic enough', and he claimed that the 'Communist states as a group' would begin to shift to net importer status by the end of the year.(21) As Director of the CIA, Turner predicted that Communist exports of 0.8 million barrels per day in 1979 would decline to the point were these same states would collectively have to import one million barrels per day by 1985.(22)

Meanwhile at the height of the second energy crisis the Japanese had committed themselves to a long-term economic agreement and a new treaty relationship with the PRC, which included a compromising statement regarding the need to resist 'hegemonism' in the Asia-Pacific region. Ironically, no sooner had the Japanese tilted towards the Chinese when the PRC embarked on a new economic programme. The disclosures which came to light with Chinese 'national economic readjustment' in the spring of 1979 underlined the significance of China's domestic energy shortage as well as the protracted time-frame for the actual development of China's uncertain offshore resources. The so-called 'petroleum faction' was discredited under a new regime of financial and economic austerity which resolutely cut capital construction and revised import policy so as to emphasise the selective importation of key technology as opposed to the wholesale import of 'turn-key projects'.

The Soviet press happily pronounced the 'end of the Chinese oil bluff', and the research of the World Bank and CIA both projected significant declines in China's energy production and exports during the 1980s. As is detailed in Chapter One the Chinese were not able to meet the early expectations which had buoyed the original long-term economic agreement with Japan. Some of the intervening international factors of recession and slumping energy demands were beyond Chinese control, but throughout the rigours of 'readjustment' the Chinese maintained their oil-export status and the success of 'readjustment' coupled with an associated 'economic reform' has already confounded the late 1970s early 1980s projections of precipitous decline in Chinese primary energy production through the 1980s. The episode of the early 1980s process of 'readjustment and reform' is important to our understanding of China's capacity as a developing nation to meet the new needs for energy generated by the domestic process of modernisation while sustaining a programme of energy exports for the purpose of gaining greater foreign capital and technological inputs to insure an expansion of the country's industrial base.

Discussion in Chapter One suggests that there are grounds for cautious optimism regarding the generation of further Chinese energy exports. Certainly, it cannot be overstressed that the PRC's energy strategy must be placed in the context of China as a developing nation, which is still quite self-conscious about the history of Twentieth Century 'imperialism' in China. A recent American study which suggests that the Chinese will eventually become hostage to US companies which can provide the critical energy technology necessary to development appear to have grossly underestimated the Chinese sense of national interest.(23)

Potentially, the USSR and PRC are the two greatest sources of regional energy surpluses; however, there has been continuing controversy as to the degree to which the exploitation of their respective reserves will depend on Western capital and energy-related technology.(24) The CIA has often raised alarm over possible Soviet manipulation of the international energy trade, but the prospects for the future export of East Siberian resources do not appear to be significant. Professor Rodgers' analysis in Chapter Two suggests that not only is there little prospect for the future development of East Siberian resources, but also that the development of West Siberian crude oil reserves has not really been sufficient to offset declining production in the Volga-Urals region. The CIA projection of 1980 may have been a bit too pessimistic; it projected that Soviet production would decline from 12 to 8 million barrels a day by 1990. This projection contrasts with that of the European Economic Commission which had anticipated that Soviet production would climb to 14 million barrels per day in the 1980s. During 1984 Soviet oil production fell only slightly for the first time since the Second War from 12.32 in 1983 to 12.26 million barrels a day in 1984.(25)

However even the CIA in its worst moments of strategic pessimism has underlined the point that the Soviet problem does not necessarily lie in the non-availability of resources.(26) The world's largest oil producer has significant untapped resources, but it has difficulties in developing new reserves. Protracted declines in Soviet energy production would adversely affect the Soviet ability to generate foreign currency earnings, especially in consideration of the continued deterioration of the market price for oil. The Soviet ability to influence the regional energy picture will also ultimately depend upon the Soviet ability to manage its problems of industrial organisation and on its ability to achieve a new leadership dynamic.

As for the Chinese, they are at a lower stage of economic development. They have not even finished surveying their extensive hinterland resources. Their offshore is generally acknowledged as quite important to future development in the 1990s. The Chinese, themselves, expect to have continuing problems in the provision of the population's energy needs at the local levels. The rate of decline at their established oil fields in the north and in the northeast has not been as precipitous as expected, but eventually reserve depletion there will place a greater emphasis on the offshore and on a westward shift of technical resources in order to open up untapped reserves in the vast hinterland. In contrast with the more developed countries in East Asia the PRC did not experience to the same degree the pattern of the 1960s and 1970s whereby inexpensive international oil reserves were used increasingly in the drive for industrialisation. The strongly performing economies of Japan, Taiwan and the ROK all developed a much greater dependence on international oil while the Chinese continued to emphasise 'self-reliance' and had to rely to a much greater extent on domestic coal reserves. The Chinese had an advantage in the early 1980s when they began switching back to coal-fired plants; they had gigantic coal reserves, and they had not gone as far down the road of oil dependence in industry. On the other hand, the export of 127 million tons of crude oil and petroleum products in 1973-83 helped to generate the foreign exchange needed to expand the programme for the importation of foreign technology.(27) However, the further development of China's hardpressed transportation network and the rapid development of new energy technologies will require massive capital inputs.

While the pace of changing internal domestic consumption may yet be significantly altered in a process of modernisation, the Chinese leadership to date has demonstrated an impressive organisational capability during the course of 'national economic readjustment'. Given China's tremendous unexploited resource base as well as organisational flexibility and growing technological ability, there is no compelling need to subscribe to a 'worse-case' scenario with respect to future Chinese energy development. There is not only the definite possibility of an internally rationale interrelationship of resource development and consumption, but also a definite possibility of a greater pattern of energy exports.

The PRC's ability to influence the regional pattern of energy trade will, to a considerable extent, depend on the timing and extent of offshore oil development. While the PRC's national energy programme is discussed in general terms in Chapter One, special attention has been paid to aspects of Chinese offshore development in Chapters Seven and Eight. At the Third UN Conference on the Law of the Sea, the PRC proposed that the joint development on the continental shelf might proceed on an interim basis even without agreement on maritime boundaries.(28) Professor Hungdah Chiu, however, examines closely the legal issues, which have emerged with the new law of the sea especially with reference to the resolution of conflicting maritime jurisdictions in the East China Sea and the comparative legal positions of the PRC, Taiwan, Japan and South Korea. Of special interest is the extent to which the relatively new emphasis on the exclusive economic zone has complicated the claims which were previously based on an exclusive reading of international law regarding the continental shelf. Also, given the continuing controversy over the role to be played by Western technology in the exploration and development of offshore resources, Kim Woodard and Alice Davenport of China Energy Ventures, Inc. of Washington D.C. have put together an analysis of the economic and security dimensions of the Chinese development of South China Sea resources.

Chapters One through Six of this volume attempt to describe the multifaceted national energy policies and related resource diplomacies of the PRC, the USSR, Taiwan, the ROK, Japan and the Socialist Republic of Vietnam. In each case the national reactions to the energy crises of the 1970s are reviewed in terms of the attempt to secure and protect domestic programmes for economic development against the uncertainities of changing economic and geopolitical realities. In the regional profile of resource dependency and self-sufficiency there is of course the potential for both mutually beneficial co-operation and calculated obstruction between states which are all seeeking to realise their national priorities of economic development.

While the Chinese have emphatically rejected the verticalisation of trade, they have insisted that the exchange of Daqing and Bohai Gulf oil reserves for Japanese capital and technology is mutually advantageous. Chinese resource diplomacy has acted to preclude major Japanese investment in Soviet Siberian resource development and has been particularly sensitive to the negative strategic implications of such development. The latter not only raises the possibility of greater Soviet influence in the regional energy trade, but also raises the level of logistically sustained Soviet military and naval presence in the region.

The Japanese remain acutely aware of their own vulnerability. They are suspicious of increased Soviet naval activity in nearby waters, the deployment of approximately 30 per cent of Soviet ICBMs and SLBMs in the Far East, and the continuing deadlock over the Northern Territories issue has negatively influenced the pattern of Japan's commercial and economic relations with the Soviet Union. While the Japanese have been reluctant to become involved in expensive energy ventures in the Soviet Union, they have, despite the initial misunderstandings of Chinese 'readjustment', steadily expanded their involvement in China's modernisation programmes.

As for the South Koreans, their energy dependence is at least as great as that of Japan, and in fact Thomas Stern suggests their energy-import dependence may well increase to over 90 per cent of total national energy requirements by the 1990s. Like Japan, South Korea is intimately tied to the US in security terms, but also like Japan, South Korea moved closer to Arab producers during the two international energy crises of the

1970s, and South Korea has embarked on an international investment programme in overseas resource development. The South Koreans would like to deny the North Koreans access to established Middle Eastern energy markets, and they would like to foster energy trade with the PRC in order to generate geopolitical pressure on the North.

As for Taiwan, Dr. Chi-yuan Liang points out that it is presently 88 per cent dependent on external commercial energy supplies. Taiwan too has undergone strenuous effort to cope with the impact of the energy crises of the 1970s through multifaceted programmes of energy-switching and conservation. In this new industrialising context, final energy consumptiton in 1965-83 increased almost five times, and between 1970-80, Taiwan's imports from the Middle East climbed from 3 to 20 per cent of total imports.(29) Both Taiwan and South Korea have placed great emphasis on nuclear power generation in their energy planning for the future.

The following chapters will examine the potential for a greater pattern of domestic resource development and regional energy trade in East Asia. The ability of the PRC and USSR to influence this pattern is highlighted. In response to international energy crises the resource deficient states have often made significant advances in the rational and integrated management of resource development and consumption as well as in the field of international trading and investment strategy; however, the historical levels of energy dependence in these same states have not been fundamentally altered. Such exaggerated levels of dependence will insure a more complicated pattern of economic and strategic co-operation and competition within the East Asian region.

NOTES

1. 'Sinochem's Official on Petroleum Export Prospects,' China Economic News, 22 February 1982, p. 3.

2. Subcommittee on International Trade, Finance, and Security Economics, Joint Economic Committee, US Congress, Energy in Soviet Policy (US G.P.O., Washington, D.C., 11 June 1981), p. 1.

3. According to Arkady Shevchenko's account, Kosygin warned against the 'squandering' of Soviet natural resources which would be used to buttress the Western economies and to increase Soviet dependence on Western markets. Arkady Shevchenko,

Breaking with Moscow (Alfred Knopf, New York, 1965), p. 213.

4. Energy in Soviet Policy, pp. 162-3.

5. Ronald C. Keith, 'China's Modernisation and the Policy of "Self-Reliance"', China Report, Vol. XIX, No. 2, March/April, 1983, pp. 19-34.

6. In his analysis of the Chinese use of fossil fuels Vaclav Smil emphasised the comparatively low rate of liquid as opposed to solid fuel consumption. Vaclav Smil, 'Energy in China: Achievements and Prospects', China Quarterly, March, 1976, p. 58.

7. Deng Xiaoping's speech at the Sixth Special Session, UN General Assembly, in King C. Chen, ed., China and the Three Worlds (M. E. Sharpe, White Plains, New York, 1979), p. 93.

8. See Martha Caldwells' discussion of the origins of 'Japanese oil diplomacy' in her chapter, 'The Dilemmas of Japan's Oil Dependency', in Ronald E. Morse, ed., The Politics of Japan's Energy Strategy (Institute of East Asian Studies, University of California, Berkeley, 1981), p. 67.

9. Ibid., p. 68.

10. For example Herschede and Kadhim note the 'overly enthusiastic' report of H. C. Ling. Fred Herschede and Minssen Kadhim;, 'China's Petroleum Production and Reserves: Domestic and International Significance', Journal of Energy and Development, Vol. 5, No. 1, (Autumn, 1979), p. 57.

11. See Yuan-li Wu's analysis of Hasegawa's emphasis on Chinese capacity to generate significant oil exports. Yuan-li Wu, Japan's Search for Oil (Hoover Institution Press, Stanford, California, 1977), p. 51.

12. At least this was the allegation of James R. Schlesinger, former US Secretary of Energy and Director of the CIA. See Schlesinger's comments before the Committee on Energy and Natural Resources, US Senate, Geopolitics of Oil, Part 1, (US G.P.O. Washington, D.C., 1980), p. 55.

13. Ch'ang Ch'ien, 'Behind the So-Called "Energy Crisis"', (from Hongqi, No. 2, 1 February 1974) in Chen, ed., China and the Three Worlds, p. 298. More recently there have been reports that beginning in 1982 the Soviets started swapping goods, and arms for oil from Libya, Iran and Iraq. While these suppliers thus evaded OPEC's 'minimum price', the Soviets either re-traded the oil to Finland for Finnish goods, or they sold the oil on Western spot markets for US dollars. See 'OPEC Members Barter Oil with the Soviet Union', Durrant's, London, 24 January 1984.

14. 'Third World Struggle Against Hegemony in the Economic Sphere', from Peking Review, No. 39, 26 September 1975, and reproduced in Chen, ed., China and the Three Worlds, p. 310.

15. Henry Kissinger's address to the National Press Club, Washington, D.C., 3 February 1975 as quoted in Yuan-li Wu, Japan's Search for Oil, p. xiii.

16. In his contribution to a Library of Congress study, Johnathan Stern, the London Representative of Conant Associates Ltd., took issue with this popular assumption arguing that the recent history of international relations suggests that the Soviets have 'more limited objectives' in the Middle East. This study suggests that the Soviets are more likely to attempt to assert political influence to gain commercial access to oil rather than employing 'massive military forces in an invasion to secure a country's oil...' See Energy in Soviet Policy, p. 81.

17. Senator Jackson's opening statement to 31 July 1980 hearing of the Committee on Energy and Natural Resources, US Senate, Geopolitics of Oil, Part 2 (US G.P.O., Washington, D.C., 1980), p. 1.

18. Statement of Professor Henry Rowen, Geopolitics of Oil, Part 1, p. 139.

19. Energy in Soviet Policy, pp. 1 & 3.

20. See John Hardt's review of the 'worse' and 'best cases' in Ibid., p. 3. For a critique of the CIA's 'worse case' see Marshall Goldman, The Enigma of Soviet Petroleum: Half-Empty or Half-Full? George Allen & Unwin, London, 1980), passim.

21. Statement of Admiral Stansfield Turner, Director, CIA, Geopolitics of Oil Part 1, p. 70.

22. Ibid., p. 74.

23. Thomas Fingar, Energy in China: Paradoxes, Policies, Prospects (The China Council of the Asia Society, New York, 1983), pp. s-2, s-7 and 21.

24. See fn. 26.

25. See Table 2.1: Soviet Energy Production, 1960-84 in this volume.

26. For example, a study prepared for Senator Jackson's Committee by Fern Gold and Melvin Conant argued that the USSR had an abundance of oil, gas, coal and uranium, but that the reasons for the Soviet failure to realise the potential of these resources lie in timing, policy priorities, technological development and the application of resources to energy development. See Committee on Energy and Natural Resources, US Senate, Access to Oil -- The United States Relationships with Saudi Arabia and Iran, (US G.P.O., Washington, D.C.,

1977), p. 7. Dienes and Shabad argued that geographically iirrational relation of regional energy resources to the historical pattern of Soviet industrialisation posed the most significant problem. See Leslie Dienes and Theordore Shabad, The Soviet Energy System: Resource Use and Policies (John Wiley & Sons, New York, 1979), and also Gordon B. Smith, 'Soviet Energy: Prospects, Problems and Policies', The Journal of Energy and Development, Vol. VII, No. 2, (Spring, 1982), pp. 397-415.

27. Ta Kung Pao, 13 January 1983, p. 6.

28. 'Oil Under Troubled Waters', Far Eastern Economic Review, March 1984, p. 30, and Mark Valencia, 'Joint Development is Key to South China Sea's Oil', The Asian Wall Street Journal, 8 March 1984.

29. As cited in Roy Mathews' discussion of Taiwan's import trade. Roy Mathews, Canada and the Little Dragons (Institute for Research on Public Policy, Montreal, 1983), p. 65.

Chapter One

CHINA'S 'RESOURCE DIPLOMACY' AND NATIONAL ENERGY POLICY

Ronald C. Keith

INTRODUCTION

The Chinese exercise of 'resource diplomacy' depends upon the domestic economic capacity to generate potential and real energy reserves and exports, and therefore, it is tied to the formal objectives and practical consequences of China's national energy policy. In 1980 this policy was summed up as 'placing equal emphasis on conservation and development, with main efforts on the latter in the near future', kaizhan yu jieheng, jinchi yao ba jieneng fangzai youxian diwei.(1) Generally, this policy must be placed within the larger context of the Chinese approach to economic development particularly as this approach has recently encompassed developing emphases on 'economic readjustment' and 'economic reform'.

The complex study of Chinese 'resource diplomacy' is multifaceted as it correlates factors of domestic and international policy. Internal energy mix and planning, patterns of industrial and agricultural energy usage and the interrelated rates of reserve discovery and exploitation are among a series of domestic factors which can be related to the Chinese assessment of commercial trends and opportunities in the international energy market, conflicting national security interests and emerging geopolitical alignments. Obviously, leadership dispute over the nature and extent of foreign participation in domestic economic development must be considered as critical to the determination of energy policy in its relation to Chinese participation in international energy trading. However, the relevant aspects of domestic politics are also inclusive of variables such as the national will and the organisational ingenuity of the Chinese in their response to the continuing energy shortages affecting industry and agriculture in a time of rising consumer expectations.

National energy self-sufficiency has been and still is a serious national political commitment, and the extent to which vital energy resources will be released to facilitate developing political and commercial relations with other states largely depends upon the developing policy balance between interrelated, and sometimes competing priorities of national security and economic development. On the one hand, Deng Xiaoping has insisted that China must apply the historical principle of 'self-reliance', zili gengsheng, in the ultimate realisation of 'socialism with Chinese characteristics', and thus the Chinese leadership is committed to Zhou Enlai's goal to create a comprehensive and self-reliant industrial base in China by the year 2000.(2) On the other hand Deng has committed the Party to the long-term acceptance of an 'open door policy', kaifang zhengce, which seeks to facilitate the process of domestic modernisation through a larger pattern of foreign capital investment and technological input.(3)

Chinese scholarship has described China's 'national power' in terms of 'the economic ability to sustain a huge growing population and a self-supporting capability for continuous economic growth on the basis of a comparatively low level of development'.(4) Hence, China's ability to shoulder 'protracted strategic burdens' is self-consciously viewed as proportional to the rate of domestic economic development.

In the planning of China's Sixth, and in the scheduling of the Seventh Five-Year Plans, energy development has been singled out as the 'strategic key link' or the 'material foundation' for the enlivening of all sectors of the national economy.(5) Specifically, the doubling of current energy production is officially regarded as pivotal to the larger national goal to quadruple the value of industrial and agricultural output by the year 2000.

Energy policy attempts the dialectical integration of emphases on 'self-reliance' and the 'open door'. 'Development', when 'placing equal emphasis on development and conservation', embodies emphases on the domestic refining of China's natural resources and the reproduction of foreign energy technology, as well as an emphasis on the continued expansion of indigenous intermediate technologies in the generation of rural residential energy. 'Development' especially features the use of foreign capital and technology in the achievement of greater rates of efficient energy usage through the general upgrading of industrial plant and the more sophisticated surveying and large-scale extraction and mining of energy resources. Hence China's door is particularly open to foreign capital and technology in areas such as enhanced oil recovery, deep-sea drilling technology, large-scale open-pit mining, sophisticated hydro-electric transmission and nuclear-power plant construction. The parameters of foreign participation have been progressively expanded, and the Chinese have not hesitated to exchange natural resources for technology and equipment.

The 'conservation' side of energy policy has not only involved an elaborate scheme of rationing, but also conservation through the introduction of more energy efficient plant. 'Conservation' is also inclusive of a strategy of rationing which reserves major energy resources for large-scale urban industry while attempting to meet the needs of local consumption through the more efficient maximisation of local resources in the creation of local energy projects. Perhaps 'conservation' as opposed to 'development' more obviously invokes a well established and distinctively Chinese economic regime which since the mid- to late 1950s has responded to the twin factors of labour abundance and capital scarcity. In the context of economic reform Deng Xiaoping has stressed 'studying new situations and solving new problems';(6) however, the course of national economic readjustment since spring, 1979 has also highlighted the notion of 'self-reliance' as it invokes familiar themes emphasising 'walking on two legs', 'local expediency' and 'combining small, medium and large'. The late 1950s emphases on decentralisation and the simultaneous and complementary exploitation of foreign and domestic technologies in a multidimensional strategy to achieve national and local increases in industrial productivity are even now evident in the projected development of small-scale coal mining and hydro-electric generation.

In energy policy the synthesis of 'self-reliance' and the 'open door' has been complicated. The apparent contradictions within oil export policy of the early 1980s offers a ready example of this complexity. In response to the decline in total primary energy production the Chinese nonetheless acted to protect their newly won oil export status by adopting the 'squeeze principle'. Domestic consumption of crude oil was rationed to insure sustained levels of domestic refining and a minimal level of exports to established customers. While this policy tactic may have cramped energy-starved domestic industry, the 'squeeze' was nevertheless rationalised as part of the total programme for self-reliance, for the oil, which was used to achieve the quick generation of foreign exchange, facilitated the greater purchasing of foreign technology and the accelerated modernisation of China's industrial base.

In this particular case the Chinese may have demonstrated flexibility in their application of the principle of 'self-reliance'; however, they remain very jealous of their own national security. They seldom neglect the lessons of recent world politics. In responding to the 1973 international oil crisis, for example, the Chinese focused on the 'oil hegemonism' of the superpowers in the Middle East. In the context of ongoing UN debate concerning the New International Economic Order, China's diplomats emphasised the importance of Third World countries maintaining political and economic control over their own natural resources for purposes of domestic economic development. While expressing national pride in their own story of self-sufficiency, they endorsed OPEC price controls and production cuts as legitimate expressions of Arab national independence vis-a-vis the allegedly marauding transnationals and the 'power politics' of their state patrons in the industrialised West.

Chinese resource diplomacy was, especially in the late 1970s, conditioned by the fear of Soviet 'oil' and 'gas hegemony' as it has threatened adversely to affect East Asian geopolitical relations; and thus the Chinese closely monitored the development of Soviet Siberian and Far Eastern natural resources particularly as they became relevant to Japanese energy investment and supply. The Sino-Japanese energy trade became an increasingly critical component of the developing Sino-Japanese economic relationship as a whole. The schedules of the Sino-Japanese Long Term Agreement of 1978 (LTA) largely depended on the exchange of Chinese natural resources for Japanese technology, equipment and capital. In their diplomatic interaction with the Japanese the Chinese made very shrewd use of the certainties of established crude oil reserves at Daqing and the future potential of the Bohai Gulf, as against the financial and production uncertainties of Japanese involvement in the Soviet Tyumen fields.

Over the last several years China's relationship with the Western industrialised economies has represented a growing dynamic; however, the Chinese still insist that China will establish 'socialism with Chinese characteristics' and will not follow the 'big powers' in an 'external-oriented road in the form of industry-foreign trade.'(7) With reference to China's national energy programme, Professor Thomas Fingar's 1983 study concludes that even though 'self-reliance' still complicates emerging Sino-foreign co-operation, inevitably '... China's search for new supplies of energy promises to tie the country to the United States.'(8) As for the Chinese they have occasionally slapped the wrists of 'inept strategists' who think that China can be '... brought into the sphere of influence of certain economic forces.'(9)

Currently, the Chinese are emphasising the importance of a creative response to the changing conditions of socialist development, and they are moving into a new era of economic reform and international economic participation. Recent history, nevertheless, provides some important clues as to the future evolution of China's economic and foreign policies as they are relevant to national energy development and resource diplomacy. In the first half of this chapter the historical dimensions and underlying strategic motivation of China's resource diplomacy will be discussed. There is a critical chronology which interrelates resource diplomacy and domestic economic development as the Chinese moved away from the 1970s emphasis on rapid modernisation through the exponential development of China's oil resources, to a more balanced and conservative emphasis of the early 1980s which in the energy sector was exemplified in the 'equal emphasis' given to development and conservation. The second half of the chapter will extend the discussion of resource diplomacy with more detailed coverage of domestic energy strategy. Despite continuing domestic energy shortages the Chinese have consistently achieved an exportable surplus of crude oil and coal to meet externally entwined strategic and commercial commitments. This organisational achievement, when placed in the context of China's tremendous reserve potential and relatively late start in the exploitation of primary energy, should inform any tentative conclusions concerning the PRC's future participation in the East Asian energy trade.

'RESOURCE DIPLOMACY' AND THE STRATEGIC IMPLICATIONS OF 'SELF-RELIANCE'

Chinese oil exports currently account for almost 25 per cent of China's foreign exchange earnings. The PRC exports petroleum to at least 42 countries including Japan, France, the US, West Germany, Romania, Switzerland, Denmark, Thailand, Malaysia, Egypt, Syria, Nepal, Spain, Pakistan, Tanzania, etc. China's remarkable ascent from oil dependence to self-sufficiency and export status can perhaps best be explained in terms of domestic policy changes as they relate to the Sino-Soviet dispute of the late 1950s, early 1960s.

Energy policy of the 1950s was in part shaped by the internal response to capital scarcity and labour abundance and by an external reliance on Soviet and East European technology and imports. The internal consumption of liquid fuels was restricted, and the first years of planning stressed the development of abundant coal and hydro-electric resources. The lack of accessible oil reserves in the urban coastal areas encouraged the regime to adopt expensive shale-oil and coal-oil methods of petroleum extraction. However, as a result of the discovery of new fields in late 1957 and the failure to achieve the petroleum production targets of the First Five-Year Plan, state planners began to invest more heavily in the expansion of conventional reserves.

Domestic crude oil production jumped from 1.16 million metric tons in 1957 to 2.6 million metric tons in 1958. In the late 1950s the import of petroleum products mainly from the Soviet Union and Romania was quite high; however, there was some moderation of this pattern even by 1960. While imports accounted for 57 per cent of total consumption in 1958, this level dropped to 50 per cent in 1959 and 42 per cent in 1960.(10)

In the context of the late 1950s Sino-Soviet dispute the Chinese were more forthcoming about the shortcomings of the Soviets. Originally in 1950, under heavy pressure from Stalin, the Chinese leaders had agreed to the formation of several joint companies including the Sino-Soviet Oil Corporation, which targeted the exploration and development of the Karamai oilfield in Xinjiang. The Soviets apparently had hoped to compensate for an apparently declining reserve situation at Sakhalin Island through the establishment of a significant petroleum base inside China which would facilitate the future supply of the Amur-Ussuri Valleys. The Chinese, however, regarded such co-operative ventures as too one-sided and exploitative.

In 1958 Mao Zedong issued his famous directive, 'self-reliance is primary while striving for foreign assistance is supplementary', '*zili gengsheng wei zhu, zhengqu waiyuan wei bu*', and Mao more clearly articulated an indigenous Chinese as opposed to a Stalinist model of socialist economic development.(11) As Premier Zhou Enlai explained, due to China's huge land mass, great population and rich resources, participation in international exchange could only be supplementary to the indigenous solution of China's enormous developmental problems. Mao noted in 1958: 'It is necessary to win Soviet aid, but the most important thing is self-reliance.'(12) The latter became even more important in the context of the 1960 unilateral withdrawal of 1390 Soviet experts and the reduction of Soviet oil supplies.

The crash programme to develop newly discovered domestic crude oil reserves at Daqing was subsequently politically immortalised. At Daqing the Chinese believed that they had triumphed over both the US 'imperialist' trade embargo and Soviet paternalism. Production miracles at Daqing were cited to disprove early American geological assumptions that China was 'oil poor' due to the prevalence of 'continental' as opposed to 'marine formations'.(13)

The PRC achieved basic self-sufficiency in crude oil production by the end of 1963 and in 1964 Mao moved politically to extend the Daqing lesson in 'self-reliance' to all of China's industry in the national campaign called 'In Industry Learn From Daqing'. Soviet resource diplomacy had failed in its political objective, as Mao attacked Soviet products as 'heavy, crude and highpriced'. Complaining that 'they always hold something back', Mao claimed that he would rather deal with the '... French bourgeoisie, who still have some notion of business ethics.'(14)

During the subsequent years of Cultural

Revolution radicalism, Chinese foreign policy stridently emphasised class struggle as a universal factor in international politics, and in 1967 Chinese analysis treated the Six-Day War in the Middle East as an 'oil war' which had its origins in the 'neo-colonialist Policy' of the US.(15) In its support for Israel, the US allegedly acted to neutralise the growing force of Arab nationalism and to maintain its strategic control over the region's oil supplies.

The Chinese highlighted the collusion between the US and the USSR in their attempts to maintain the status quo. The Soviet leadership was castigated for having betrayed Arab nationalism. In fact, its revisionism was apparently so perfidious that the Soviet leaders even went so far as to betray the national interest of the Soviet people. In 1967, the Chinese denounced the Soviet-Japanese Joint Economic Committee and its plans for the joint development of Siberian and Soviet Far Eastern natural resources. The Soviet 'revisionists' in collusion with the 'Japanese monopolist group' were allegedly engaged in an insidious manoeuvre to engage American 'monopoly capital' in the exploitation of Siberian resources.(16)

During the subsequent Middle Eastern crisis of 1973-4, the Chinese began to export significant amounts of oil. Their exports went to trusted allies, North Korea and North Vietnam, and they subsequently began modest exports to the Philippines and Thailand at 'friendship prices.'(17) Whereas in 1967 Chinese analysis emphasised US-Soviet collusion, in 1973 the crisis was characterised in terms of superpower rivalry for 'Middle Eastern oil hegemony.'(18)

The Chinese had little sympathy for the West's energy predicament; the ensuing energy crisis was viewed as politically contrived. According to Chinese analysis world energy supplies were actually abundant, and the crisis was the inevitable result of the internal contradictions of a profit-driven, wasteful 'monopoly capitalism' which treated Middle Eastern reserves as a 'money-producing tree.'(19) Chinese Communist Party analysis argued that half of the energy consumed in the US was wasteful and explained the crisis as follows:

> In view of the economic and strategic value of petroleum and the greater profits gained by seizing the petroleum of foreign countries, the monopoly capitalists have competed in seizing

> the land and oil of the Third World countries rather than extracting the petroleum in their own countries. Particularly they covet the Middle East, which has rich petroleum reserves and holds an important strategic position politically and geographically.(20)

At the UN General Assembly in 1974, Deng Xiaoping personally called upon Third World countries 'to terminate imperialist economic monopoly.'(21) He asserted: 'The oil battle has broadened people's vision.'(22) OPEC actions to control the production and pricing of oil were viewed as the politically necessary response to 'neo-colonialism'. In defining 'self-reliance' at the UN, Deng emphasised that Third World countries must exercise direct control over their natural resources. However, while he attacked the trading practices of the multinationals and the superpowers, he also emphasised the need for international exchange in his distinction between 'self-reliance' and 'autarchy' as 'self-seclusion' or 'rejection of foreign aid'. Deng urged greater exchange on the basis of 'equality and mutual benefits' and 'the exchange of needed goods to make up for each other's deficiencies.'(23)

Deng's constructive synthesis of 'self-reliance' and international exchange was essentially orthodox in the theoretical terms of 'Mao Zedong Thought'; however, in so clearly raising the issue Deng exposed himself to domestic criticism which at the polemical level focused increasingly on the theme of 'national betrayal'. In so far as Deng was concerned, the use of China's natural resources in fair international exchange for the purpose of accelerating the 'four modernisations' made patent common sense. Deng, for example, supported the export of coal on a long-term contractual basis, arguing the advantages of Chinese coal in exchange for foreign equipment and technology included the generation of greater foreign exchange earnings, the technological transformation of the coal industry and the greater employment of domestic labour.(24)

If leaders such as Deng were prepared to sell China's natural resources, they were also quite conscious of the underlying political and strategic motivations which seemingly characterised international exchange. Resource diplomacy in the mid to late 1970s became an increasingly important aspect in the mix of strategic and economic interests in East Asia. In light of the Shanghai

Communique of February, 1972 and the first tentative steps towards Sino-American normalisation, international speculation focused intensively on Chinese offshore oil potential, and China's role as a major exporter was then greatly exaggerated.

The Communique was a setback for the Soviets, but they still hoped to regain the strategic initiative through the creation of an effectively anti-Chinese system of 'Asian collective security'. Thus they needed to arrest the process of Sino-Japanese normalisation, which had been promised in the Zhou-Tanaka statement of 29 September 1972.(25) However, the Japanese government had had to issue on 22 November 1973 an embarassing declaration calling for the Israeli withdrawal from all Arab occupied territories. Japan's dependence on foreign oil appeared to offer a strategic opening, as Japanese foreign policy struggled to maintain its traditional distinction between the political and economic spheres of international politics.

Energy dependency threatened to undermine the Japanese policy of 'equidistance' which had worked to avoid the political costs of taking sides in the Sino-Soviet dispute.(26) The Soviet offer of extensive economic co-operation in Siberian energy projects came at a time when the Japanese were especially anxious to diversify their external sources of oil supply away from the Middle East. In return for Japanese capital and technology, the Soviets preferred a 'carrot' in the form of an annual stable supply of 40 million tons of Tyumen crude oil. The Chinese were apprehensive lest the accelerated development of Soviet Siberian oil and gas, coupled with the projected development of supporting communications and transportation infrastructure, might result in greatly improved Soviet logistical capacity to wage war in the Far East.

On 17 January 1975, the Chinese National People's Congress approved a new state constitution which raised the struggle against 'the hegemonism of the superpowers' to the ethereal heights of fundamental ideological principle, and in February Chinese diplomacy pressed hard for the inclusion of an 'anti-hegemony' clause in the yet to be drafted Sino-Japanese peace treaty which was to symbolise the culmination of the normalisation process between the two countries. The Japanese, however, feared that the inclusion of such a clause would compromise their 'equidistance' and alienate the Soviet

Union.(27)

Initial Soviet-Japanese negotiations required that the Japanese invest 3.2 billion US dollars in Tyumen in return for a stable supply of oil for twenty years. In a time of Western financial crisis the Japanese may have had some qualms about tying up so much capital in a Soviet mega-project, particularly when there was a Chinese alternative close at hand. The Soviets dropped the projected annual delivery from 40 to 25 million tons, and this may have raised questions in Tokyo as to the viability of the project and the extent of the prospective Soviet reserves. Also, the project's compatibility with the requirements of Japanese-American security arrangements was at issue. The Soviets responded by welcoming American investment in the project; however, in the context of growing American suspicion of Soviet foreign policy objectives, tight money and domestic recession, the Americans refused to participate.(28) Also, the Soviets may have had their own reservations about committing so much of their new oil wealth to long-term exports to Western markets.(29)

The situation was ripe for Chinese intervention. The Chinese offer of at least ten per cent of national crude oil output for export to Japan did not entail the same kind of investment complications which appeared to dog the Tyumen project. The latter required expensive logistics. Even while the Soviet ambassador to Japan was vigorously pushing for Japanese investment in Tyumen, the Japanese Minister of International Trade and Industry, Yasuhiro Nakasone, was engaged in discussions with Premier Zhou Enlai over potential increases in China's oil exports to Japan and the possibility of Japanese participation in China's offshore oil development.(30) The Japanese were especially receptive as the USSR had rebuffed the Japanese Prime Minister's attempt to link investment in co-operative energy ventures with Soviet concessions on the Northern Territories issues.

One observer summed up the situation as follows: 'The oil strategies of China, Japan and the Soviet Union were dominated by the sober reality that as a resource-poor 'Big Power' Japan had to walk a tightrope between the two resource-rich Big Powers ...'(31) According to Taiwanese intelligence, Premier Zhou Enlai in a report to senior cadres had explained the interrelation of these 'oil strategies' in the following way:

> To Japan, the Soviet revisionists use the exploitation of Tyumen oil field as a lure to better relations with her. However, [the Soviets] will not yield the request for the return of the four islands north of Japan. Under Japan's strategy of 'separation of politics and economics', it is impossible to make any progress in the relations between Japan and the USSR. The Soviet revisionists also attempt to win over the US to open up Tyumen oil field, but the US capitalists do not show great interest. First, the USSR uses the capital of the US to promote construction and her own capital to amplify her armaments. Second, it will require five years after investment to produce petroleum products and who knows what will happen in the world during the five years.(32)

Whereas in 1967 the Chinese may have been overly concerned over the prospects concerning the participation of American 'monopoly capital' in Siberian natural resource development, in the early to mid-1970s Zhou Enlai was reasonably confident that neither the US nor Japan could afford involvement in such development. Zhou might have added that there was so much more potential in the Sino-Japanese trading relationship given the different, but complementary stages of Chinese and Japanese economic development.

In 1976, while the Miki government was reeling from the fallout associated with the 'Lockheed payoff scandal', the Chinese were plunged into yet another round of debilitating leadership disputes. Even in death, Zhou Enlai was maligned as the leader of a 'foreign affairs faction', yangwu pai, and his protege, Deng Xiaoping, came under direct public attack in April.(33) Deng was accused of denigrating Mao's principle of 'self-reliance' and of practicing a 'slavish comprador philosophy' which sought to transform China into a 'raw material base' and an 'investment center' for foreign capital.(34) Subsequent to the arrest of the 'Gang of Four' in October, 1976 the issue of 'national betrayal' became a dead-letter, as the Chinese leadership progressively acted to reconcile 'self-reliance' with an emphasis on the 'open door'. The supporters of the 'Gang of Four' were villified in turn for failing to observe Mao's instruction 'to make foreign things serve China'.

Meanwhile with rising expectations concerning

China's offshore oil wealth and antagonistic relations with the Soviets over the Northern Territories issue, which of course drew attention to the potential Soviet military threat to Japan, the business leaders of the Keidanren, the Japanese Federation of Economic Organisations, pushed more vigorously for a breakthrough in Sino-Japanese negotiations which had stalled over the issue of the anti-hegemony clause and Japan's commitments to Taiwan. Regardless of the formal separation of politics and economics in Japanese policy, the potential of the China market offered an especially comforting respite in an increasingly gloomy international scene, marked by a developing Western antagonism over the issues of reciprocity and Japan's successful penetration of Western markets. The extent of China's crude oil exports was the key to future Sino-Japanese trade.

In the spring of 1977 an agreement in principle for long-term trade was worked out between Li Qiang, China's Minister of Foreign Trade and the representatives of the Keidanren. These negotiations culminated in the Long-Term Trade Agreement of 16 February 1978, which outlined the schedules for the Chinese export of crude oil and coal in exchange for Japanese technology, equipment and machinery. On May 25th Vice-Premier Kang Shi'en requested Japanese technological and financial co-operation in the development of offshore oil and gas resources, and his request was followed up in July with an agreement to promote joint oil development in the Bohai Gulf and Pearl River Estuary.

On the twelfth day of August Foreign Ministers Huang Hua and Sunao Sonoda signed the long awaited Sino-Japanese Peace and Friendship Treaty. Japanese diplomacy claimed success in watering down the Chinese wording of the anti-hegemony clause in Article II and in the inclusion of a qualified reference to 'third countries', meaning the USSR; however, the Soviet press dismissed such quibbles as an 'illusion' and darkly warned of 'the revival of Japanese militarism.'(35) Regardless of the established requirements of Japanese 'equidistant' or 'omnidirectional diplomacy', in the practical terms of international perspective Japan had tilted to the PRC, and the politics of oil were integral to this transition. On September 9th just prior to the final ratification of the treaty in the Japanese Diet, the Chinese announced: 'China will co-operate with other countries in the development of offshore oil, and will choose Japan before other partners, if all conditions are the same.'(36)

The ambitious and new framework of resources for capital and technology was, however, almost immediately bogged down in the complexities of domestic Chinese politics. A major shift in economic thinking and political alignment was brewing to the disadvantage of the new Party leader, Hua Guofeng. Under his leadership the Party had rushed headlong towards an immediate and sweeping modernisation under the Great Leap Forward banner of 'going all out, aiming high and achieving greater, faster, better and more economical results in the building of socialism.'(37) In his ill-advised enthusiasm, Hua ordered the building of 'ten Daqings', the raising of annual steel production to 60 million tons and 85 per cent mechanisation of all the major processes of farmwork by 1985.

The theme of 'readjustment' emerged at the third plenum of the Eleventh CCP Central Committee in late 1978 with the return of Chen Yun to direct the national economy.(38) The Japanese immediately felt the consequences when the China National Technical Import Corporation suspended Baoshan equipment contracts along with 21 other contracts with Japanese companies worth 1.5 billion US dollars.(39) The scheme for a massive integrated steel works at Baoshan came under attack in the context of sustained political attack on the 'erroneous' line of 'taking steel as the key link'. The principle of 'self-reliance', a principle which Hua Guofeng had himself identified, came into even greater vogue as Chinese policy emphasised a reduction in the import of complete sets of technology, the contraction of capital construction in favour of existing production facilities, the maximum usage of scarce indigenous resources and a balanced budget.

In March, 1979 the Chinese and Japanese agreed to extend the LTA to 1990. While 'readjustment' was formally endorsed at the Second Session of the Fifth National People's Congress in June, 1979, Chinese leaders such as Hua Guofeng and Deng Xiaoping reiterated China's long-term commitment to the 'open door'. Party dialectics presumed that the 'open door' and 'self-reliance' were part and parcel of the same positive synthesis. Deng later explained to delegates from Japan's House of Councillors that 'readjustment' was necessary to avert escalating prices and financial deficits which threatened to undermine the Party's attempt to raise the standard of living. Deng believed that 'readjustment' was only in appearance a 'temporary retreat', whereas 'in essence', it was a progressive step towards establishing the 'four modernisations' on 'a more stable and solid basis.'(40)

Part of the economic problem originated with an overestimation of the immediate oil production capabilities which were expected to help fuel accelerated modernisation of Chinese industry. The political emphasis on the production miracle at Daqing was perhaps counterproductive in this respect. Even the Party could not build ten Daqings overnight, and Chinese planners had to modify their projections of future oil wealth in relation to actual contemporary production capabilities.

'Readjustment' affected Sino-Japanese trade. Whereas the Japanese enjoyed a trade surplus of US $754.9 million in 1980, this historical pattern of surplus was reversed in 1981 primarily due to decreased Chinese purchases of Japanese steel and increased Japanese importation of Chinese crude oil. Even in the context of softening world oil prices and the growing pattern of recession in the West, the Chinese engaged in the fulsome frankness of 'readjustment' to reveal the extent of China's domestic energy shortages. Soviet analysis gleefully predicted the end of the so-called Chinese 'oil bluff', and upbraided the Japanese for having helped to create a false euphoria over China as a 'second Saudi Arabia'. Western observers were criticised for having projected China's 'rapid advance into the ranks of the leading oil exporters' and for their fool-hardy assumption that China could be used as a 'new lever for exerting pressure on the OPEC countries'. Soviet analysis incidentally claimed that Beijing used 'oil diplomacy' to support Thailand and the rebel bands of 'Khmer reactionaires' and to establish behind-the-scenes contact with Taiwan and South Korea.(41)

Chinese press reports focused in turn on the Soviet's 'southward strategy' which would use Afghanistan as a stepping stone for the project of Soviet influence into the vital Persian Gulf.(42) The Chinese also warned against Western European involvement in the construction of a transnational pipeline and the long-term purchase of Yamal Peninsula gas reserves, claiming that the Soviet notion of joint development was malicious in its hidden strategic agenda. This analysis concluded:

> There are two aims behind this. It wants Western capital and advanced technology to open up Sibera and then [it would] make Western Europe and Japan rely on it for part of their energy wants. The other aim the Soviet Union has in mind is political, to pry these countries away from the United States.(43)

The Chinese stressed that the Soviet 'southward strategy' was essentially designed to 'outflank' Western Europe in the Middle East and that it was linked to a secondary strategic thrust in the Pacific, which they dubbed the 'dumb-bell strategy.'(44) This secondary refinement (see Figure 1.1) recalled the strategic significance of Siberian resource development for Soviet expansionism in the Far East, and it placed the Strait of Malacca at the middle point of a bar which strategically joined Soviet naval activites in the Indian and Pacific Oceans. With the Soviet access to military facilities in Vietnam's Cam Ranh Bay and Danang bases this 'dumb-bell strategy' had particularly serious implications for Japan.

The Soviets attempted in turn to malign the Chinese export of scarce oil reserves as detrimental to China's economic 'self-reliance'.(45) The Chinese were only too well aware that they could indeed use all the oil which they produced for domestic consumption. On the other hand, the use of oil to earn foreign exchange allowed a wider purchasing power which could facilitate the improvement of the technological basis of Chinese industry at key points nationwide. Oil was China's number one earner of foreign exchange, and despite the downward pressure on oil prices, oil exports could still generate a higher rate of exchange than the export of agricultural commodities and sideline specialties. Thus the 'squeezing' out of an artificial export surplus was regarded as 'objectively' necessary and ultimately consistent with 'self-reliance'.(46)

China's status as an exporter of oil is also fundamentally a matter of national prestige and Chinese analysis has tried to suggest that despite over-supply and softening international oil markets '... the export of petroleum and coal has many advantages for strengthening bilateral co-operation and alliances against hegemonism between us and the Third World countries and some Second World countries.'(47)

However, in their conservative emphasis on

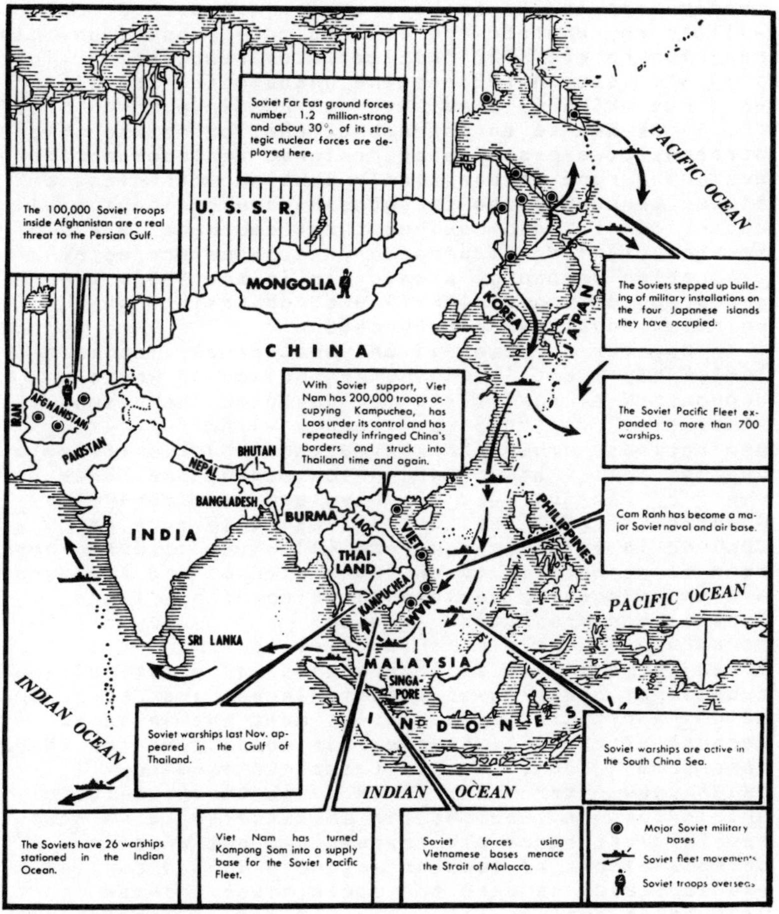

Figure 1.1: Growing Soviet Military Presence in the East

'readjustment' the Chinese became more cautious in their energy projections for the 1980s. Western analysis followed suit and was perhaps overly pessimistic in its focus on China's short-term ability to generate new oil and coal production. In reaction to the difficult years of readjustment in 1979-81, Western forecasting highlighted production declines which were expected to continue throughout the 1980s due to an untenable relation between the patterns of extraction and reserve replacement and a declining rate of elasticity in the coefficient of energy production to the gross value of industrial output due to aged equipment and backward levels of technological development. In sum the projected stagnation of energy production in the 1980s was expected to impose significant constraints on China's industrial growth.(48)

However Chinese oil and coal production in 1983-4 has outstripped the assumption of Western econometrical analysis which accepted the dismal statistics of 1980-81 as the base-line for projections throughout the decade.(49) The effect of Chinese policy and organisation during the first years of readjustment may have been seriously underestimated. The anticipated steep rate of decline in established crude oil production has not been borne out due to the expansion of old fields and the discovery and exploitation of new fields in established production areas.

Even in the difficult years of early 'readjustment' the Chinese were still politically capable of creating an exportable surplus of crude oil. Exports to Japan did not meet the inflated targets of the LTA; however, in absolute terms they rose from 13,009,000 metric tons in 1980 to 13,754,000 metric tons in 1981 and to 15,204,000 metric tons in 1982.(50) In 1982-4, the two sides were able to negotiate downward adjustments in China's export of coal and crude oil.(51) Earlier export schedules were too steep given Chinese production difficulties, the pattern of recession in the West and the short-term success of Japanese economic adjustments and energy policy.

The Chinese do not operate in an international environment free from the larger constraints and vicissitudes of the international market place. They have become more flexible, for example, in contract negotiations concerning foreign investment in both offshore and onshore exploration and development; however, Chinese analysis expects a very modest strengthening of world oil markets in the second half of the 1980s at a time when China's offshore wells are expected to come on stream. The current picture of over-supply is regarded as a temporary phenomenon largely induced by policy adjustments precipitated by the prevailing pattern of recession in the early 1980s. Song Baoxiang, for example, in his futurist study of oil pricing in the 1980s and 1990s suggests that sudden disruptive increases, such as was the case in 1973, are not likely in the developing context of competition between different forms of energy supply. However, he also rules out steep declines as just as unlikely, as not only the interests of producers, but also the world commodity and exchange markets would be drastically affected. Song's rather optimistic projection expects oil prices to stabilise between twenty-five and thirty US dollars per barrel.(52)

Chinese research has also argued that regardless of conservation and energy-switching by the Western industrialised states, the number of Third World countries requiring greater external energy supplies will increase and will negatively affect the international pattern of energy availability. Citing the findings of the 12th World Energy Conference , Zhang Yan of the Chinese Ministry of Petroleum Industry, has argued that the Third World share of total world energy consumption will increase by 33 per cent by the year 2000, when the Third World will account for over 50 per cent of the international oil trade.(53) The Chinese media has also singled out OPEC projections which assume an increase in Third World oil imports from 5.3 million barrels per day in 1980 to 26 million per day in 2000.(54) This last projection also assumed that even given relatively successful conservation and energy switching the industrialised states would still need to import the present level of 20 million barrels per day of oil equivalent.

Prediction as to the future levels of Western importation is difficult; however, the present slowdown in the Japanese programme for switching from oil to coal consumption is perhaps suggestive of future difficulties. In 1975-82 the Japanese succeeded in modifying the pattern of supply dependence on the Middle East, bringing down the level of dependence from 78 to 69 percent of domestic consumption , but Japan still relies on foreign supplies for 99 per cent of its crude oil.(55)

The LTA appears to have survived the trauma of

Chinese 'readjustment' as both sides have tolerated annual trading imbalances. The trend of Chinese coal and crude oil exports to Japan, which is depicted in Table 1.1, reflects the modified domestic and international expectations of the early years of 'readjustment'.

Table 1.1 The Sino-Japanese Energy Trade and 'Readjustment'

Year	Commodity	Quantity (MT/KL)	Value $1000	Annual %Change	Export Share
1979	Coal	2,407,123	69,098		
	Crude Oil	8,506,183	1,003,522		
1980	Coal	2,070,831	116,519	47.1	2.7
	Crude Oil	9,147,305	1,949,172	7.5	45.1
1981	Coal	2,790,595	118,676	34.8	3.6
	Crude Oil	10,288,654	2,332,960	12.5	44.1
1982	Coal	3,116,628	212,537	11.7	4.0
	Crude Oil	10,592,433	2,340,918	3.0	43.7

Source: JETRO, China Newsletter, No. 31, Mar/Ap., 1981, p. 35, No. 37, Mar/Ap., 1982, p. 31, No. 43, Mar/Ap., 1983 p. 25

In 1979-82 there was a downward trend in the percentage increase of export volume in crude oil shipped to Japan. There was a perceptible decline in oil's percentage share of total exports, and there was a slight increase in coal's percentage share of total exports in 1982. The 1983 JETRO figures indicate that although volume of crude oil exports dipped slightly, oil's export share remained at the 1982 level.

OPEC price reductions and declining domestic Japanese demand helped to push down the percentage increases in both volume and value of Chinese oil exports. A variety of factors affected the revision of LTA scheduling, including overall lower economic growth in Japan, a more effective manipulation of Japan's domestic energy mix, the decline in the Japanese production of high energy-consuming steel production and the slackening of coal-fueled elected power generation.(56)

The trade figures for 1983 and 1984 show a positive modification of earlier restrictive patterns with increasing Chinese import activity, including steel imports from Japan. Japanese exports to China in the first half of 1984 stood at US $2,884,700,000, an increase of 37.1 per cent over the first half of 1983. At the same time Japanese imports registered a total of US$2,952,080,000 an increase of 22.4 per cent. There were sharp increases in the Chinese import of Japanese machinery, (74.8%), steel, (21.5%), and there were also sharp increases in the Japanese import of Chinese textiles, (48.4%) and crude oil, (16.2%). (57)

With respect to Japan, the opportunity for Chinese 'resource diplomacy' under current circumstances is only very modest. The Chinese supply to Japan may have helped to decrease Japanese reliance on the Middle East, but China acts as only one component in the Japanese strategy for diversification of supply. The PRC is presently the fifth largest crude oil supplier to Japan following Saudi Arabia, Indonesia, the United Arab Emirates and Iran. In 1982, Daqing, for example, only accounted for five per cent of Japan's total crude oil imports; whereas, this amount accounted for 60 per cent of China's total oil exports.

The Japanese are still modestly engaged in Soviet economic development; however, it appears that they did accept the LTA as a positive alternative to massive involvement in Soviet energy and resource development. The PRC is emerging as a more important trading partner than the USSR. In 1983, for example, Sino-Japanese trade declined only slightly whereas Japanese exports to the Soviet Union collapsed by 27.6 per cent to US $2.82 billion and Japanese imports from the Soviet Union dropped 13.4 per cent to US $1.46 billion.(58)

Given the potential of Japan's already burgeoning economic relationship with China, the Soviet-Japanese deadlock over the Northern Territories issue, and the hostile Japanese view of the Soviet-Vietnamese military relationship, the Vietnamese position within Kampuchea and the positioning of Soviet SS20 missiles in the Soviet Far East, the strategic possibilities of 'omnidirectional diplomacy' appear to be moot. On the other hand, the Chinese strategy for the 'four modernisations' which has sought a positive correlation of 'self-reliance' and the 'open door' has perhaps achieved its greatest success in the realisation of the LTA, whereby Chinese resources are exchanged for Japanese capital and technology.

At least since its formal inclusion in the new state constitution of 4 December 1982 the Chinese have summed up their foreign relations in terms of 'independent foreign policy', duli zizhu waiguan zhengce, and under this formulation they have adopted a complex position.(59) This position has abandoned earlier emphasis on the imminence of world war in a search for a more stable strategic environment conducive to domestic modernisation and international trade. This position, however, attempts a synthesis of competing emphases, for on the one hand, the Chinese seek bilateralism and normal state-to-state relations with both the US and the USSR, but on the other, the Chinese insist that they will continue to oppose American and Soviet 'hegemonism' mainly through diplomatic multilateralism in the Third World.

Under 'independent foreign policy' the Chinese are still sensitive to the strategic implications of the Soviet 'dumb-bell strategy'. The 'three obstacles', relating to the Soviet involvement in Kampuchea and Afghanistan and the Soviet force levels on the Sino-Soviet border, are still very critical to Chinese strategic thinking, but the Chinese are not constrained in developing greater commercial and economic ties with the Soviets. The latter even includes Soviet involvement in open-pit coal mining in Inner Mongolia. The Chinese are perhaps less vitriolic, but nonetheless, serious in their calculation of the Siberian factor in regional energy relations. Chinese analysis has, for example, expected that the completion in 27 October 1984 of the Soviets' Baikal-Amur Mainline will contribute to the development of Soviet ocean shipping to countries in the Pacific Rim as well as in Europe. A significant improvement in the Soviet military logistical capacity in the Far Eastern Soviet Union is also expected.(60) Even given the economic and political challenges of Siberian development the Chinese are prepared to expand Sino-Soviet trade.

The last several years of Chinese energy development have been more positive than Western analysis originally anticipated, and the PRC has proven that despite formidable domestic difficulties it can maintain its status as an oil exporter. However, it is possible that the commercial factors of China's 'resource diplomacy' which seek to facilitate the goals of the 'four modernisations' might become more important and the geopolitical variables concerning energy supply for military logistics less important in the context of 'independence and self-reliance', which seeks a normalised bilateralism with the Soviets. With the development of Sino-Soviet commercial relations the Chinese would not be in as strong a position to pressure against Japanese involvement in Soviet energy projects, but then the Japanese, themselves, are trying to hold the line on domestic energy consumption and external capital investment in energy projects. There is yet another unknown variable, namely, the impact of Sino-Soviet bilateralism and trade on the Vietnamese-Soviet economic and geopolitical relationship.

Any assessment of the trend of Chinese 'resource diplomacy' must necessarily encompass a complex variety of domestic and international factors such as foreign participation in domestic energy development, the Chinese capacity to apply new technology to their energy problems within the time-frame of the Sixth and Seventh Five-Year Plans, and a measure of the Chinese political and organisational ingenuity in carrying out current policies for energy conservation and development.

THE 'FOUR MODERNISATIONS' AND THE NATIONAL ENERGY PROGRAMME

The current national energy programme formally gives 'equal emphases' to conservation and development. In an attempt to facilitate this programme the 'open door' has been opened still wider, but foreign investment and technological imports act as only one significant element in this complex policy of conservation and development. Energy policy has emerged within a specific framework of economic 'readjustment' and 'reform'. In this evolving context both 'economic' and 'administrative' mechanisms are at work. 'Economic' factors have become significant in new ways relating to energy pricing and contractual relations governing capital construction and regional energy supply. However, Chinese energy planning in meeting the energy requirements of rural China have also continued to emphasise an earlier organisational experience which originated in the Great Leap Forward strategy of 'walking on two legs'.

The problems of China's energy sector are well known. Over 50 per cent of the current crude oil production is located in the Daqing area of the northeast.(61) As of 1984 some 770 billion tons of proven coal reserves, or 60 per cent of total reserves, are located in North China. At least 80 per cent of China's natural gas production is concentrated in the one province of Sichuan. China has the world's largest theoretical reserves of hydro-electric power, but more than 70 per cent of China's 380 million kilowatts of exploitable water reserves are remotely located in the mountainous regions of the southwest. Northeastern industry has had significant access to energy resources, but this has not been the case in the coastal areas in and around Shanghai. The development of significant oil and coal reserves in the Northwest has, hithertoo, lacked economic feasibility given the unevenness in regional transportation facilities, the historic lack of major capital investment and the distance from industrial centers in eastern China.

Also, Chinese planning has had to contend with the spatial inequalities which have arisen with regional variations in industrial development and the standard of living. Chinese planning is like no other planning in that it must meet the energy needs of a rural population of over 800 million people. In fact the policy connotations of 'self-reliance' have become especially explicit in 'national economic readjustment' as a whole and more specifically in the strategy for rural energy development. The Chinese do not expect to find a comprehensive external solution to domestic energy deficiency either in the loans and services of World Bank or in the larger pattern of international investment and technological transfer.

Perhaps it is ironic that during a period of relative isolation in the politically tumultuous years of the Cultural Revolution Chinese energy output annually grew by 9.2 per cent. The production of crude oil in particular climbed from 14.55 million tons in 1966 to 87.16 million tons in 1976. However, during the period subsequent to Mao's death, when the Party leadership enthusiastically committed itself in the long term to the 'policy of the open door', the coal and oil industries began to experience serious difficulties. Li Chengrui, Director of the State Statistical Bureau, has argued that the big increase in oil production during the Cultural Revolution was largely responsible for boosting the total product of society by an annual 6.8 per cent. However, he has also contended that, while the accelerated development of energy resources filliped the national economy through supplying more raw materials to the petrochemical industry and encouraging the development of light industry, national energy policy failed to achieve a rational balance between the extractions of established reserves and the generation of new reserves. Thus the energy dilemma, which assumed public policy significance at the time of 'national economic readjustment' in 1979 had originated with the accelerated exploitation of scarce resources during the 1960s.(62)

The imbalance within the energy sector was part of a larger deteriorating situation within the economy as a whole, which had been increasingly characterised by imbalances between heavy industry, light industry and agriculture. Generally, at the level of self-perception, the Chinese leadership had at least since 1958 emphasised a native Chinese as opposed to a Stalinist model of economic development. This model has many variables including an organisational emphasis on complex patterns of decentralisation and centralisation, an emphasis on 'industry serving agriculture', as well as on the carefully crafted dialectical interrelationship of the economic interests of the individual, the collective and the state. However, the June, 1979 decision calling for 'readjustment' revealed imbalances in the Chinese economy, which despite the reoccuring assertion of 'Maoist' themes in 1966-76 were suggestive of a Stalinist recidivism. The lop-sided development of heavy industry, for example was supposedly a Soviet and not a Chinese vice, but the June decision repudiated 'taking steel as the key link' and forced Chinese planners to return once again to the dialectically balanced reasoning of Mao's 'On the Ten Major Relationships'.(63)

In 1979 the targets for the 'four modernisations' were modestly re-stated. At the moment of China's entry into the qualitatively new world of international economic exchange, Chinese policy appeared to dredge up old revolutionary adages, such as 'self-reliance' and 'develop the economy and insure supplies'. In the financial emphasis on the accumulation of revenue through increases in production and in the conservative readjustment favouring production increases at existing facilities over the creation of new industry through extended capital investment, there were traces of the early 1950s conservative budgetary philosophy of leaders such as Chen Yun and

Bo Yibo, who had so decisively beaten back spiralling inflation.

The Second Session of the Fifth National People's Congress in June, 1979 adopted what some Western analysis might have to regard as a rarified position. The Chinese leadership claimed that the policies of 1977-8 had, instead of concentrating China's meagre resources to fight the classic guerrilla action or 'battle of annihilation' at one or two weak spots in the economy, impetuously unfurled the banner of the 'four modernisations' along an excessively 'long front' of capital construction.(64) The practical policy implications of such polemical metaphor were conveyed in the more pedestrian instructions of the State Council to shift from the earlier emphasis on 'extensive reproduction on an expanded scale' to 'intensive reproduction on an expanded scale'.(65) The government faced a serious national deficit which in 1979 totalled 17 billion yuan. It had earlier overspent in the purchase of complete sets of technology from abroad, and officials had paid too little attention to how the inpouring technologies would fit into China's relatively weak infrastructure characterised by communications and energy restraints.

The economic conservatism, which sustained 'readjustment' called for greater emphasis on the expansion of the latent potential of established enterprise as opposed to an emphasis on large-scale capital investment in new enterprise. The shopping-spree for complete technologies and turn-key projects was abruptly called off, and new policy emphases required a direct correlation of the scale of imports to China's ability to expand exports. NPC legislation attempted a more refined synthesis of 'self- reliance' and the 'open door'. The Law on Joint Ventures, The Income Tax Law of the PRC , the Regulations of the PRC on the Exploitation of Offshore Petroleum Resources in Co-operation with Foreign Enterprises all reflected the Chinese policy priority to insure that foreign participation in the Chinese economy would contribute to domestic development through training programmes, the use of the most advanced technology in joint enterprise, and the resort to domestic logistical and ancillary services by joint enterprise for supplies and raw materials.(66)

In the energy sector 'readjustment' ended the euphoria of 1977-8. The export of oil was important, but it was not an overnight panacea for the rapid acceleration of the total modernisation process. No one could pretend that China would achieve an annual production of 400 million tons of crude oil in the early 1980s, and throughout the whole of the energy sector the buzz word was 'conservation', as Chinese planning focused on the task of appropriately limiting the domestic use of crude oil while maintaining an annual output of approximately 100 million tons.

Officials' 'self-criticism' revealed that energy policy has been characterised by the 'unilateral pursuit of output' and a comcomitant 'irrational ratio' between established coal and oil outputs and the generation of new reserves. Impressive production gains at Daqing did not compensate for the fact that between 1965-79 the ratio between extraction at old sites and the development of new reserves dropped fourfold. The same story was essentially repeated with respect to coal. During the first Five Year Plan, 1951-5, the ratio between extraction at established sites and the generation of new reserves was 1:1, but by 1976-8 this healthy ratio declined to 3.18:2.(67)

In relation to 1979, total Chinese primary energy production in 1980 dropped by 1.3 per cent and a further 0.8 per cent in 1981. Aggregate electricity production continued to make very modest gains; however, the coal industry suffered a serious setback. While coal and crude oil production figures for 1980-1 showed a marked propensity for production decline, the figures for 1982-4 suggest a quicker recovery than Western analysis had anticipated. Coal production in 1981 declined to 620 million tons, or 2.4 per cent less than in 1980. In 1981 crude oil production declined to 105.95 million tons, or 0.2 per cent less than 1980. In 1982, crude oil production slumped to 102.12 million tons while coal production edged upwards to 666 million tons, a 7.1 percentage increase over 1981. In 1983 coal production moved beyond the 1979 figure to 715 million tons, or 7.4 per cent over 1982 production, while crude oil production rose to 106 million tons, or the highpoint of 1979.(68) By 1983 the Chinese had already achieved maximum production figures for coal and crude oil which had been originally set for 1985. The production of 114 million tons of crude oil and 770 million tons of coal belied gloomy Western predictions, and the Chinese became quite bullish as to their long-term prospects.(69) Hu Yaobang, the Party's Secretary-General, predicted that China's offshore wells alone will produce 150 million tons per annum by the end of the 1980s.(70)

The revivification of China's energy production has to be explained with reference to policy forumulation and execution. In the summer of 1980 energy policy was formulated as 'placing equal emphasis on development and conservation, with main efforts on the latter in the near future'. The tactical implications of 'self-reliance', namely, 'rely mainly on the existing foundation and fully tap the potentials', became explicit in the revisions to national energy policy. Earlier projections of oil production increases were scaled down, and the Chinese moved decisively to emphasise the industrial use of coal.

Coal took center stage as the backbone of the national energy programme. Oil remained as a critical component of the government's strategy to secure foreign exchange, but from within the new regime of 'readjustment' planners became much more involved in the systematic manipulation of the national energy mix for purposes of conserving oil in relation to other forms of energy. National planning highlighted technical renovation and'intensive reproduction', and a high budgetary priority was assigned to the shift from coal to oil-fired industrial plant. Of the 1303 energy-saving projects cited in the Sixth Five-Year Plan, 195 were listed as costing over ten million yuan each.(71)

While the conservation programme called for the saving of crude oil for export and for domestic refining, it also reflected a greater commitment to changes in the national energy mix which progressively gave greater weight to the exploitation of renewable resources. Unlike oil and coal production, there were still modest increases in annual electricity generation during the tough years of early 'readjustment'. National policy has stressed that where possible thermal electric generation is to be located at coal pitheads and that where possible hydro as opposed to thermal generating capacity will be increased. Revised planning priorities insisted upon a closer co-ordination to insure that thermal generation will be reduced during periods of heavy rainfall and greater hydro-generating capacity.(72) The planned seasonal adjustment of thermal electric peak loads was designed to facilitate conservation and the more efficient use of non-renewable coal reserves.

Hydro-generating capacity has steadily

increased, but it is still a scarce resource. In May, 1982, the State Council established fixed volumes of electricity for all provinces, municipalities and autonomous regions. The new regulations allowed the 'method of forced deduction' whereby any administration which attempted to exceed its quota would face either restriction or outright cessation of supply. Limits have also been imposed against high-energy consumers producing commodity-type electrolytic aluminium, pig iron and yellow phosphorus. Electricity was more generously supplied to priority industries whose products were high in quality and low in energy consumption and cost.(73)

The dimensions of conservation were clearly spelled out in Premier Zhao's December 1, 1981 government work report. The report required quotas for different products, the shutting down of energy-guzzling factories whose products did not meet significant social needs, the substitution of coal for oil and the technical improvement of production facilities. Zhao Ziyang described the annual burning off of 40 out of 106 million tons of oil for fuel as a 'shocking waste' of 'an immense item of wealth '. Zhao told those, who had pessimistically assumed that China's oil output would drop to the point where China would become an oil importer, that they were dead wrong. He summarised national energy policy: 'Our policy ... is to lay equal stress on exploiting energy resources and on practicing economy in its consumption, while giving priority to saving energy now and in the future.'(74)

Energy planning thus focused on the scheduled reduction of inefficient energy use as critical to the success of 'conservation'. The issue of ' conservation' is in fact intricately linked to the issue of 'development ' in that it requires greater technological innovation and the selective importation of advanced technology in order to reduce the excessively high rates of energy usage in industry. China's present energy utilisation rate is about 40 per cent lower than that of economically developed countries, and the current energy target for the year 2000 requires not only a doubling of total primary energy production, but also a 50 per cent reduction in energy consumption per one-per cent increase in the total output value of production.(75) As approximately 60 per cent of China's machines and technologies are still of 1940s and 1950s vintage, these long-term goals would seem to reinforce arguments in favour of the 'open door' and the consequent technical renovation of Chinese industry at least on the 'intensive' basis of purchase of selective technologies. Under 'readjustment', 'conservation' has encompassed a positive functional correlation between 'self-reliance' and the 'open door'.

The 'squeeze principle', which in the difficult years of 'readjustment' played such a prominent role in China's 'resource diplomacy', was largely dependent upon a more efficient energy utilisation rate in industry through technical renovation and the switch from oil to coal. As of November, 1980, the Chinese ceased to design new petroleum-fueled equipment. Although the 1982 rate of 1.9 tons of standard coal equivalent consumed per ton of steel is not regarded as satisfactory, there was in 1978-82 a 24 per cent reduction in energy consumption per ton of steel.(76) To promote conservation of coal and the replacement of inefficient coal boilers in industry the State Council introduced a strict system of rationing as of 1 January 1983. Enterprises draw their coal supplies against ration books, and once these are exhausted, they are either refused supplies, or they are forced to face higher prices for additional amounts of coal.(77)

As of late 1984 the State Economic Commission ordered its Energy Bureau to monitor the energy consumption of all factories which consume more than the equivalent of 50,000 tons of coal per annum.(78) Also, the Chinese expect that through conversion from oil to coal they will eventually achieve a saving of 20 million tons of petroleum per year. This will result in 7 to 8 billion yuan of direct income going to the state, not to mention the social benefits which are expected to originate with the production of finished petroleum products, as opposed to the burning off of such tonnage in industrial boilers and furnaces.(79) The Chinese are presently studying a number of ways to facilitate oil-to-coal conversion. A special oil-to-coal funding agency has, for example, financed techniques for the burning of coal-oil mixtures in cases where the conversion to coal has been difficult.(80)

One of the most significant policy components of the conservation programme relates to the state's political ability to manage residential energy consumption, particularly in the rural areas. The rural population relies on non-commercial energy sources for up to 80 per cent of daily household needs, and the state cannot, without jeopardising the present targets of energy planning, increase the supply of energy resources to the rural areas before the end of this century. The state has, therefore, continued to apply the principle of 'self-reliance' to the energy problems of the localities, placing a greater emphasis on the local mobilisation of capital and intermediate technologies as opposed to central investment in large-scale rural energy programmes.(81)

'Self-reliance' has historically sustained a multidimensional strategy which attempts to achieve simultaneous production increases at different levels of organisation. This response to China's economy, characterised by labour abundance and capital scarcity, represented an ideal attempt to bring together all positive factors in the economy through central investment in large-scale modern technology and local investment in intermediate technology. Small-scale enterprise of course was more labour intensive but less costly to start up. Politically, this strategic interrelationship of indigenous and external variables was summed up as 'walking on two legs', and its policy implications have been analysed in the research of Carl Riskin, Jon Sigurdson and the American Rural Small-Scale Industry Delegation.(82)

The terms of this strategy have been refined over time in response to political controversies over the correct application of the principle of 'self-reliance', but the related policy connotations such as 'local expediency' yindi zhiyi the 'strategy of combining large, medium and small' dazhonqxiao xiangjie di fangzhen have survived into the new era of the 'open door', particulary as national energy policy relates to the supply of residential energy requirements. While the 'development' half of the current energy policy requires state capital investment and foreign technological inputs in key large-scale energy and transportation projects, the 'conservation' half requires the continuing popularisation of small-scale energy technologies in the countryside.

The energy demands of China's vast rural population have thus far been largely met through local initiative in the development of both traditional and modern fuels. Presently, over 60 per cent of China's rural production brigades are supplied with electricity and roughly eleven per cent of national electricity supplies are consumed for household lighting and agricultural purposes.

(83) There are of course significant regional variations. The lowest rate of brigade electrification is to be found in the southwest where theoretically the hydro-electric potential is the greatest, whereas brigade electrification in the Northeast is the highest at 94.5 per cent compared to 46.9 per cent in the southwest.(84)

According to a 1983 estimate, 180 million tons of fire-wood and 223 million tons of vegetation, which together represent 220 million tons of standard coal equivalent, are burned off every year to meet rural household needs. (85) Contemporary policy recommends the increased use of fire-wood as opposed to the use of straw, as the uncontrolled consumption of the latter results in the reduced availability of fodder necessary to the production of organic fertiliser. On a lesser scale than is the case with fire-wood, the use of biogas has been encouraged as a cheap method of providing energy, which is not only hygienic but also linked to the inexpensive production of high-quality fertiliser byproducts.

To insure local energy requirements, cadres were instructed to adopt the strategy of 'suiting measures to local conditions, multiple energy sources supplementing each other, comprehensive utilisation and attention to practical results'.(86) This strategy recommends a complex energy mix whereby one or more energy forms are identified as the 'key link' and then supplemented with other energy resources in a multifaceted scheme to achieve comprehensive energy efficiency and sufficiency. The Chinese appear to have had some success in reducing rural energy costs; for example, a Chinese survey of peasant income and expenditure has indicated that, while in 1978 average expenditure for fuel was 8.28 yuan out of total yearly per capita consumer expenditure of 112.9 yuan, in 1982 fuel costs averaged 12.36 out of 215.23 yuan. Thus the share of fuel costs to total peasant consumer expenditure dropped from 7.14 to 5.61 per cent.(87)

The seriousness with which the State Council views the problems of planned rural energy development is manifest in the 19 May 1984 creation of a rural energy leading group, headed by Vice-Premier Li Peng and supported by the China Rural Development Research Centre. Chinese planning is becoming more attuned to the pressures of rural demography and the energy requirements of agricultural mechanisation. Under 'readjustment', for example, stress on conservation has led to some criticism of the lop-sided use of foreign methods requiring 'oil-based agriculture'. Referring to the importance of 'local expediency', some Chinese energy experts have contended that the continued use of small tractors and draft animals would be preferable to the use of oil-consuming machinery in hilly and mountainous areas. The same emerging conservatism militates against the heavy, exclusive use of chemical fertilisers, which not only require greater oil consumption, but also pose a threat to soil fertility.(88)

National energy policy also reflects the continuing emphasis on the simultaneous development of 'large, medium and small' enterprise. While rural industrialisation is commonly regarded as a signficant approach to raising the standard of living in the hinterland, small-scale production has often been singled out by Western critics as inferior. It appears, however, that such technologically backward production is necessary to economic growth and the conservation of scarce energy resoures, for it frees the state to concentrate more efficiently on large-scale production.

The small coal mine, for example, continues to play a positive role not only in sustaining and bolstering national production, but also in addressing the difficulties of social and economic transition in the countryside. With the movement of significant numbers of rural peasantry away from agriculture, which is becoming more efficient due to rural economic reform, coal mines will help soak up some of the underutilised labour in the countryside. China's labour policy has been brought into line with energy policy emphasising the development and expansion of the small mines so that peasants may more freely enter these mines under contract.(89)

In 1983 the State Council approved measures to accelerate the growth of the small mines. Re-tooling of some of these mines was an inexpensive means of achieving an additional 23.3 million tons of coal production. The contribution of the small mines is not viewed as a temporary palliative. In 1982, 22,000 small mines produced 146 million tons or 20 per cent of national production. With the 1983 measures the number of small mines climbed to approximately 40,200, and these produced 169 million tons of coal, or approximately 25 per cent of national production. In 1984, foreign-financed, large, new operations were responsible for an aggregate production of 25 million tons.(90)

Mechanised operations only account for 40 per cent of national output, and while there is a long-term planning commitment to develop more open-pit mining, 96 per cent of China's current production comes from underground operations.(91) Despite plans to increase mechanisation and develop large open-pit mines, it is estimated that by the year 2000 open-pit production will only account for one-sixth of the projected estimate of 1.2 billion tons. It is estimated that at this time small-scale production will produce 500 million tons or approximately 40 per cent of the total.(92)

Surprisingly, the local mines of Shanxi's Datong region act as one of the main sources of supply to Japan. This factor was raised in the negotiations which led up to the signing of the 23 September 1982 memorandum adjusting the terms of the LTA. The Japanese were unhappy with such coal exports due to local variations in sulfur content and ash melting rate.(93)

Not only coal production, but also hydro-electric generation has been organised on the basis of 'combining large, medium and small'. In response to the Party's call for the quadrupling of agricultural and industrial output by the year 2,000, the Party group within the Ministry of Water Resources and Electric Power identified the following key question for study: 'How to build more power stations with less investment, and how to substantially shorten project construction periods?'(94) The Party group insisted on an allocation of capital resources which would insure the more rational siting of large hydro-electric stations 'along successive river sections as opposed to arbitrary siting at separate spots'.

The central government has carefully husbanded its capital to invest in several large-scale key projects such as the largest hydro-electric facility in the country at Gezhouba. Even at Gezhouba there has been a policy stress on 'rely mainly on our own efforts and regard foreign aid as subsidiary'. With the exception of some imported heavy-duty trucks, bulldozers and excavators, most equipment was China-made, and the project was entirely designed by Chinese engineers and technicians.(95) However, 1,100 out of China's approximately 2,000 counties have small-scale hydropower stations, each capable of generating over 10,000 kilowatts, and ideally these units are to adhere to a policy of 'self-construction, self-management and self-use'. (96) Sixty per cent of the funding for such units is

(96) Sixty per cent of the funding for such units is raised locally. Generally, these units are owned by the brigades and the electricity produced is to serve the specific brigades and townships involved and not the large power grids, which service the larger industrial centres. 'Combining large, medium and small' was endorsed in a national power industry conference in 1983 which set out five principles: 'exploit hydro-electric potential...; accelerate the construction of thermal power plants in coal mining areas; develop nuclear power stations in a proper way; develop power grids in a big way, and develop small hydro-electric stations and tap other energy resources in rural areas according to local conditions'.(97)

Western research has drawn attention to Chinese attempts to create positive organisational linkages between 'large, medium and small'. Such a complex strategy has posed difficulties of interfacial rationalisation between different levels of administrative organisation and technological expertise. Ideally, this strategy allows greater flexibility in the design of a more rational energy mix which, with minimal investment, will serve to alleviate rural energy deficiencies, but the Chinese have traditionally emphasised that such 'walking on two legs' must be qualifiied with important reference to 'unified management' under state planning. 'Self-reliance' cannot be rationally oppposed to the cost efficient regional division of labour necessary to the effective generation of energy. Chinese planning has sought to avoid the problems of 'large and complete and small and complete' which have so adversely affected the industrial division of labour in other sectors of the economy.

In the transmission of electric power, for example, 'unified management' is asserted against irrational exchanges between large and small hydro-electric grids. Cadre rectification has focused on small-scale units which produce surplus electricity in the rainy season. Such seasonal small-grid transmissions to surfeited larger regional grids often forced the latter to reduce their own capacities. Whereas in the dry season, the small grids suffering from accutely diminished reservoir capacity apparently made urgent and irrational demands on the larger grids which had to repay earlier rainy-season transmissions with more expensive thermoelectricity.(98)

Chinese planning has, therefore, earmarked the

improvement from within an integrated scheme which measures the local strengths and weaknesses of hydro and thermal electric generation. While 'self-construction, self-management and self-use' are emphasised with reference to 'objective' local conditions, 'unified management' is viewed as necessary to the rational, rather than random, local exploitation of the water systems.

In coal-deficient areas, the small thermoelectric power station is regarded as a liability as it not only consumes two to three times the coal used per unit of production at the larger thermoelectric stations, but it also incurs higher costs due to the shipment of coal over long distances. Under these circumstances 'unified management' finds small-scale hydro-electric generation to be more cost efficient. Although the number of years for the recovery of investment in a small-scale hydro-electric plant with an effective reservoir regulation capacity may be approximately the same as the time needed to recover investment in a new medium-scale thermoelectric plant, Chinese planning tends to favour the former over the latter, as the latter's long-term operating costs are considered to be higher.(99)

Under 'readjustment' the themes of 'self-reliance' and 'conservation' became explicit in the organizational strategy of 'combining large, medium and small'; however, in pursuit of 'development' the Chinese also responded to the possibilities of greater foreign capital investment and technological transfer, which is expected to facilitate the cost effective generation of energy. While 'readjustment' has generally called for the 'tapping of existing potentials', the energy and transportation sectors (and the latter is especially important to the delivery of new reserves) have been favoured in the state allocation of funding for 'development'. In order to redress the declining ratio of resource extraction to the generation of new reserves, these sectors were given greater privileged access to meagre central capital resources. Zhao Ziyang in his 1982 report on the Sixth Five Year Plan insisted that, while these sectors were pivotal to the development of the national economy as a whole, they were in fact the 'two weakest links in our national economy'.(100) Zhao reported that the 890 large and medium-sized construction projects in the plan included energy and transportation projects which accounted for 38.5 per cent of the total capital construction budget of

per cent of the total capital construction budget of 230 billion yuan. This percentage included 17.9 billion yuan for the development of 28 large coalfields, as well as another 15.4 billion yuan for investment in the petroleum construction industry. The latter included provisions for the exploration of the Sungliao Basin, the Bohai Gulf, the Puyang area of Henan, the Erlian Basin of Inner Mongolia as well as increased funding for the surveying and exploration of Xinjiang's Junggar Basin, Qinghai's Qaidam Basin and the older gas and oil fields of east China. The plan also allocated 20.7 billion yuan for the continued development of the hydro-electric resources of the upper Yellow River, the middle and upper Yangtze River and the Hongshui Basin, the construction of several large-scale hydro-electric stations and the construction of pit-mouth stations in Shansi, eastern Inner Mongolia, the Huaibei-Huainan area, west Henan, Weibei and Guizhou and the high energy consuming areas of Liaoning, Shanghai, Jiangsu, Zhejiang, Guangdong and Sichuan.(101)

In 1984, 79 of China's 123 top-priority construction projects were listed as in the energy and transportation sectors. This list was inclusive of 14 coal mines with a total annual production capacity of 89.59 million tons, 26 power generating projects capable of producing 15.17 million kilowatts, and six petroleum projects which are to add 7.7 million tons to the annual production of crude oil.(102)

Within the energy sector the emphasis on 'readjustment' and organisational reform has been progressively linked to economic reform measures calling for more rational pricing, (a point which the World Bank has emphasised in its recommendations), the introduction of contractual economic relationships between enterprise and production units and a responsibility system. This system, with its decentralised emphasis on unit responsibility for profits and losses, attempts to conform to the larger tendency favouring 'economic' as opposed to 'administrative' control over industrial enterprise. The pattern of decentralisation is expected to vary significantly throughout the energy sector, but there is a general mandate for the gradual transformation of companies into 'economic entities'.

In responding to the Party leadership's goal of 'doubling of output to insure a quadruple output', or doubling national energy output to insure a quadrupling of agricultural and industrial output by the year 2000, the Minister of the Coal Industry, Gao Yangwen, in October, 1983 insisted that the coal industry would have to be more flexibly managed.(103) This meant a further relaxation of policy towards small-scale coal mining in the localities and a further implementation of systems of economic responsibility. The concurrent decentralisation and economic reform is, for example, being applied in some of the state-owned large mines such as the Dongmei Company and Anhui Coal Industry Company, which are to be transformed from administrative organs into 'economic entities' responsible for their own profits and losses.(104)

During a rectification meeting of the leading party groups of the Ministries of Communications, the Petroleum Industry, Water Conservancy and Electric Power, the Party Secretary-General, Hu Yaobang, addressed the problems of lingering 'leftism' and outlined the interrelated factors of national energy policy. In calling for the opening of more channels to raise funds for energy development, Hu criticised 'the traditional practice of power departments' which hitherto had refused to involve regions and departmental units in their operations. Hu instructed party cadres 'to fully arouse the initiative of various regions, departments and units in building big, medium and small power stations through the concerted efforts of the state, enterprises, collectives and individuals'.(105) Hu Yaobang also emphasised the deployment of local funds in energy development particularly in the industrially strong regions of the east coast. He encouraged these energy deficient areas to invest in the resource rich hinterland and to participate in joint ventures in 'conducting energy development and producing energy-intensive products'.

The state has ambitious plans for increasing energy production, but it has insufficient funds to insure the planned rate of development. While the state has established an energy development fund, it is focusing more intensely on the 'self-reliant' capacity of the energy industry at the local level. 'Conservation' is reinforced through taxes levied on the use of limited energy supplies in some areas of production, and the Party is even considering the issuance of 'energy development shares' among the peasants to encourage their participation in private investment. The evolving strategy in the energy sector extends the historical emphasis on 'combining large, medium and small', but it is also breaking new ground in encouraging contractual relations between industrial users and energy producers. The President of the China Energy Research Society, Lin Hanxiong, succinctly summed up the necessity of such an approach: 'In the past, funds for energy development were borne by the state. It seems that this method can no longer raise sufficient funds for energy development.'(106) Lin concluded:

> Therefore, it is necessary to adopt suitable policies to ensure reasonable returns for the investors and to decide on reasonable methods of distributing products and to calculate output value to inspire the localities enthusiasm.(107)

In 1983 the central government invested 470 million yuan in local mines, while local authorities raised another 700 million yuan. In the energy deficient areas of Zhejiang and Jiangsu alone, enterprises raised 360 million yuan to invest in the Shanxi mines over a three year period in return for the supply of 18 million tons of coal over ten years.(108)

In his meeting with the party groups in the energy ministries, Hu Yaobang urged the transfer of 'enterprises in a pure sense' to 'key cities' where they would become 'real economic entities'. He further instructed that development should be accelerated through the use of foreign funds. Hu intended to solve the transportation difficulties in the energy sector through a shake-up of the communications management system:

> ...it is necessary to institute multiple management and encourage competition allowing all departments, trades and professions, and localities to vie with each other in using state run, collectively owned, or private transportation vehicles.(109)

The Ministry of Communications was thus obliged to transfer control of some of its enterprises to municipal governments.

In the area of capital construction energy policy tends to reflect the larger trends towards enhanced economic responsibility and administrative decentralisation. The Ministry of Water Resources and Electric Power, for example, is reforming its traditional system of funding allocation, which had failed to make allowances for interest payments or price increases during periods of capital construction. New projects, funded on a reformed basis, are to be kept on a strict schedule through a system of financial sanctions. Hydropower construction companies, which assume the status of independent economic accounting units will thus incur interest penalties in the event of construction postponements.

In this more complex environment of administrative decentralisation and economic reform, the State Planning Commission must struggle to insure a positive interface between centrally funded construction projects and a host of local projects which may compete for control of the same resource potential. In the early 1980s, for example, the central government focused on the 'maximising' function of economic centres and the transfer of key projects to the major cities; however, more recently there has been a swing back to an emphasis on 'unified planning.'(110) In his government work report of 27 March 1985, Zhao Ziyang warned the major cities against 'blindly pursuing a higher rate of development' without regard for the limitations of infrastructure in energy and transportation. In the following excerpt from his report Zhao advises against a focus on the 'quadrupling' of the value of industrial output:

> Even if, with strenuous exertion, an excessively high rate of development were attained...this rate would be difficult to maintain due to an inadequately developed infrastructure especially in energy and transport... This would severely damage the entire economy. ...major cities have the important task of supporting national or regional economic construction in many respects. They should not focus on quadupling their industrial output value, but should do more to rationalise the structure of production, promote socialised production, accelerate technological progress and vigorously develop the tertiary industries...(111)

Central planners have warned against the proliferation of local projects outside the state plan. The state, in other words, has to be protected against bad business ventures which have resulted in shortages of building supplies and rising prices. Projects, using self-collected funds and bank loans, which have resulted in such consequences, are pejoratively called the 'two runaway horses'.(112)

Central planning, inspired by the stock notion of 'taking the whole country as a single chessboard', quanguo yibanqi, must ideally seek a balance between 'self-reliance' and 'unified management'.(113) Under the former such planning must exploit the differences in the natural economic conditions of China's several regions, emphasising 'the fullest utilisation of the strong points of the localities', but under the latter it must foster a cost efficient division of labour between economically interdependent regions. The simultaneous, comprehensive economic development of the several regions is not possible given the variations in natural conditions and economic history. As is particularly the case with the distribution of energy resources, China's natural resources map in significant instances fails to correspond with the map of industrial development. Uneven patterns of industrialisation and urbanisation have consistently favoured the economic development of the east, northeast and northern regions. Figure 1.2 indicating major coal-producing areas and Figure 1.3 indicating major land-based oil and gas fields demonstrate this traditional bias. The same appears to hold true for Figure 1.4 which indicates the distribution of all key capital construction projects in 1984.

An heavy emphasis on offshore development along China's east coast is certainly a very positive aspect in the overall scheme to exchange natural resources for foreign capital and technology; however, it may reinforce the uneven east-west axis in national economic development. The recent willingness on the part of the Chinese government to introduce foreign capital and technology into hinterland energy development is important for long-term economic development, especially given the inevitable decline at established oil fields in the northeast and north of China.

There is a central problem of spatial equity that originates in a 'readjustment' strategy that tends to favour central investment in key capital construction and practice of local 'self- reliance' under a regime of scarcity in the far western hinterland. There is the danger of proportional imbalances within and between regions and the national energy programme is part of this planning

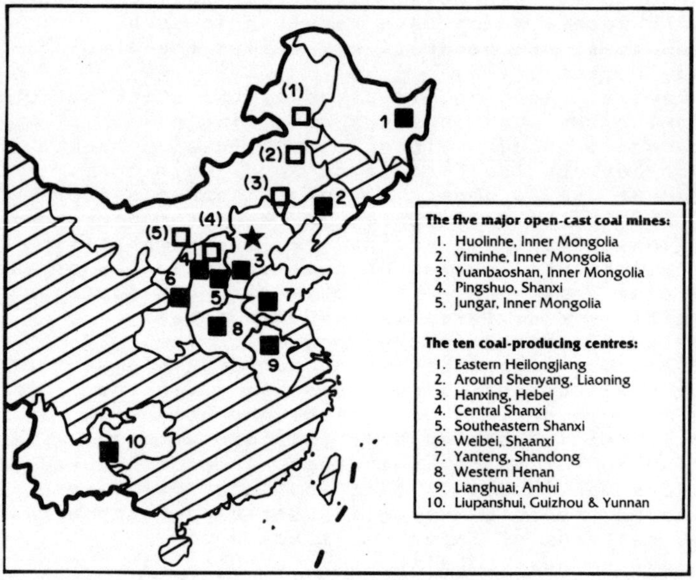

Figure 1.2: China's Major Coal-Producing Centres

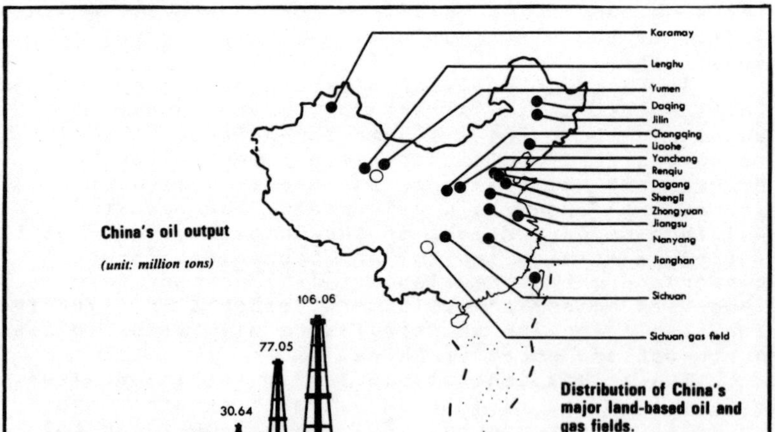

Figure 1.3: The Distribution of China's Major Land-Based Oil and Gas Fields.

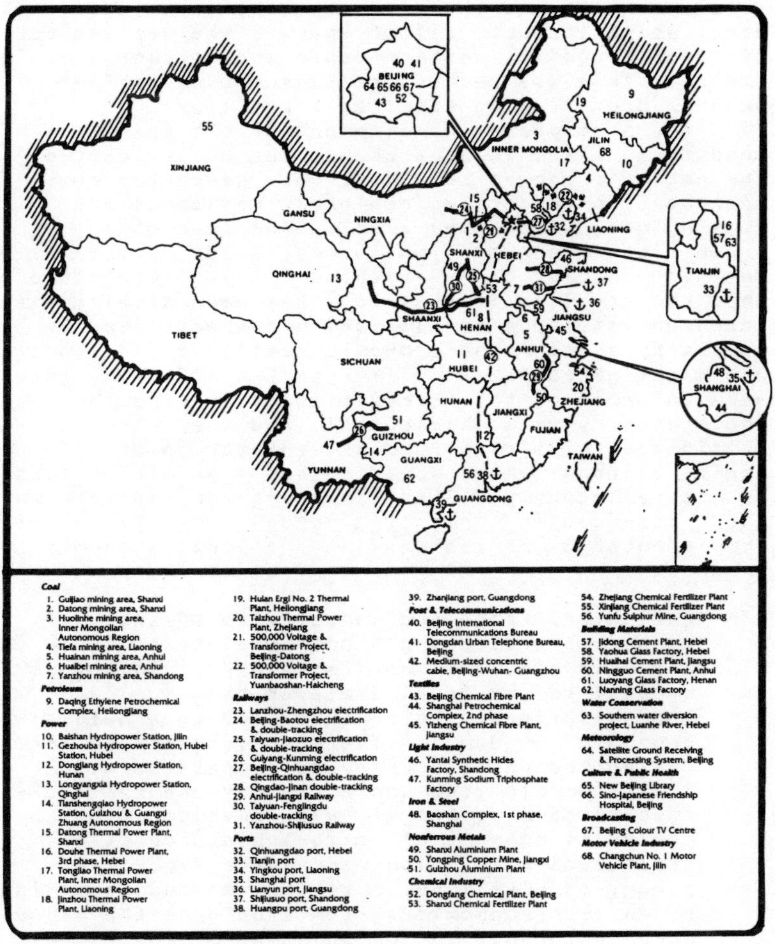

Figure 1.4: The Distribution of China's Key Capital Construction Projects

dilemma. There was, for example, serious debate over planning objectives in relation to the development of the Shanxi energy-chemical-industrial base, which includes all of Shanxi, the western part of Inner Mongolia, western Henan and northern Shanxi. This was perhaps reminiscent of earlier debates over 'taking steel as a key link'.

The accelerated development of the Shanxi industrial base, which accounts for 60 per cent of the nation's proven coal reserves, generated some apprehension concerning regional imbalances and 'taking coal as the key link'. The fear of proportional economic imbalances, based on the one-sided notion of 'everything falling into place once the key link is grasped', has been dismissed as inappropriate to a new situation characterised by the Party's new found economic realism.(114) Those who highlighted Shanxi's 'low self-sufficiency rate' were informed of the necessities of 'taking the whole country as a chessboard', and they were criticised for a distorted interpretation of 'self-reliance' which would foster a primitive form of natural economy. Shanxi's energy development was then presented in terms of a mutually beneficial complementarity of regional and national economic interests:

> Were every trade and industry to advance evenly, practice small but complete or large and complete...we most certainly would not be brought to the ideal state of the four modernisations. This would lead to a natural economic kingdom... Therefore, adherence to taking the whole country as a chessboard, Shanxi helping the whole country and the whole country helping Shanxi, with development of a commodity economy of large-scale production, great coal production, and large exports of energy to give impetus to the rational building of an open economic system should be the major guiding thought in the building of energy, heavy industry and chemical industrial bases.(115)

This rebuttal suggests the need to accommodate an emphasis on 'self-reliance' with emphases on the importance of an 'open economy' and a 'commodity economy' in the relations between regions. The pursuit of 'combining large, medium and small' is still necessary to the planned coal production of Shanxi, and in this there is an element of 'local expediency'. But on the level of comprehensive regional economic development, there is an emphasis on maximising Shanxi's special economic conditions within the framework of a national division of labour which expects the rational exchange of goods and services between regions. That the independent economic relations of China's several regions are to be more vigorously pursued on the basis of a law of value, within the central government's planning, suggests the extent to which 'readjustment' in the national energy sector has become progressively associated with the wider process of economic reform.

The planned resolution of conflicting priorities, expressed in principles such as 'taking the wole country as a single chessboard' and 'local expediency', is to take place at different levels and in different areas of energy development. Levels of decentralisation and 'unified management' will vary, but there is the central premise of positive interdependence such as in 'Shanxi helping the whole country, and the whole country helping Shanxi'.

In the planned generation and transmission of electricity, for example, Chinese planning has begun to stress the necessity of national interrelationships between the several large regional electricity grids. The Northwestern regional grid is awash with water resources and is comparatively more self-sufficient, while neighbouring grids in central, north and southwest China have been more regularly exposed to seasonal shortages in the transmission of electricity.

Officials in the Northwest have of course stressed their region's stable hydro-electric capability and the necessity of their 'transmitting electricity across zones for the benefit of the whole country'. Their argument focuses on the co-ordinated development of coal mining and thermal generation. It follows that with greater investment in Northwestern coal mines that there will be less need for the expensive transportation of coal to the Northwest for thermal generation. The argument further suggests that, while Northwestern cross-regional transmissions of electricity can be increased, industries which have a high energy consumption capacity, such as electric-furnace steel production and electrolytic aluminium production could be transferred to the Northwest from the coal and power deficient localities in other regions of China.(116)

The long-term development of China's energy resources, based upon a positive ratio of resource extraction to reserve creation would appear to depend upon a political commitment to develop the rich resources of the hinterland in the northwest and southwest.

The strategic emphasis in energy policy has thus far largely conformed to the historical economic map of China, and the weight of foreign investment has also conformed to that map. Foreign investment, for example has focused on the offshore oil potential of the Bohai Gulf, the Pearl River Delta, off Shanghai in the East China Sea and in the Beibu Gulf and Yinggehai areas. World Bank loans are now in place for the technological reinforcement of enhanced recover at Daqing and the development of the Wenliu fields of Zhongyuan. Since the late 1970s, the Japanese have become progressively involved in the Bohai Gulf and in many other projects in several regions of China. Occidental has more recently become involved in a significant way in the Shanxi energy-chemical-industrial base. There is, however, a growing foreign interest in the oil and gas resources of the Junggar, Erliau and Tsaidam Basins and the Chinese appear to be moving toward a dual strategy which would more rationally capitalise on the contemporaneous development of new onshore oil reserves. The development of the hinterland is bound to be an expensive and relatively slow process given the extensive nature of regional transportation and communications problems. The future potential production of the hinterland should not, however, be overlooked in the long-term calculation of Chinese ability to meet growing domestic requirements of modernisation and export commitments.

Even within the context of China's industrially advanced areas, existing infrastructure has been overtaxed. For example, in 1984 coal transportation, which has yet to facilitate all the demands of the coastal industrial areas, swallowed up 43 per cent of national railway capacity and 47 per cent of national water transport capacity.(117) The Japanese were anxious during the 1982 negotiations concerning the long-term supply of Chinese coal and sought re-assurances from the Chinese that they would more closely co-ordinate coal development, transportation and trade. Both sides agreed to earmark a large portion of the Japanese yen credit (worth two billion US dollars) for upgrading the capacity of the Datong-Beijing and

Beijing-Qinhuangdao railroads, as well as for expanding terminal capacity at Qinhuangdao Port and second-phase railway construction such as double-tracking.(118) The Chinese claim that with the 1987 inauguration of their first special doubletrack electrified line from Datong to Qinhuangdao they will acquire an extra capacity of 100 million tons. Shanxi's governor has optimistically predicted that by 1990 the Shanxi railway system will be able to handle an annual capacity of 400 million tons.(119)

The problem of transportation surfaced again during the difficult negotiations with Occidental Petroleum for the development of the world's largest open-pit mining area at Pingshun. Occidental was concerned about declining coal prices and possible bottlenecks in the Shanxi transportation system. They reportedly attempted to get the Chinese to guarantee any difference in foreign exchange earnings should they drop below expected revenue levels which were to be generated by the export of 50 per cent of the coal from proposed mining at Antaibao.(120) The 30 year Sino-American joint venture to develop China's largest opencut coal mine was not signed until 29 June 1985.

While the level of foreign participation in energy projects was somewhat restricted in the hard years of 'readjustment', over the last few years even while central aspects of the 'readjustment' policy have been continued, the rate of foreign participation has improved together with the rate of economic growth. According to the China International Trust and Investment Corporation a target of US $6 billion was originally set for the Sixth Five-Year Plan of 1981-5; however as of 1984 the figure of US $8 billion was reached due to an upward spiral of foreign investment which is reflected in the increased formation of joint ventures. Between May 1980 and December 1982, 83 such ventures were formed; and, between January, 1983 and June 1984, 279 ventures were established. (121)

Between 1979 and June, 1984, the PRC used US $15.8 billion in foreign funds. The larger proportion of this amount, US $12.5 billion, originated with loans from foreign governments, international financial organisations and buyers' credit loans. Direct investment by foreign firms including joint ventures, co-operative production and exploration enterprise accounted for US $3.3 billion.(122) During the hard years of 'readjustment', foreign companies invested US $490 million in the exploration of Chinese off-shore resources, and in fact the Chinese government in this period was slow to commit credits which had been extended for offshore development and exploration.(123) During the Sixth Five Year Plan, 1981-5, the central government put aside approximately one-fourth of all capital investment funds or approximately 610 billion yuan for energy exploitation.

While foreign investment has been a definite advantage, it is still 'supplementary' or subsidiary to the domestic effort based upon the policies of 'readjustment' and economic reform, as these relate to a national energy policy summed up in 'placing equal emphasis on development and conservation with main efforts on the latter in the near future'.

'Self-reliance' underlies the theme of 'conservation', and local funding and supply are still basic to the Chinese approach to rural energy deficiency. 'Readjustment' has required the careful husbanding of central capital resources, the selective approach to project development and 'unified management' in planning which insures the rational 'combining of large, medium and small', while current emphases on economic reform call for new contractual relations, creative funding techniques between consumers and producers and the cost efficient organisation of capital construction.

CONCLUSIONS

China's response to the international energy crises of the 1970s reflected her position as a developing country with a potentially strong resource base. The Chinese must 'sustain a huge growing population' and they must achieve 'a self-supporting capability for continuous economic growth on the basis of a comparatively low level of development. The complexity of the Chinese response to this 'low level of development' is understood in the 'equal emphasis' given to 'conservation' and 'development' in national energy policy. The Chinese approach is a multidimensional synthesis which operates at different levels of organisational response. The conscious synthesis of the 'open door' and 'self-reliance', for example, endorses the rational substitution of labour for capital at the local levels, but it also welcomes any advanced external inputs favouring the generation of modern energy technology and energy efficient industrial machinery within China.

The energy production figures for 1983-4 suggest that Western projections of China's primary energy production, which perhaps overestimated the intractable nature of Chinese energy difficulties and underestimated the effect of 'readjustment', were somewhat misleading. In the hard years of 'readjustment', 1979-82, the Chinese demonstrated policy ingenuity in manipulating the national energy mix, a disciplined approach to 'conservation' and 'development' and political resolve in maintaining modest levels of crude oil exports. In future, as they move towards the dual strategy of development of both off-shore and hinterland new reserves, they will undoubtedly make more effective use of foreign capital and technology, and the 'squeeze principle' of the early 1980s may no longer be necessary, for the Chinese will likely be in a more positive position to create a genuine export surplus.

Those, who in the late 1970s speculated that China would in very short order become a 'Second Saudi Arabia' were misinformed; however, this is not to gainsay the fact that China is indeed blessed with an abundance of natural resource riches, which the Chinese have only very recently begun to exploit in a systematic and technologically sophisticated way. Potentially oil-bearing sedimentary layers, for example, account for a total of 4.2 million square kilometres of China's onshore territory. Two-thirds of this area has hardly been seriously surveyed and explored. Also, offshore oil reserves are likely to be discovered in over one million square kilometres of China's continental shelf.(124)

The Chinese have had to cope with a historical pattern of capital scarcity and significant demographic pressure. However, even without the benefit of a significant and sustained programme based upon foreign capital and technology and despite serious political upheavals, the Chinese have in the past met these liabilities with organisational creativity, which more recently has encompassed significant economic reform. The Chinese, themselves, are quite aware of the difficulties which lie head. They can only in the short-term arrest declining oil production in the Northeast. The major industrial centres in East China will have to be increasingly supplied by new offshore and hinterland oil reserves as future energy production centres move westward. A recent research report, 'China by 2000', which summarised the findings of a research programme backed by the

State Council and the Chinese Academy of Social Sciences recommends the installation of more petroleum-processing facilities in central, south and southwest China, the increased transmission of thermal and hydro-electric power from north and central China to the east and northeast, the expansion of hydro-electric and nuclear power capacities and further economic reform to rationalise pricing and to generate local investment in energy development.(125) There are signs of continuing dispute over economic policy, but the PRC is currently enjoying a period of relatively stable political leadership. 'Readjustment' has been declared a success and has been extended with modifications to the 1990s. There is a greater predispostion to further the domestic process of economic reform and to encourage a larger pattern of foreign involvement in the energy sector.

The progressive development of the national energy structure within the overall context of the 'four modernisations' will be accompanied by an evolution in China's 'resource diplomacy', as well as by changes in the East Asian energy trade. In a regional context, marked by significant variations in national energy dependence, a modernised Chinese economy with an exportable energy surplus may react against the logistical implications of the Soviet 'dumb-bell strategy'; however, with the strengthening of bilateralism under 'independent foreign policy' not only Sino-American, but Sino-Soviet economic ties may expand considerably. The Chinese have continued to emphasise 'the three obstacles' to Sino-Soviet normalisation, but they have also downgraded the Soviet threat in the East Asia-Pacific region in a re-evaluation of the global 'balance of forces' which stresses the comparative improvement of the US military position under the Reagan administration, and one should not dismiss the possibility of expanded Soviet involvement in Chinese energy projects.(126) Also, a modernising China may progressively challenge the energy deficient, but strongly performing economies of Japan, South Korea, Singapore and Taiwan for a greater share of international markets.

Chinese involvement in the regional energy trade may affect the interests of traditional suppliers of raw materials and energy. China's export potential in coal, for example, became the subject of controversy during the recent negotiation of Occidental's involvement in Shanxi, as questions were raised within the Reagan administration as to whether it would indeed be appropriate to sell advanced mining technology to the competitive Chinese, so that they could in future dramatically increase their coal exports at the expense of US interests.(127)

The prospect not only of increases in China's energy exports, but also of an expanded trading position resulting from the success of the 'four modernisations', has some ASEAN interests worried over the possible flooding of their traditional markets with cheap Chinese products. From within ESCAP and elsewhere, the Chinese have attempted to assuage such anxiety by arguing that their primary concern is filling the needs of their own very large consumer markets and that new production resultiing from the 'four modernisations' will for the most part be internally oriented.

While there may indeed be some prospect for competition, particularly as Chinese policy insists upon paying for expanded technological imports through compensatory trade or expanded exports, there is also the attractive opportunity of investing in the Chinese modernisation process; for example, the Malaysian Foreign Minister Tan Sri Ghazali Shafie, during discussions with Hu Yaobang in May, 1984, indicated Malaysia's desire to become involved in Chinese modernisation. The visit resulted in the signing of a letter of intent to build an international trade centre in Beijing and was followed up by the Chinese awarding the Malaysian Overseas Investment Corporation a US $690 million turnkey project for the development of integrated rubber and timber plants in Xiamen.(128) These headlines may help to explain the subsequent positioning of the Indonesian Foreign Minister who urged Indonesia's parliament to open direct trade links with China.(129)

The Malaysians, themselves, however, were not entirely convinced of the benign nature of Chinese modernisation. In fact the Malaysian Prime Minister, Mahathir bin Mohammed, during the July 1984 visit of US Secretary of State Shultz, categorically rejected American arguments to the effect that an economically strong China would serve the interests of world peace. The Malaysian Prime Minister insisted that an economically strong China would be 'equally a militarily strong China, which could then revert to the politics of hegemony, which from a historical perspective in this part of the world has always been found to be a serious concern'.(130)

Japan, Singapore and the United States have traditionally been key export markets for both Indonesian and Malaysian crude oil, and these countries may face the implications of increased Chinese exports.(131) The prospect for their involvement in China's economic modernisation may be commercially alluring; however, these countries are obviously ambivalent, if not hostile, to the strategic implications of China's 'four modernisations'.

In so far as foreign involvement in Chinese economic modernisation is concerned, Japan has an obvious edge. Despite the revisions to the scheduling of Chinese oil and coal exports, the LTA has been a relatively successful vehicle for the exchange of Chinese resources for Japanese capital and technology. Japanese success was perhaps confirmed in the late 1982 warning of the US State and Commerce Departments against Chinese favouritism towards Japan in the bidding for Bohai Bay offshore oil concessions.(132)

Even in Japan there is the occasional anxious expression of concern regarding the future role of a modern, energy rich Chinese economy in the East Asian region. An editorial in the Japan Economic Journal, for example, speculated that with China's likely emergence as the world's 'No. 2 Oil Power' the existing regional markets of Indonesia, Malaysia, Brunei, Thailand, Australia and New Zealand would be threatened.(133) The editorial joined issue with those who would become so heavily involved in Chinese resource development without a more deliberate consideration of the future strategic consequences for Japan and other states in the Pacific area.

China's future status as 'No. 2' is obviously very controversial; however, even assuming that the Journal's analysis is correct in its assumption that the Chinese will raise daily crude oil production from the present figure of two million barrels a day to three million barrels a day, one cannot assume that other producers in the region will stand still in their efforts to improve upon production.

The recent record of 'readjustment' and 'economic reform' suggests that the Chinese do have the political and organisational ability to achieve a larger pattern of national energy development even in the face of demographic pressure and rural energy deficiency. They have consciously made use of 'strong points' such as labour abundance, the lower cost of living and rich natural resources in order to enter the international market place. Such 'strong points' are deliberately manipulated to compensate for 'weak points', such as the 'lack of funds, and a low level of technology and management skills'. 'Self-reliance' has, despite the conservatism of 'readjustment', been functionally combined with the 'open door' in order to gain foreign exchange and technology through the export of natural resources. While foreign capital and technology are concentrated at key points in the energy and transportation sectors, the Chinese can be expected to continue to develop labour-intensive, small-scale industries in the rural areas.

In such a context the important example of the Sino-Japanese LTA stands out. The Japanese remain fearful of Soviet strategic intentions in the Pacific and still need to diversify their energy sources away from the Middle East. Also, participation in China's 'four modernisations' may provide a hedge against growing protectionist trends in the West; although one might expect strenuous efforts to prevent protectionism from fundamentally disrupting the Japanese-American security arrangement.

The LTA has demonstrated the Chinese ability to structure a relatively rational symmetry between the domestic requirements of the 'four modernisations' and the regional dictates of 'resource diplomacy'. However, the Chinese in manipulating their 'strong points' against their 'weak points' are not interested in creating a structure of dependence. The current policy allowing greater emphasis on the export of coal, crude oil and light industrial and agricultural goods is regarded as consistent with 'self-reliance' in so far as it facilitates the creation of a comprehensive industrial base within China. Hence, the Chinese are interested in exploring horizontal forms of co-operation, such as co-operative production and operations and the transfer of the most advanced technology in such a way as to obviate any tendencies toward a vertical structure of trade which would force China into the permanent role of raw materials exporter. 'Self-reliance', as it remains explicit in a strong notion of independence and national security, insists that even in the context of greater participation in international exchange, there must be a greater emphasis on the domestic as opposed to the international market, and there must be a relative degree of security against the fluctuations of the international market-place.

NOTES

1. See Luo Hongda, '_Tantan Woguodi nengyuan zhengce_', (Talks on national energy policy) in _Nengyuan_ (Beijing), No. 1, (1982), p. 1.

2. Deng Xiaoping, _Deng Xiaoping wenxuan_, (Deng Xiaoping's selected works), (Renminchubanshe, Beijing, 1983), p. 370.

3. For further discussion of 'self-reliance' and the 'open door' refer to Ronald C. Keith, 'China's Modernisation and the Policy of 'Self-Reliance', _China Report_, New Delhi, Vol. XIX, No. 2 (1983), pp. 19-34, and to Sameul P. Ho and Ralph W. Huenemann, _China's Open Door Policy_ (The University of British Columbia Press, Vancouver, 1984), passim.

4. 'National power' or _guojia quanli_ is discussed more fully in Zhou Zhixian and Chen Qida, 'Some Points of View on Assessing China's National Power', unpublished paper, Pacific Rim Conference, Vancouver, Canada, April 1982, p. 15.

5. Vice-Premier Li Peng in a discussion of the strategic development of hydropower refers to energy as the 'strategic key point' for the next 20 years. See 'China's Policies for Hydropower Development' in Joint Publications Research Service, (hereinafter cited as JPRS), Econ 398, 84737, 14 November 1985, p. 17.

6. Deng Xiaoping, _Selected Works of Deng Xiaoping, 1975-82_ (Foreign Languages Press, Beijing, 1984), p. 264.

7. Zhou Zhixian and Chen Qida, 'Some Points of View', pp. 12-13.

8. For Thomas Fingar's discussion of China 'biting the bullet' see 'Energy in China: Paradoxes, Policies, and Prospects' (The China Council of the Asia Society, New York, 1983), pp. S-2, S-7, and 21.

9. Zhou Zhixian and Chen Qida, 'Some Points of View', pp. 12-13.

10. US Department of State, Bureau of Intelligence and Research, Intelligence Report No. 8458, 24 May 1961, pp. 2-5. For discussion of the Chinese desire for independence from Soviet energy see _Petroleum Economist_, 'Special Report on China', prepared for Offshore Oil Exhibition and Conference, Guangzhou, November 1981, p. 471.

11. Mao gave the date for the inception of this formulation as 'major policy' during his '7,000 cadres speech' of 1962. See Stuart R. Schram, ed., _Mao Tse-tung Unrehearsed_ (Penguin, Harmondsworth,

1974), p. 178.

12. Ibid., p. 126.

13. Chiang Shan-hao, Impression of Taching Oilfield (Foreign Languages Press, Peking, 1978), p. 17.

14. Schram, ed., Mao Tse-tung Unrehearsed, p. 199.

15. Chou T'ien-chih, 'The Lesson of the Arab War Against Aggression', in Hongqi No. 13, 1967 in US Consulate General, Hong Kong, Selections from China Mainland Magazines, (SCMM) No. 593, 19 September 1967, p. 3.

16. For Renmin ribao commentary on the 'Soviet Revisionsist Clique's Sell Out of Soviet Sovereignty' see US Consulate General, Hong Kong, Survey of the China Mainland Press, (SCMP), No. 4025, 21 September 1967, pp. 34-5.

17. Choon-ho Park and Jerome Alan Cohen, 'The Politics of China's Oil Weapon', Foreign Policy, 20, (Fall 1975), p. 46.

18. Xue Yuan, 'Mei-Su liangba jiajin zhengdao zhongdong shiyou baquan', (The US and USSR are intensifying their rivalry for Middle Eastern Oil), Xuexi yu pipan, (Study and criticism), No. 3, 1973, p. 48. This analysis describes the Soviet 'southward strategy to breakthrough at the middle', zhongjian tupodi nanxia zhanlue, in terms of the threat to Western Europe and the Soviet attempt to interdict European oil supplies in the Middle East.

19. Ch'ang Ch'ien, 'Behind the So-Called "Energy Crisis"' in King C. Chen, ed., China and the Three Worlds (M.E. Sharpe, White Plains, New York, 1979), p. 297.

20. Ibid., p. 297.

21. Deng Xiaoping's speech at the Sixth Special Session of the UN General Assembly in Chen, ed. China and the Three Worlds, p. 92.

22. Ibid., p. 93.

23. Ibid., pp. 94-5.

24. Selected Works of Deng Xiaoping, 1975-82, p. 44.

25. Refer to the following analyses: Hiroshima Kimura, 'Failure of Soviet Policies Towards Japan', Asian Pacific Community, No. 16, (Spring 1982), p. 1; Institute for the Study of Conflict, 'Japan's Triangular Diplomacy', Conflict Studies, No. 129, (April 1981), pp. 5-6; Yueng H. Park, 'The "Anti-Hegemony" Controversy in Sino-Japanese Relations', Pacific Affairs, Vol. 49, No. 3, (Fall, 1976), p. 479.

26. For the Japanese connotations of the

policy of 'equidistance', kokyori gaiko, see Joseph Cheng, 'China's Japan Policy in the 1970s: The United Front and the "Four Modernizations"', Asia Quarterly (Brussels), No. 1 (1980), p. 21 fn. 4. 'Equidistance' was subject to very different interpretations, but the one connotation implying 'friendly relations with all countries' apparently was the precursor to the later Fukada formulation of 'omnidirectional diplomacy' which required that Japanese diplomacy direct itself equally to all nations. Refer to Chae-Jin Lee, 'The Making of the Sino-Japanese Peace and Friendship Treaty', Pacific Affairs, Vol. 52, No. 3 (Fall, 1979), p. 424 and Michimasa Irie, 'The Politics of the Peace and Friendship Treaty', Japan Echo, Vol. V, No. 4 (1978), p. 72.

27. Hong N. Kim, 'The Fukada Government and the Poltics of the Sino-Japanese Peace Treaty', Asian Survey, Vol. 29, No. 3 (March 1977), pp. 298-9.

28. Allen Whiting has argued that the Chinese hinted that they would find the project more acceptable if the Americans would become involved in Siberian Development and East Asia (Stanford University Press, Stanford, 1981), p. 144.

29. Dev Murarka, 'Growth Pace Curbed', Far Eastern Economic Review, (hereinafter cited as FEER), 31 January 1975, p. 62.

30. See William Tow, 'Sino-Japanese Security Cooperation: Evolution and Prospects', PA, Vol. 56, No. 1 (1983), pp. 58-9. Randall Hardy argues to the contrary suggesting that Chinese oil did not play a significant role as the PRC's oil exports were not sufficient to gain leverage over Japan. See Hardy, China's Oil Future: A Case of Modest Expectations (Westview Press, Boulder, 1978), p. 57.

31. John P. Puthenveetil, 'Strategic Options Behind Sino-Japanese Trade Relations', International Studies, June 1978, p. 551.

32. Zhou Enlai's report on the international situation of March, 1973 in Issues and Studies, Vol. XLII, No. 1 (1977), p. 125.

33. Study Group of the Ministry of Light Industry, 'Zili gengsheng yang wei chongyong', (Self-reliance and making foreign things serve China), in Jianjue yonghu lingxiu Hua zhuxi fennu shengtao sirenbang (Firmly support our leader Chairman Hua in angrily condemning the Gang of Four), (Sanlianshudian, Hong Kong, 1977), p. 119.

34. Fang Hai, 'Criticize the Slavish Comprador Philosophy', Hongqi, No. 4, 1 April 1976 in US

Consulate General, Hong Kong, Survey of the People's Republic of China Magazines, (SPRCM), No. 867-8, 20-6 April 1976, pp. 22-3.

35. Supplementary Materials, New York Times, (NYT), 13 August 1978, pp. 118, 119, 122.

36. See Table 1: Chronology of Japan-China Negotiations on Joint Oil Development in JETRO, China Newsletter, (CNL), No. 24 (December 1979) p. 28.

37. Hua Guofeng, 'Unite and Strive to Build a Modern Powerful Socialist Country', National People's Congress, People's Republic of China, Documents of the First Session of the Fifth Session of the Fifth National People's Congress of the People's Repubic of China (Foreign Languages Press, Beijing, 1978), pp. 35-42.

38. Refer to Martin Weil's analysis, 'The Baoshan Steel Mill: A Symbol of Change in China's Industrial Development Strategy', US Congress, Joint Economic Committee, China Under the Four Modernizations, Part I, (US GPO, Washington, D.C., 1982), p. 375.

39. For a report on the initial Japanese reaction see 'Japan Reassessing Projects in China', NYT, 16 February 1981, pp. D1, D5.

40. Beijing Review, (hereinafter cited as BR), No. 4, 26 January 1981, p. 8.

41. For example see Sergei Manezhev and Vladimir Potapov, 'End of the Oil Bluff', New Times,(Moscow) Vol. 43, October 1981, pp. 26-8.

42. Huai Chengbo, BR, No. 19, 11 May 1981, p. 12.

43. 'Building Up the Siberian Base', BR, No. 19, 11 May 1981, p. 13.

44. 'Moscow's "Dumb-bell" Strategy', BR, No. 8, 25 February 1980, pp. 8-9.

45. Manezhev and Potapov, 'End of the Oil Bluff', pp. 27-8.

46. Liu Yuejing, 'Why Export Coal When There Is Still an Energy Shortage', from Shijie jingji dabao, Shanghai in JPRS, Econ 323, 83162, 30 March 1983, p. 12.

47. Ibid., p. 11.

48. Robert M. Field and Judith A. Flynn, 'China: An Energy-Constrained Model of Industrial Performance Through 1985', China Under the Four Modernizations, Part I, pp. 335-64.

49. Ibid., 342-3. Also the World Bank's 'tentative' forecast suggested that oil production would fall to 100 million tons by 1985. The World Bank, China. Socialist Economic Development, (A

World Bank Country Study), Vol. II, (Washington D.C., 1983), p. 225.

50. Table 14, Production, Trade and Consumption of Crude Petroleum, in UN, Energy Statistics Yearbook (United Nations Publication, New York, 1982), p. 280.

51. The late 1982 Sino-Japanese memorandum covering 1982-5 trimmed Japanese import ceilings to 8.0-8.6 million tons of crude oil and 7-8 tons of coal per year. See China Economic News, No. 38, 4 November 1982. In December, 1985 the Chinese were unable to persuade the Japanese to increase their oil imports by 600,000 tons. See Dow Jones News Service, 32 February 1984 and the Japan Economic Journal, 1 November 1984, p. 9.

52. Song Baoxiang, 'Youjie dongdang ji qi yingxiang' (Drastic changes of oil prices and their impact), Guoji maoyi wenti, No. 2, 1984, p. 23.

53. Zhang Yan, 'Oil: Leader in World's Energy Consumption', Intertrade, July, 1984, p. 13.

54. For example, see 'Third World to Import More Oil', China Daily, (hereinafter cited as CD), 10 November 1983, p. 4.

55. Mike Tharp, 'Still 99% Dependent on Foreign Sources for its Crude', FEER, 25 August 1983, p. 66.

56. See JETRO, CNL, No. 47, Nov.-Dec., 1983, p. 21 and Swadesh de Roy, 'Energy Targets Trimmed Under Revised $60 Billion 12 Year Agreement', China Business Report, December 1984, p. 23.

57. JETRO, CNL, No. 51, July-August, 1984, p. 23.

58. 'Japan-USSR Trade Off', CD, 27 February, 1984, p. 2.

59. For an extended discussion see Ronald C. Keith, 'The origins and Strategic Implications of China's "Independent Foreign Policy"', International Journal, Winter 1985-6.

60. Shan Cheng, '"Second Siberian" Provides Vital Link', BR, No. 12, 25 March 1985, pp. 12-13.

61. The regional variations in the production of crude oil are striking; for example, out of the total annual 1980 production of 105.94 million tons, the Northeast produced 58.59, the North 19.11, the East 17.92, the Northeast 6.06, the Central-South 4.16 and the Southwest 0.10 million tons of crude oil. See Table 3.1, World Bank China, Vol. 11, p. 224.

62. Li Chengrui, 'Are the 1967-76 Statistics on China's Economy Reliable', BR, No. 12, 19 March 1984, pp. 23-4.

63. Ronald C. Keith, 'China's Modernization and the Policy of "Self-Reliance"',pp. 28-9.

64. See Liu Xin, 'The Inside Story of Economic Readjustment in Communist China', Zhengming (Hong Kong), No. 19 (May 1979), pp. 9-13; Shi Zhengwen, 'Readjusting the National Economy: Why and How?', BR, No. 26, 29 June 1979, p. 22; Tian Yun, 'One Step Back, Two Steps Forward', BR, No. 29, 21 July 1980, pp. 15-19.

65. See Sueo Kojima's analysis of the State Council's view in 'Japan-China Economic Interchange and Enterprise Reform', JETRO, CNL, No. 40, (September/ October, 1982), p. 18.

66. Gu Ming, 'Plans Readjusted, Policy Unchanged', BR, No. 30, 27 July 1979, pp. 9-11.

67. Hao Bin, 'The Present Status and Future Outlook for China's Energy Structure', in JPRS Econ 323, 83162, 30 March 1983, pp. 2-4.

68. These production figures originate with the annual communiques usually released in May to cover the production of the preceding year. See BR, No. 19, 12 May 1980, p. 13; BR, No. 19, 11 May 1981, p. 24, BR, No. 19, 9 May 1983, Supplement, p. V; BR, No. 22, 28 May 1984, p. 18.

69. See Zhao Ziyang's government work report in BR, No. 16, 22 April 1985, Documents, p. IV.

70. Song Ping's speech at a work conference, Foreign Broadcast Information Service, Daily Report: China (hereinafter cited as FBIS, I), 10 September 1984, p. K1.

71. BR, No. 19, 9 May 1983, Supplement, p. XIII.

72. '1983 is Record Year for the Production of Hydroelectricity', from Shuili fadian, No. 1, 12 January 1984, p. 2 in JPRS, CEA, 84026, 29 April 1983.

73. 'Regulations for Planned Power Generation and Supply', Peking Home Service, 24 May 1982, Summary of World Broadcasts, (hereinafter cited as SWB), FE/703/c/3.

74. Zhao Ziyang, 'The Present Economic Situation and the Principles for Future Economic Construction', in China's Economy and Development Principles (Foreign Languages Press, Beijing, 1982), p. 30.

75. BR, No. 9, 23 February 1983, p. 15.

76. 'Efficient Economical Management Key to Conservation in the Steel Industry', Neng Yuan (Beijing), No. 5, 25 October 1983, pp. 38-9 in JPRS CEA, 84032, 30 April 1984, pp. 85.

77. Ta Kung Pao (Hong Kong), 19-25 August

1982, p. 6.

78. Barry F. Neal and Associates ltd., Australasian Report, 4, 1984, p. 12.

79. 'China's Energy on Track', Petroleum News, June 1984, p. 57.

80. Li Renjun, 'Oil-to-Coal Conversions Could Reduce Oil Consumption Dramatically', in JPRS, CEA, 84014, 12 February 1984, p. 72.

81. Wang Qingyi and Gu Jian, 'How Will China Solve the Energy Problem', BR, No. 35, 29 August 1983, p. 14.

82. Carl Riskin, 'Small Industry and the Chinese Model of Development', China Quarterly, (hereinafter cited as CQ), No. 46, April-June 1971, pp. 245-73; Carl Riskin, 'China's Rural Industrialization: Self-Reliant Systems or Independent Kingdoms', CQ, No. 73, March, 1978, pp. 78-98; Dwight Perkins, ed., Rural Small-Scale Industry in the People's Republic of China (University of California Press, Berkeley, 1977), passim; Jon Sigurdson, Rural Industrialization in China (Harvard University Press, Cambridge, Mass., 1977).

83. See Robert Taylor, 'Decentralized Renewable Energy Development in China,' World Bank Staff Working Paper, No. 535, 1982, pp. 1-2. Also see Lu Qi, 'Energy Conservation and Its Prospects', BR, No. 46, 21 November 1984, p. 20.

84. Table A.20, World Bank, China, Vol. II, p. 264.

85. BR, No. 35, 29 August 1983, p. 14.

86. SWB, FE/W1222/A/9, 9 February 1983, pp. A9-A10.

87. 'Sample Survey of Peasant Household Incomes and Expenditures', BR, No. 43, 24 October, 1983, p. 23.

88. Hou Xueyu, 'Comprehensive Solution to the Rural Energy Issue', JPRS, CEA, 84032, 4 April 1984, pp. 72-4.

89. CD, 10 April 1984, p. 1.

90. CD, 2 April 1984, p. 3.

91. Li Cheng, 'Capital Sought for Development', World Mining Equipment, New York, March, 1984, p. 48.

92. China Economic News, 28 March 1983, p. 3.

93. Kenji Hattori, 'Trends in China's Coal Development and Japan-China Trade', JETRO, CNL, No. 43, March/April 1983, pp. 14-20.

94. Xin Fengbing, 'Ministry of Water Resources and Electric Power Studies Way to Build More Power Stations with Less Investment', JPRS, CEA, 84032, 30

April 1984, p. 22.

95. 'China's Largest Hydropower Project', BR, No. 35, 31 August 1982, p. 23.

96. Li Peng, 'China's Policies for Hydropower Development and Strategic Measures for Speeding Up Hydropower Construction', in JPRS, Econ 398, 14 November 1983, pp. 19.

97. 'Priority to Developing Energy', BR, No. 45, 7 November 1983, p. 23.

98. Wang Juchen, 'Problems in Development of Small-Scale Hydropower Analyzed', Neng Yuan, No. 6, 25 December 1982, pp. 5-8 in JPRS, CEA, 83757, 24 June 1983, p. 46.

99. Ibid., p. 43.

100. Zhao Ziyang, BR, No. 51, 1982.

101. 'Energy and Transportation Are the Focus of Investment', in JPRS, CEA, 83162, 30 March 1982.

102. 'Transport and Energy Projects Get Priority', CD, 20 March 1984, p. 2 and also BR, No. 2, 9 January 1984, pp. 26-7.

103. 'Coal Minister on Comparison, Examination Work', in FBIS, I, 20 April 1984,p. K10.

104. 'Coal Ministry Broadens Authority of Some Major Mines', in JPRS, CEA, 84014, 21 February 1984.

105. 'Hu Yaobang Presides Over Ministry Briefings', FBIS, I, 10 September 1984, p. K2.

106. 'Meeting Energy Goals Requires Rethinking of Investment Policy', in JPRS, CEA, 84040, 1 June 1984, p. 1.

107. Ibid., p. 2.

108. 'Coal Mines to Get Local Building Funds', CD, 18 June 1983, p. 3, and 'Enterprises Help Boost Coal Output', CD 26 April 1983, p. 2.

109. Hu Yaobang, FBIS, I, 10 September 1984, p. K3.

110. 'Three Key Reforms', BR, No. 3, 27 January 1985, p. 4.

111. Zhao Ziyang, 'The Current Economic Situation and Reform of Economic Structure' in BR, No. 16, 22 April 1985, Documents, p. XIII.

112. For example, refer to 'Key Projects During the Sixth Five-Year Plan', BR, No. 2, 9 January 1984, p. 26.

113. For further discussion of this formulation and others relating to centralisation and decentralisation refer to Ronald C. Keith, 'The Relevance of Border Region Experience in Nation-Building in China, 1949-52,' CQ, No. 78 (June 1979), p. 274-95.

114. Zhang Guoyan, 'Unify Understanding, Unify Action and Hasten the Building of Energy, Heavy

Industry and Chemical Industry Bases', in JPRS, CEA, 84014, 21 February 1984, p. 7.

115. Ibid., p. 9.

116. 'Development of the Northwest Power Grid', SWB, FE W1280, 28 March 1984, p. A10.

117. BR, No. 25, 18 June 1984, p. 18.

118. Kenji Hattori, 'Trends in China's Coal Development and Japan-China Coal Trade', p. 15.

119. CD, 13 February 1984, p. 3.

120. 'Hammering Out a Deal', China Trade Report, Vol. XXII, April 1984, p. 8.

121. 'Reforms to Boost Foreign Investment', BR, No. 47, 19 November 1984, p. 9.

122. 'China Has Used $15.8 Billion in Foreign Funds in the Past 5 and 1/2 years', FBIS, I, 7 September, 1984, p. A1.

123. Ta Kung Pao, Hong Kong, 2-8 June 1983, p. 5. Also refer to Hiroki Kawai's table of China's use of foreign capital in 'Direct Investment in China in 1983', JETRO, CNL, No. 48, January/February 1984, p. 19.

124. World Bank, China. Socialist Economic Development. Vol. 1, p. 186.

125. CD, 11 November 1985, p. 1.

126. For more sustained analysis of current Chinese strategic thinking refer to Ronald C. Keith, 'The Origins and Strategic Implications of China's "Independent Foreign Policy"' International Journal, Winter issue, 1985-6.

127. 'US Involvement Queried on China's Coal Plans', Journal of Commerce, 25 May 1984, p. 11A.

128. See BR, No. 25, 14 June 1984, p. 10 and Journal of Commerce, 18 June 1984, p. 23B.

129. Ta Kung Pao (Hong Kong), 15 November 1984, p. 11.

130. 'Malaysia, Seeing a Threat', NYT, 10 July 1984, p. A10.

131. See Tables 6 and 26 in US Energy Information Administration, The Petroleum Resources of Indonesia, Malaysia, Brunei and Thailand (US GPO, Washington, D.C., 1984), pp. 17, 51.

132. 'US Voices Alarm Over China Project', Shipping and Trade News, (Tokyo), 10 December 1982.

133. 'China May Emerge As a Big Oil Producer, Changing Its Political Stand in Asia', Japan Economic Journal 26 July 1983, p. 24.

Chapter Two

SOVIET ENERGY SUPPLY AND EAST ASIA

Allan Rodgers

INTRODUCTION

The Soviet Union continues to be the world's leader in energy production. It ranks first in the production of petroleum and natural gas, and stands third after the US and China in coal output! Then too, the USSR is the world's leading exporter of energy products. Its exports feed Eastern and Western Europe, and to a far lesser degree, they serve East Asian markets.

However, the past few years have witnessed a crunch in energy production because of stabilised oil and coal extraction, although natural gas output continues its rapid growth. The lack of significant growth in oil and coal production has placed increasing pressure on internal consumption and energy exports.

My central concern in this chapter will be with the relationship between Soviet energy supplies and potential exports to East Asia. However, given the fact that such exports can only be fed by production in Eastern Siberia, much of the focus will be on that region and particularly the Far East.

The questions and topics relating to this focus fall into two groups: the first treats the energy resources of the USSR from a broad national perspective. What are Soviet energy production patterns? What is the current product mix, and what can we anticipate in the coming decade? In turn, we will treat internal energy consumption patterns and the 'energy balance'. Finally from this perspective, we will cover energy export patterns, by product and by destination.

The second group of questions is concerned with Soviet Far Eastern energy resources, especially their accessibility and economic feasibility. To what degree can the exploitation of these resources counterbalance the decline of oil and coal production in European Russia (including the Urals)? Should the US and Japan aid the Soviet Union in the exploitation of these resources through the media of credits and technology? What does the exploration and development of Far Eastern energy resources foreshadow for her current and potential trading partners in the Pacific Basin? Finally, what are the implications of the proximate completion of the BAM (Baikal-Amur Magistral) for economic development in that region and to what degree will this new artery play a role in energy exports to East Asia?

ENERGY PRODUCTION AND THE EVOLVING PRODUCT MIX

The rate of growth of energy production in recent years was half that of the previous decade. In addition to resource depletion, the diminished rate reflects insufficient investment, inadequate technology and equipment, and poor logistical co-ordination of energy supplies. Yet the overall growth pattern conceals diffentials in incremental rates among the various energy sources. The recent modest overall increase is solely attributable to continued expansion in natural gas production. Oil and coal output have remained essentially stable from 1980 to 1984.

The historical pattern of energy production is demonstrated in Table 2.1, which was derived from Hewett (1) and Shabad.(2) Unfortunately, data were not available for peat, shale, and fire-wood production in 1983 and 1984, nor were they obtainable for electricity derived from nuclear and hydro-electric power sources.

In 1960 coal still accounted for over half of the primary energy production in the USSR with oil and natural gas at respective values of 29 and 8 per cent each. By 1982 the shares of these fuels had shifted. Oil with 42 and gas with 28 per cent had climbed into the lead, whereas coal's share had declined to 28 per cent. The sectoral growth pattern changed between 1983 and 1984 as natural gas continued its rapid expansion at the expense of oil and coal.

The minor fuels like peat, shale and fire-wood declined relatively, and electrical power sources such as nuclear and hydro retained minimal shares of the overall energy mix. The latter is contrary to

Table 2.1: Soviet Energy Production, 1960-84

		millions of bbls. per day of oil equivalent							
Year	Total	Oil*	Natural Gas	Coal	Peat	Shale	Fire-wood	Nuclear	Hydro
Absolute									
1960	10.01	2.96	0.76	4.22	0.29	0.67	0.40	0.00	0.33
1965	13.99	4.85	2.10	5.78	0.24	0.10	0.47	0.00	0.47
1970	17.75	7.04	3.27	6.06	0.25	0.12	0.47	0.02	0.64
1975	22.68	9.83	4.80	6.61	0.26	0.15	0.36	0.10	0.70
1980	27.71	12.08	7.22	6.68	0.10	0.17	0.32	0.32	0.84
1982	29.12	12.26	8.29	6.70	0.12	0.16	0.33	0.45	0.80
1983	?	12.32	8.87	6.69	?	?	?	?	?
1984	?	12.26	9.71	6.65	?	?	?	?	?
Percentage Share									
1960	100	29	8	52	3	7	4	0	3
1965	100	35	15	41	2	7	2	0	3
1970	100	40	18	34	1	7	2	0	4
1975	100	43	21	34	1	1	2	0	3
1980	100	43	26	25	1	1	2	2	3
1982	100	42	28	23	0	1	1	1	3
1983		?	?	?	?	?	?	?	?
1984		?	?	?	?	?	?	?	?

* Including gas condensate

Source: Ed Hewett, Energy, Economics and Foreign Policy in the Soviet Union, Washington, 1984, pp. 32-3;
Ted Shabad, 'News Notes', Soviet Geography April, 1984 and 1985. These data are modified by conversion factors to arrive at million barrels per day equivalent.

Western experience, and is apparent despite Soviet plans to expand the nuclear base of European Russia. The shift from coal to petroleum and natural gas, however, follows the historical precedent of Western Europe and Anglo-America. Such shifts arose from lower production costs, ease of transportation, and the greater efficiency with which oil and gas can be used. The relative decline of nuclear and hydro-electric power are attributed by the Soviets to their high capital-intensity in a period when there has been fierce competition for scarce capital investment funds.

Oil production in the USSR grew at a remarkable pace from the 1960s on with increases in Volga-Urals output and later with expansion into Western Siberia. While the Soviet Union remains the world's leading oil producer and exporter, the 1980s have witnessed a stabilisation of overall output with occasional slight declines. What does this portend for oil production for the next decade?

Here we enter the realm of speculation, for the Soviets have published no data on planned targets for the late 1980s or 1990s. All that can be hoped for is an educated guess. Turning first to potential or reserves, the Soviets have published no reserve data since 1974. Such data are classified as state secrets. However, Western oil experts believe that Soviet proved oil reserves* vary between 60 and 80 billion barrels or 13 to 18 years at current output levels. Meyerhof (3) citing Dikenshtein (4) argues that proved, probable, and predicted reserves may total 441 billion barrels. There are apparently huge reserves in the Arctic (Kara and Barents Seas) and Eastern Siberia, but these have not even been minimally explored and offer no prospects for our time-frame.

It is true that by deeper drilling, secondary or tertiary recovery, more reserves can be proved. However, this would require greater capital investments to increase oil recovery and exploit offshore oil deposits. Investments in oil production are surely increasing but whether or not they are at sufficient levels to offset oil depletion is debatable. Soviet planners must decide whether increased investments in this sector merit reduced investments in other branches and a heavier strain on overall consumption.

---

* These are A, B and C. Such reserves are termed 'proved' in Soviet technical terminology.

The geographic pattern of oil production from 1940 to 1984 is demonstrated in Table 2.2, which shows the evolving regional patterns of oil output. Until 1950, production was dominated by the Caucasus (North Caucasus and Azerbaijan). In 1940, for example, 86 per cent of the overall output came from that region. By 1950 the share had declined to 55 per cent. In the late 1950s and 1960s, the Volga-Urals region came to the fore accounting for 70 per cent of the nation's output. Then that region began to decline both absolutely and relatively as Western Siberian output soared and took up the slack with 61 per cent of Soviet oil production in 1984. However, the annual rate of increase of that region began to decline in the 1980s. Gains in Western Siberia have slowed down because of the need for developing widely scattered deposits in a hostile environment. This requires major investments in the social and economic infrastructure of the region. Then too, as Ted Shabad has noted in his findings of 1984,(5) there has been a notable decline in well productivity. Western Siberian production has failed to counterbalance the decline in the Volga-Urals region. Barring major new discoveries, to meet internal consumption requirements and export goals, the Soviets must increase their capital investments in Western Siberia, Eastern Siberia, and the Arctic, otherwise the CIA's negative forecast of 1977 may still come to pass.

Turning to the geographic pattern of natural gas production over time, Table 2.3 demonstrates the recency of large-scale extraction which dates from 1970. Here, unlike petroleum, we have large annual increments in the 1970s and 1980s which show no sign of stabilisation or conceivable decline. The shares of the nation's output of oil and of gas originating in Western Siberia are roughly similar (60 and 59 per cent respectively). Unlike the oil pattern, the remaining gas production is more dispersed, notably in Central Asia, and secondarily in the Volga-Urals. The reserve pattern resembles that of production, and their proved reserves (A, B and C) would sustain the current production for over forty years. Inevitably gas production will surpass oil output in both relative and absolute terms.

As recently as 1960, coal production (standard fuel) accounted for half of the Soviet energy output. That share is now down to less than 23 per cent so that coal has declined in both relative and absolute importance. Output declined from 718

Table 2.2: Geographical Distribution of Soviet Oil Output

Regions	Millions of metric tons per year							
	1940	1960	1970	1980	1982	1983	1984	1985 (Plan)
USSR	31.1	248	353	603	613	616	613	628
Komi ASSR	0.1	0.8	7.6	19	20	19	(19)	(19)
North Caucasus	4.6	12	35	19	15	14	(12)	(11)
Volga	0.2	75	145	111	89	(81)	(76)	(71)
Urals	1.7	29	63	82	79	(77)	(73)	(69)
W. Siberia	0.5	--	1	313	353	369	(378)	402
Sakhalin	0.5	1.6	2.5	3	3	3	3	3
Ukraine	0.4	2.2	13.9	7.6	7	(7)	?	
Byelorussia	--	--	4.2	3	3	(3)	?	
Georgia	--	--	--	3.2	3.5	(3)	(2)	
Azerbaijan	22.2	18	20	14	13	12	?	
Kazakhstan	0.7	1.6	13.1	18.7	19.3	19.5	20.6	22.6
Central Asia	0.7	7.3	16.8	9.5	8.5	(7)	?	

Source: Data for 1940 and 1970 are from Shabad and Dienes (1979), while data for the 1980s were derived from Shabad (1984 and 1985).

Table 2.3: Geographical Distribution of Natural Gas Production

	billions of cubic meters							
Region	1940	1960	1970	1980	1982	1983	1984	1985 Plan
USSR	3	45	198	435	501	536	587	632
Komi ASSR	--	10	6.9	17.5	18	17	(26)	(16)
North Caucasus	0.2	13.7	47.0	14	12	11	(9)	(8)
Volga	--	8.3	14.4	8	9	8	(7)	(6)
Urals	--	0.5	2.2	52	52	(51)	(50)	(50)
Western Siberia	--	--	--	162	234	(277)	(331)	371
Sakhalin	--	0.3	0.8	6	6	(7)	(7)	(7)
Ukraine	--	--	--	52	48	45	43	(41)
Azerbaijan	--	--	--	14.5	14	14	14	(14)
Kazakhstan	--	--	--	5	5	5	5	(5)
Central Asia	--	--	--	109.3	109	108	112	(121)

Source: Dienes and Shabad (1979) for 1940-70 data and Shabad (1983 and 1984) for 1980-85 data.

million metric tons in 1982 to 712 million metric tons in 1984, far below planned levels. The Five Year Plan had called for 775 million metric tons by 1985.

Table 2.4 demonstrates the geographic pattern of coal production from 1960 to 1984. Clearly, coal extraction is more widely dispersed than oil production. The leading producer is the Donets Basin of the Eastern Ukraine. It accounted for 57 per cent of the output in 1940 and 28 per cent in 1984, while the share of the Kuznestk Basin of Western Siberia rose from 13 to 20 per cent last year. The rest is scattered in a variety of fields. Note that production during the 1980s was stable in many fields. The Donbas has moved to the mining of low-cost quality bituminous coals, and were it not for its accessibility to European markets, its relative and absolute importance might have shrunk even more. In contrast, output in the Kuznetsk Basin should have increased in the 1980s because of the quality of its product and relatively low mining costs. Increased capital investment there appears to be merited, for its higher quality coal can be delivered to European Russian markets at a price competitive with Donets coals. The most promising fields currently under exploitation are the Ekibastuz and Kansk-Achinsk basins. In the former, the coals are so low in carbon content and so high in ash and other impurities that the most feasible intermediate market for the product lies in thermo-electric generation and shipment to distant markets. The same is true of the Kansk-Achinsk deposits. This product is even more difficult to handle. Again, its use in electric power production seems most feasible. There is also talk of the use of coal slurry pipelines, but technically such long distance lines are only in the experimental stage.

Sheer reserves do not appear to be a problem. Location, accessibility and the cost and quality of the product all remain as a major issue. Here too, output has essentially stabilised.

ENERGY CONSUMPTION AND THE ENERGY BALANCE

Table 2.5 demonstrates energy balances for the Soviet Union for selected years. It details trends in energy production, net exports and consumption. Turning to the latter, it is notable that consumption increased roughly 250 per cent from 1960 to 1982. At the same time, there was

Table 2.4: Geographical Distribution of Coal and Lignite Output.

Region	1960	1970	1980	1982	1983	1984	1985(Rev. Plan)
	millions of metric tons						
USSR	510	614	716	718	716	712	726
<u>European Russia</u>							
Moscow Basin	42.8	40.8	26	24	21	?	?
Pechora Basin	17.6	18.1	28	28	28	?	?
Donets Basin	188	216	204	200	(198)	(196)	(194)
Georgia	2.8	2.3	?	?	?	?	?
<u>Asiatic Russia</u>							
Urals	54.9	46.6	41	?	?	?	?
Kuznetsk Basin	83.6	113	145	148	147	243	?
Kansk-Achinsk	8.5	18.2	35	37	38.5	?	?
Eastern Siberia	?	?	?	?	?	?	?
Neryungri (Yakutsk)	0.9	1.6	2.5	4	5	7	11
Karaganda (Kazakhstan)	25.8	38.4	48.6	48	48.9	(49)	(49)
Ekibastug (Kazakhstan)	6.0	14.3	66.8	70	73.7	(76)	(78)
Central Asia	7.8	8.3	(11)	?	?	?	?

Source: Data for 1960 and 1970 derived from Dienes and Shabad (1979); data for 1980-5 derived from Shabad (1983 and 1984).

Table 2.5: Soviet Energy Balances, 1960-82

	millions of barrels per day equivalent				
	Energy Production	Energy Exports	Energy Imports	Net Exports	Energy Consumption
1960	10.2	0.8	0.2	0.6	9.5
1965	14.2	1.6	0.1	1.5	12.6
1970	17.8	2.3	0.2	2.1	15.6
1975	22.8	3.3	0.5	2.8	19.8
1980	27.6	4.5	0.2	4.3	23.4
1981	28.2	4.5	0.2	4.3	23.7
1982	29.0	4.8	0.3	4.5	24.3

Stock changes for each of 1975, 1981 and 1982 were 0.2.

Source: Modified from Hewett (1984)

a threefold increase in energy production. The increasing gap between the two values was accounted for by net exports. These will be discussed later. They were used to serve the East European bloc and to earn hard currency from the West. The moneys earned were used mainly to purchase grain and to buy foreign technology and equipment. Exports increased sixfold from 1960 to 1982. The increased domestic consumption arose with the greater use of oil and gas in thermoelectric stations, transportation, heating and industry.

Table 2.6 shows the consumption pattern by sector for 1972. It is the most detailed pattern available. Note that 40 per cent was consumed by industry, and another 23 per cent was used for the production of electric power. I surmise that roughly the same

Table 2.6: The Structure of Energy Consumption by Sector in 1972.

(millions of tons of standard fuel)

Sectors	Absolute	Share %
Intermediate Consumers		
Industry		
metallurgy	206.5	16.5
oil products	25.9	2.1
machinery	63.1	5.0
chemicals	65.0	5.2
wood and paper	22.6	1.8
construction materials	53.2	4.2
light industry	15.9	1.3
food industry	39.3	3.1
other industry	11.8	0.8
Construction	32.3	2.6
Agriculture	73.6	5.9
Transport	77.8	6.2
Trade	11.4	0.9
Fuels and Power		
coal	19.9	1.6
oil	3.4	0.3
gas	4.8	0.4
electric power	288.9	23.1
Final Users		
Private Consumption	71.1	5.7
Passenger Transportation	22.4	1.8
Other public consumption	102.1	8.2
Other domestic final demand	39.5	3.2
Gross Consumption	1251.6	99.9

Source: These data were derived and modified from Kurtzweg and Tretyakova 'Soviet Energy Consumption', Soviet Economy in the 1980s, Joint Economic Committee, US Congress, Part 1, 1982, pp. 355-90.

Table 2.7: The Structure of Energy Consumption by Energy Source, in 1972.

Sectors in %	Coal	Oil Products	Gas	Electric Power	Total	Absolute Total
<u>Intermediate Consumers</u>						
Industry						
Metallurgy	69.2	5.2	17.0	8.5	100.0	206.5
oil products	--	21.2	42.7	37.1	100.0	25.0
machinery	18.2	30.9	31.2	19.7	100.0	63.1
chemicals	4.2	5.7	43.1	47.1	100.0	65.0
wood and paper	34.1	42.5	9.7	13.1	100.0	22.6
construction materials	30.3	6.2	45.9	17.7	100.0	53.2
light industry	16.4	7.5	16.4	59.7	100.0	15.9
food industry	28.8	39.2	17.6	14.5	100.0	39.3
other industry	25.4	7.6	44.9	22.0	100.0	11.8
Construction	23.5	59.8	6.8	9.9	100.0	32.3
Agriculture	14.0	78.5	1.8	5.7	100.0	73.6
Transport	11.8	69.2	11.7	7.3	100.0	77.8
Trade	51.8	17.5	12.3	18.4	100.0	11.4

Table 2.7: The Structure of Energy Consumption by Energy Source, in 1972.

Sectors in %	Coal	Oil Products	Gas	Electric Power	Total	Absolute Total
Fuels and Power						
coal	74.4	3.5	--	22.1	100.0	19.9
oil	--	14.7	44.1	41.2	100.0	3.4
gas	--	8.3	83.3	8.3	100.0	4.8
electric power	46.0	26.1	25.4	2.5	100.0	288.9
Final Users						
Private Consumption	30.4	8.7	17.7	43.2	100.0	71.9
Passenger Transportation	--	92.0	--	8.0	100.0	22.4
Other public Consumption	42.6	--	33.4	23.8	100.0	102.1
Other domestic final demand	5.3	91.6	3.0	--	100.0	39.5
Gross Consumption	35.7	27.4	22.1	14.9	100.0	1251.5

Source: These data were calculated from Kurtzweg and Tretyakova "Soviet Energy Consumption", Soviet Economy in the 1980s, Joint Economic Committee, US Congress, Part 1, 1982, pp.©355-90.

pattern holds true today. Clearly, the share of the various energy sources varies considerably by sector.

Table 2.7 views energy consumption in the USSR from a different perspective.
It shows the shares of coal, oil products, gas and electric power by sector. Note the ways in which those percentages vary by industrial group. Metallurgy is the sole industry whose consumption was dominated by coal. Sixty per cent of the energy consumed by light industry came from electric power. In other sectors, we find differing patterns. For example in agriculture and transport, 78 and 69 per cent respectively came from oil products. In the case of electric power, coal was the leading fuel source, while passenger transport used predominantly oil products.

EXPORTS

Tables 2.8, 2.9 and 2.10 demonstrate the patterns of oil, gas and hard coal exports for 1981. I have divided these materials, derived from UN statistics, into three geographical categories, namely, the 'Socialist Bloc' (which among other Socialist states includes Yugoslavia and Cuba), Western Europe and an 'Other' grouping. In that year exports accounted for 17 per cent of oil production, for 13 per cent of the natural gas output and 3 per cent of the production of anthracite and bituminous coals. In the case of oil the export pattern was dominated by shipments to the Socialist bloc. Almost three-quarters went there and another 20 per cent to Western Europe. The gas pattern was quite different. Roughly half of the exports were sent to the Socialist bloc and a similar share to Western Europe. On the other hand, the limited coal exports moved primarily to the Socialist bloc.

Table 2.11 demonstrates the historical trends in Soviet investment since the 1970s. What is of initial concern here is the share of energy investments. The table reveals an upward trend with nine per cent devoted to energy in 1971 and 14 per cent in 1985. If we add pipelines to the total, the share increases to 19 per cent or a fifth of total Soviet investments in 1985. The increments are attributable to increasing investment in petroleum, natural gas, and pipelines. Note the sharp rise in the share of oil and gas pipelines. Clearly, oil has a high priority in Soviet

Table 2.8: Exports of Crude Petroleum in 1981.

(thousands of metric tons)

Socialist Bloc*		Western Europe*		Other areas*	
PDR of Yemen	1710	Australia		India	2610
Cuba	5000	Finland	6520	Syria	3690
Bulgaria	11700	France	5410	Other	1030
Czechoslovakia	18220	Greece	1190		
GDR	18600	Italy	4700		
		Other	6100		
Hungary	7690				
Poland	13008				
Rumania	7500				
Yugoslavia	4500				
Other	2490				
Sub-Total	90418		25700		7330

* Countries named are those that received <u>over</u> one million metric tons of oil from the USSR in 1981.

Source: Modified and recalculated from UN, <u>Energy Statistics Yearbook 1982</u>, (1984), pp. 291-320.

Table 2.9: Exports of Natural Gas in 1981.

	000 of terajoules		
Socialist Bloc*		Western Europe*	
Bulgaria	155.6	Austria	160.0
Czechoslovakia	293.5	France	161.7
GDR	221.0	GFR	414.8
Hungary	133.1	Italy	211.6
Poland	167.3	Other	28.5
Other	131.7		
Sub-Total	1103.2	Sub-Total	976.6

*Countries are named, if their terajoules are over 100,000.

Source: Calculated from UN, Energy Statistics Yearbook, 1982 (1984) pp. 584-93.

Table 2.10: Exports of Bituminous and Anthracite Coals in 1981.

		(millions of metric tons)			
Socialist Bloc		Western Europe		Other Areas	
Bulgaria	6930	Finland	810	Japan	1410
Czechoslakia	3270	Other	1080	Other	5820*
GDR	2610				
Yugoslavia	1840				
Hungary	660				
Poland	770				
Other	800				
Sub-Totals	16880		1800		7230

Countries are named if their imports are greater than 500,000 metric tons.
* This category includes 5,800,000 metric tons unspecified.

Source: Modified and recalculated from UN, Energy Statistical Yearbook, 1982 (1984), pp. 203-220.

Table 2.11: Soviet Investments by Sector, 1971-85

(trillions of 1973 rubles)

Sector	1971-75 absolute	%	1976-80 absolute	%	1981-85 absolute planned	%
Industry	172	35	224	36	275	39
Fuel	32	6	46	7	77	11
Oil	16	3	26	4	43	6
Natural Gas	7	1	10	2	22	3
Coal	8	2	10	2	12	2
Electric Power	17	3	19	3	23	3
Machinery and Metal Fabrication	38	8	54	9		
					175	25
Other Industry	82	17	100	16		
Transportation and Communications	53	2	76	12	(100)	14
Pipelines	10	0	22	3	32	5
Other	44	2	59	9	68	10
Agriculture	99	20	128	20	138	20
Other Sectors	168	34	206	33	187	27
Total	488	100	629	100	700	100

Source: The figures for 1971-5 and 1976-80 are calculated from Hewett (1984) and Naradnoye Khozyaistsvo 1980 (Moscow, 1981). The figures for 1981-5 are in R. 'Leggett, 'Soviet Investment in the 11th Five Year Plan in Joint Economic Committee, US Congress, Soviet Economy in the Eighties, Part I, 1982, pp. 129-46.

investment policy, as does the construction of pipelines and compressors. If oil output is to rise, the priority accorded it in the eleventh plan appears to be well merited.

In the coming decade, there will be increasing pressure for energy exports. Unless oil production sharply increases, and that appears unlikely at the moment, there will be pressure on internal consumption and supplies for Eastern Europe. The need for hard currency will presumably rise, and hence exports to Western Europe must remain at least at the current level. The nations of Eastern Europe, who continue to pay in non-convertible currency, are currently being charged for oil and gas at world market prices. They could conceivably be forced to purchase oil from the OPEC group with negative consequences for their economies. However, those pressures may be eased by the continuing growth of natural gas production. With the building of a host of new gas pipelines, the discovery of new deposits and the rapid increase in gas production, the USSR, presumably will be able to offset the stabilisation of oil output.

THE SOVIET FAR EAST*

I must begin this section with a caution. Other authors, for example, Allen Whiting in 1981,(6) and Victor Mote in 1982,(7) and 1984,(8) have preferred to focus on a broader area termed Eastern Siberia. My own bias is towards a more restricted zone, which the Soviets term an economic region, for I believe that some of the administrative divisions encompassed in what the Soviets call East Siberia are not now involved in energy trade with East Asia, nor do I believe that they will be important in future exchanges with that area.

The region that the Soviets refer to as 'The Soviet Far East' is demonstrated on Figure 2.1. It includes Amur Oblast, Khabarovsk, and Maritime Krais in the south, the Yakut ASSR, Magadan and Kamchatka Oblasts in the north and Sakhalin Island (Sakhalin Oblast) in the east. The Soviet Far East has an area of over six million square kilometres or 28 per cent of the nation's territory. In contrast, its population in 1979 was less than seven million or 2.6 per cent of the total population of the Soviet Union. Its average population density then was less than eight per square kilometre. However, this value distorts the true density pattern. Vast areas in the north are virtually uninhabited. In contrast, the great majority of the population lies

---

* I have drawn freely in these sections on my chapter entitled "Commodity Flows, Resource Potential and Regional Economic Development: the Example of the Soviet Far East," in R. Jenson et al. (eds.), Soviet Natural Resources in the World Economy, (University of Chicago Press, Chicago, 1983), pp. 189-219.

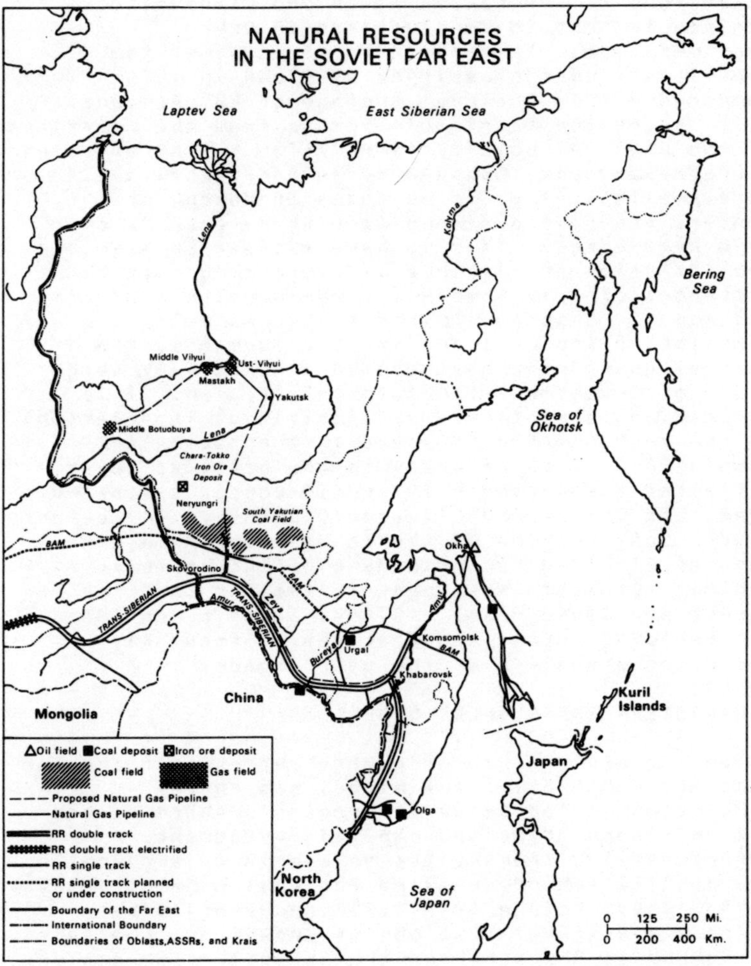

FIG. 2.2: NATURAL RESOURCES OF THE SOVIET FAR EAST

astride the Trans-Siberian railroad and its extensions to Sovetskaya Gavan and Vladivostock. The people tend to be clustered in urban agglomerations. Seventy-five per cent of the inhabitants were classified as urban in 1979 compared with a national average of 62 per cent.

The region is clearly remote from the heartland of the USSR, especially in relation to the extremes of Petropavlovsk, Magadan or Yuzhno-Sakhalinsk. More realistically, if we focus on Moscow or the Center, the rail distance from Khabarovsk is over 8500 kilometres. Thus we have a clear problem of the 'friction of distance'. Overcoming such distances clearly involves the expenditure of time and money. Despite limited funds, as well as conflicting sectoral and regional demands, the central government has devoted a relatively large share of investment funds to this region. This allocation is particularly significant in relation to the region's modest share in the nation's population. That priority in the past, at least, reflected the nation's strategic concerns vis-a-vis Japan and China. Most recently, massive investments in the construction of the Baikal-Amur Main Line have accelerated economic development in this region. Capital investment in the Far East for the latest available years, 1971-5, was 4.6 per cent of the national total, and that share presumably increased sharply over the past decade.

FAR EASTERN ENERGY DEVELOPMENT

In this overview, proved energy reserves in the Far East are comparatively limited, and energy production is far below the region's share of the nation's population and capital investment. Unfortunately, the Soviets have by and large ceased the publication of detailed regional economic data. My analysis, beyond 1975, will necessarily be speculative. The locations of known gas, coal and oil deposits are shown on the natural resources map, captioned Figure 2.2.

Oil is a commodity in short supply in the Soviet Far East. With the exception of Sakhalin, there are no proved deposits in the region. However, the geology of the Far East is such that the Far North may be an important zone of oil deposition. Most authorities argue that such exploration and exploitation must await, at least, the 1990s, if not later. The most promising areas appear to be the Arctic coast and offshore deposits

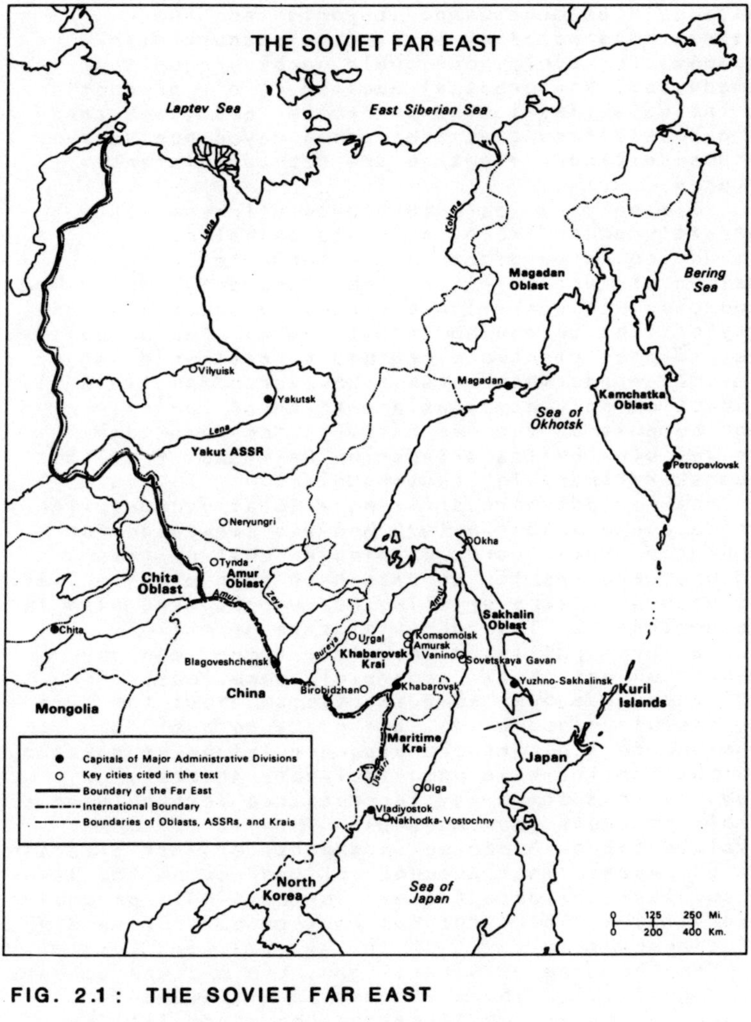

FIG. 2.1: THE SOVIET FAR EAST

in the Laptev, East Siberian and Chukhotsk Seas. The exploitation of these areas would require massive investments, and it would face the restrictions posed by an extremely short open season. Certainly, one could hardly argue that the remedy for the potential decline in oil production in the USSR lies in the Soviet Far East, but there is a possibility that the region may conceivably become self-sufficient in the not-too-distant future.

The only region with proved oil reserves currently under exploitation is Sakhalin. Production there began in the 1920s reaching a maximum of three million tons in recent years. The producing wells are concentrated in and around the city of Okha on the northeast coast. The product is then shipped via two pipelines to refineries at Komsomolsk and Khabarovsk. However, Sakhalin's production only provides one-fifth of the oil requirements of the Far East.(9) The remainder arrives via the Trans-Siberian Railroad, from the Angarsk refinery in Irkutsk Oblast.

As for offshore drilling a joint venture with the Japanese began in 1975 and was scheduled for completion this year. Barring renewal of this venture, the results to date have been mixed. There has been promising drilling off Odoptu, and also in the northeast. The potential size of the oil pool has not been published, nor have there been any reports on potential commercial operations. Then too, there has been some skepticism about the size of possible discoveries, and plans to build a pipeline to the northern Japanese island of Hokkaido via the Kuriles have been shelved. At best, expanded production may serve to reduce the imports of oil products from Angarsk. Thus it may be possible for an increase in exports of west Siberian oil to Japan. That depends, of course, on the level of surplus available there. The oil would probably move via the BAM to the Far Eastern port of Vannino for transhipment.

In the case of natural gas, the picture appears more promising. There already is a limited production of gas on Sakhalin, whose use is restricted to island markets. An expansion of that output by the 1990s now appears to be in the offing. More important, however, is the relatively recent opening up of gas fields in southern Yakutia. One author considers these deposits second only to fields in west Siberia in potential.(10) What is important, however, is the fact that, other than

in eastern Siberia. However, the proved deposits (A, B and C) are still very limited, although the prospects are truly promising. The Soviet Union persuaded the US and Japan to enter into a joint venture in 1976 to exploit these deposits. The agreement initially called for the purchase by both countries of ten billion cubic metres annually for a period of at least 25 years. US participation ended as a result of constraints imposed by the Trade Act of 1974 and its amendments, while Japanese involvement will only come when at least one trillion cubic metres are proved. By the spring of 1979, some 850 billion cubic metres were proved. Presumably, the remainder will have already been confirmed.

The field is located in the Viliui River watershed. Its center is Kysyl-Syr which is located about 400 kilometres northwest of the regional capital of Yakutsk and its output of 500 million cubic meters in 1975 was sent by pipeline to the capital to be used in a thermo-electric facility there. However, as noted earlier, the Soviets have more ambitious plans for the Viliui deposits. These call for the building of a large diameter pipeline and compressors for a distance of 3500 kilometres to Olga, a deep water ice-free port located in the southern part of Maritime Krai about 320 kilometes northeast of Vladivostock. The gas field location, the projected pipeline and the respective cities are all shown in Figure 2.2.

The second phase of the Yakutian project would be the construction of facilities at Olga for the liquefication and storage of liquified natural gas (LNG), the building of reconversion plants and storage facilities in Japan coupled with the construction of a number of LNG carriers to service the flow between the Soviet Far East and East Asian markets. Estimates of 1974 indicated that the ultimate cost of the project might be US $8.5 billion. That value is outdated because of inflation since 1974. What is important is the long-term viability of the project. In the simplest sense, the question is would the cost of delivered natural gas be competitive with that of petroleum delivered to the same market by the 1990s. Several authorities believe that the plan is currently dormant. Soviet press accounts speak of increased activity at Kysyl-Syr and the fact that the design of the pipeline is still underway despite environmental hazards. The Soviets argue that barring Japanese participation, they will still go ahead, but obviously at a much slower pace. It is difficult to rationalise their purported optimism. It appears inconceivable that markets in the Soviet Far East could absorb more than a fraction of the planned gas output of southern Yakutia. Then too, the sharp competition for scarce investment funds does not augur well for the project's future. Yet even given those obstacles, with the probable pressure on Soviet energy supplies by the late 1990s, the future delivery of Yakutian gas to markets in eastern Siberia is not unthinkable. However, such deliveries must inevitably be at a scaled-down level.

Far more is known about the coal reserves of the Soviet Far East than is true of the other energy sources. A 1966 estimate of coal reserves reported that the region accounted for roughly 5 per cent of the Soviet proved coal supplies (A, B and C) of this fuel or eleven billion tons.(11) Table 2.12

Table 2.12: Coal Reserves and Production of the Soviet Far East

(in millions of tons)

Region	Proved Reserves 1966	Production 1975
Amur Oblast	419	13.5
Kamchatka Oblast	67	13.5
Khabarovsk Krai	807	1.5
Magadan Oblast	1068	2.2
Maritime Krai	2450	10.1
Sakhalin Oblast	1073	5.0
Yakut ASSR	4580	2.0
Far East	11464	34.3
USSR	237200	701.0

Source: For the 1966 figures see <u>Energeticheskiye resursy</u> SSSR (Moscow: 1968) includes lignite coals. For the 1975 figures see L. Dienes and T. Shabad. <u>The Soviet Energy System</u> (Washington: 1979) includes lignite coals.

demonstrates the reserve and production values by political division. These data do not distinguish between bituminous, anthracite and lignite coals. The latter are of low calorific value and contain high levels of impurities like ash and sulfur, thus they are only useful for the production of steam or electricity. The largest known reserve areas are plagued by extremely low temperatures for extended periods of the year and very deep permafrost. However, these problems are offset by their shallow depth which makes them feasible for strip mining. Although there are significant supplies in every political subdivision of the Far East, because of physical problems and poor accessibility, the major areas of production are found in the southern part of the region and on Sakhalin. These serve mainly the larger urban nodes of the Soviet Far East. The region produced 34 million tons of coal in 1975 or 4 per cent of the nation's output. As indicated in Figure 2.2, the key bituminous coal centres are located at Urgal, Sakhalin and Southern Yakutia.

The coal deposits of the Yakut ASSR appear to offer the best prospects for the production of quality bituminous coals in the Far East, and it is the southern part of that political division which is currently under development. The proven reserves of Yakutia are the largest in the Soviet Far East. The South Yakut deposits constitute the largest reserves of quality coal in this broad region. They are also the only coals suitable for the production of metallurgical coke located east of Lake Baikal. Within the South Yakut field, one deposit, Neryungri, is outstanding. Its proved reserves were over half a billion tons in 1966. They are shallow (60-150 metres); the seams average 25 metres in thickness; and they are low in sulfur and phosphorus. One undesirable impurity, ash, must be removed by washing and cleaning. A more serious problem is the presence of a thick oxydised layer in the overburden. Thus thirty million tons must be removed before the quality coals are exposed.

Mining began in 1974 as part of an economic accord with Japan. The Soviets were to export five million tons a year, commencing in 1985, and the Japanese provided in return excavators, cranes, dump trucks and consumer goods. To facilitate the movement of coal, a spur, termed the Little Bam, was built south from the BAM to the Trans-Siberian long before the completion of the main line. The development has lagged behind plans, but the pace of mining has accelerated. The CIA estimates that 12 million tons will be produced this year. Then too, a coal cleaning plant was to be completed this year. There is however no news on the completion of this facility. Production problems in the mines have proved more difficult than foreseen, in part due to adverse temperatures and the escalation of mining and infrastructure costs. There is clearly ample coal for decades to come, but its costs will be much higher than originally envisaged. The main competition will presumably be from the PRC. There, mining costs are lower, but their coals are far inferior to the Neryungri product; however, transport costs would be clearly lower for Chinese shipments.

THE BAIKAL-AMUR MAINLINE

This line, whose construction began in 1974, has been one of the 'giant' Soviet construction projects of the post-war era. Part of the line, as far as Ust-Kut on the Lena River, was completed in the 1940s. The section between that centre and Komsomolsk (3148 kilometres) was to be completed in 1983. However, only this year was the major construction work finished. Apparently, the building of tunnels and bridges and the laying of track was completed in early 1985. Parts of the route are now in operation, and the remainder should be functioning within two years. The rationale for the huge investment of scarce resources and manpower appears to be have been twofold: one was strategic and the other economic.

The Soviet high command has always been conscious of the vulnerability and logistical weakness of the Trans-Siberian Railway. In strategic terms, the BAM offers adequate assurance against interdiction by Chinese ground forces. Its closest point to the border is 200 kilometres, but the largest share of the line lies about 260 kilometres north of the Chinese frontier. In addition, terrain barriers would impede any attempt to interdict the line by Chinese forces. However, the BAM is still vulnerable to air and missile attacks focused on choke points such as bridges and tunnels.

The economic circumstances that influenced the construction of the BAM and the Little BAM are clear. The railroad is viewed as a way of expediting the exploitation of eastern Siberia's resources to serve primarily the Japanese market. Initally, in the 1970s, it was thought that the BAM could serve as a funnel for oil shipments from Western Siberia to East Asian markets. Such shipments now seem unlikely. There will be a larger labour force to help exploit the BAM's service area. The resource base of the BAM hinterland, from Ust-Kut eastward, is extraordinarily rich and diverse. Yet only ten per cent of the most promising areas have been explored. Among undertakings underway or projected are the development of mines for the production of copper, asbestos, molybdenum, and probably apatites plus lumber industries and wood processing.

SIBERIAN ENERGY EXPORTS TO EAST ASIA AND THE POTENTIAL FOR GROWTH

The question of Soviet exports to East Asia has been thoroughly explored in the aforementioned volume on Soviet natural resources.(12) However, with the exception of Mote no one has focused directly on the present and prospective trade of the Soviet Far East with regard to the theme of energy development. Tables 2.13 and 2.14 provide a summary of Soviet trade with East Asian nations in oil and hard coal for 1981.

Table 2.13: Oil and Oil Product Exports of the USSR in 1981

Country	000 of metric tons	000 of rubles
Vietnam	?	213,808
Korean	400	67,708
Mongolian PR	?	87,324
Japan	90	125,750

Source: UN, Energy Statistics Yearbook 1982, New, York, 1984, and Vneshnaia Torgovlya SSR 1982, Moscow, 1983.

Table 2.14: Hard Coal Exports of the USSR in 1981

Country	000 of metric tons	000 of rubles
Korea NDR	?	19,903
Japan	1,410	57,073

Source: UN, Energy Statistics Yearbook 1982, 1984 and Vneshnaia Torgovlya SSR 1982, Moscow, 1983.

In overall trade, Japan was clearly the Soviet Union's leading trade partner in East Asia, but in energy trade the pattern evidenced in these tables was clearly more diverse. Then, too, there was a variety of transit movements relating to West Siberian petroleum and Kuznetsk Basin coals.

There were clearly transit movements of coal from the Kuzbas. Neryungri has not yet begun to fulfill Soviet commitments to Japan. Recent accounts make it appear that such shipments may be finally underway. This, of course, depends on the completion of the coal cleaning plant scheduled for operation in 1985. Coal exports to East Asia in value terms amounted to only 7 per cent of the Soviet total. The exports of oil were more diverse, but it should be understood that the exports to Japan were oil products, not crude oil. In contrast, the shipments to Vietnam, North Korea, and Mongolia represented a mixture of petroleum and petroleum products. Oil exports to the countries of the Pacific rim amounted to only two per cent in value terms of Soviet outbound flows.

We now turn to the most cogent question. What are the prospects for expanded energy exports to East Asia? We have already seen that possibilites for the near future are limited. Mote has made a statistical estimate of those prospects, and he was clearly not optimistic. In a recent article on Soviet-Japanese relations in which he drew on his observations during a ten-month visit to the region, Dienos also indicated his pessimism regarding the prospects for increased Soviet energy exports to Japan.(13)

This discussion has stressed the importance of

Neryungri as a coal mining centre, since the other coal fields, with the exception of Urgal, are scattered deposits of low-quality lignite. Neryungri now appears to be not only the best field in the Far East, but one of the very best in the USSR. Were it not for a recent slump in demand, I would project exports, via the BAM, of at least ten million tons a year. Much depends, however, on the completion of the coal cleaning plant. Also the Soviet Union will face increased competition from China, Australia , and the US in Japanese markets.

As for natural gas, the Yakutian project is dormant except for the movement by pipeline of gas to local markets. I believe that these deposits are potentially so rich that ultimately pipelines will be built to serve Soviet markets, particularly as production stablilises in western Siberia. The prospects of LNG gas exports to Japan or even the US seem so remote that they do not deserve consideration. The oil picture is more clouded. Conceivably, oil deposits currently under exploration in Sakhalin's offshore waters may prove to be fruitful. There is still a possibility the planned pipeline from the Kuriles to Hokkaido will be revived, spurring Japanese imports. Production from offshore deposits in the East Siberian Sea awaits the next century.

The foregoing analysis agrees with Victor Mote that an increase in energy exports from the Far East to East Asia awaits the distant future.

NOTES

1. Ed Hewett, Energy, Economics and Foreign Policy in the Soviet Union (Washington: 1984) pp. 32-3.

2. Ted Shabad, Soviet Geography April, 1984 and April, 1985.

3. A. Meyerhoff, 'Soviet Petroleum: History, Technology, Geology, Reserves; Potential and Policy', in Jensen, et al. (eds.) Soviet Natural Resources in the World Economy, (University of Chicago Press, Chicao, 1983), pp. 189-219.

4. Dickenshtein, et al, Neftogazovnye Provintsii, (Moscow: 1977) p. 96.

5. Ted Shabad, Soviet Geography, April, 1984.

6. Alan S. Whiting, Siberian Development and East Asia (Stanford University Press: Stanford, 1981).

7. Victor Mote, 'The Baikal-Amur Mainline and

its Implications for the Pacific Basin', in Jensen, R., et al (eds) Soviet Natural Resources in the World Economy pp. 134-188.

8. Victor Mote, 'Transport Aspects of Pacific Basin Prospects for the USSR' in Pacific Basic Transportation Prospects, Soviet Transport Project Working Paper 87 (Washington: 1984) pp. 24-125.

9. Leslie Dienes, and Ted Shabad, The Soviet Energy System, (Washington: 1979).

10. Mote, Transport Aspects, 1984, pp. 24-125.

11. Department of International Economic and Social Affairs, United Nations, Energy Statistics Yearbook 1982, (New York, 1984).

12. Jensen, et al., Soviet Natural Resources, 1983.

13. Leslie Dienes 'Soviet-Japanese Relations: Are They Beginning to Fade?' Soviet Geography (New York, September 1985), pp. 509-25.

Chapter Three

ENERGY SUPPLY AND THE VIABILITY OF THE ECONOMY OF TAIWAN, THE REPUBLIC OF CHINA

Chi-Yuan Liang

INTRODUCTION

The energy resources in Taiwan, Repubic of China, (ROC), are almost negligible.* Imported energy accounted for 88 per cent of total commercial energy supply in 1984. However, during the past decade of 'energy crisis', the ROC has performed quite well. The ROC achieved impressive real GNP growth rates of 8.3 per cent per annum during the period 1973-84. There were over the same period relatively low, 8.4 per cent per annum, increases in domestic wholesale prices. The ROC did not establish a trend of external indebtedness for oil import financing. In fact, the country's foreign exchange reserves increased from US $1.55 billion in 1974 to US $16.67 billion in 1984. The ROC's experience and governmental policies might well be useful for reference by other energy-importing countries.

This chapter will attempt to encompass a review of the supply and demand situation in Taiwan, ROC during the period 1965-83, a related examination of the impact of the two oil crises on the economy, a retrospection of the macroeconomic and energy

---

* The author is indebted to Professor R. C. Keith of the University of Calgary, Dr. Chen, the President of National Taiwan University, Mr. J. Yager of the Brookings Institution, Dr. V. V. Desai of the Asian Development Bank, Professor Kao-Chao Lee, Ms. Shiow-jiin Choiu of the Council for Economic Planning and Development, Mr. T. T. Feng, and Mr. H. T. Yih, the Executive Secretary and their colleagues of the Energy Committee for their valuable advice and assistance.

policies which emerged after the energy crises, a forecast of future energy supply and a consideration of the policy options for coping with the energy challenge in the future.

This Chapter is inclusive of the following sections: Introduction; Energy Resources, Supply and Demand; The Impact of Two Oil Crises on the Economy; Macroeconomic and Energy Conservation Policies After the First and Second Oil Crisis; Planning for Future Energy Supply and Energy Policies; Conclusion.

ENERGY RESOURCES, SUPPLY AND DEMAND

Domestic Deposits of Energy Resources

Taiwan is not well endowed with abundant deposits of fossil fuels. Proven domestic reserves amount to 1,400 thousand kilolitres of oil, 22,000 million cubic metres of natural gas, and 200 million metric tons of coal. The coal is mainly found in the northern part of the island; both the natural gas and the oil are found in the island's north-central region.

The oil reserves of the ROC are a negligible component of the total oil reserves of the Asian Pacific region. Similarly, the ROC's natural gas accounts for 0.6 per cent of the total regional reserves and its coal reserves account for 0.12 per cent of the total regional coal reserves. In 1983 the production of crude oil was 134.6 thousand kilolitres; the production of natural gas stood at 1470.8 million cubic metres; and the production of coal was 2.236 million metric tons.

Other domestic energy resources include hydro, geothermal, and biomass forms of energy supplies. Total proven hydro potential is estimated to be 5,300 megawatts, of which 1,430 megawatts have already been developed along several major rivers. Geothermal power is estimated to have a potential of 1,000 megawatts. The utilisation of this power source is in its incipient stage, however, to date, only a single three megawatt geothermal power plant in northern Taiwan is in operation. In the biomass energy sphere, anaerobic digestion of hog wastes has been used for many years to generate methane gas. Current biomass output is estimated at 390 thousand kilometres of oil equivalent, which is less than one-third of the estimated potential output of 1,300 thousand kilometres of oil equivalent.

Changes in Energy Supply

Table 3.1 shows the changes in Taiwan's energy supply situation during the period 1965–83. In 1965 the commercial primary energy supply in Taiwan totalled 6,061 thousand metric tons of oil equivalent. By 1983, the total commercial primary energy supply had increased to 31,878 thousand metric tons of oil equivalent. Prior to the first oil crisis (1965–73), the average annual growth rate of the total commercial primary energy supply was 12.4 per cent. The growth rate remained steady at 12.2 per cent per annum during the period of adjustment between 1974–9, but it then tailed off sharply following the second oil crisis to just 1.1 per cent during the period 1980–3. Between 1974 and 1983, then, the commercial primary energy supply grew on average at a rate of 8.67 per cent.

The commercial primary energy supply was increased at such a rapid pace in order to meet the soaring demand caused by rapid economic growth averaging 8.9 per cent, during 1965–83. Domestic manufacturers were forced to rely on imported energy because of the inadequacy of the indigenous energy supply.

Due to the deficiency of the indigenous energy supply, during the last 20 years Taiwan has become increasingly dependent on foreign primary energy sources. In 1965, 66 per cent of the commercial primary energy supply was indigenous energy. By 1983, only 12 per cent of the commercial primary energy supply came from domestic sources, with the remaining 88 per cent coming from imports. More specifically, 99 per cent of oil, 75 per cent of coal and 100 per cent of nuclear energy were imported in 1983. Even if nuclear energy is taken as an indigenous source, as it is reported in Japan's Aggregate Energy Statistics indigenous energy still only accounts for 26 per cent of the commercial energy supply, while the remaining 74 per cent originates with imports.

The composition of the primary energy supply has also changed a great deal during the last two decades. Coal, which had contributed 52 per cent of the commercial primary energy supply in 1965, dropped to 13 per cent in 1979, but then rose again to 17 per cent in 1983. The share of oil in the commercial energy supply rose dramatically between 1965 and 1979 from 34 to 72 per cent, but it dropped back to 61 per cent in 1983. In contrast, the contribution made by natural gas fluctuated

Table 3.1: Primary Energy Supply by Sources and Energy Types in ROC (1965–83)

	(000 MTOE)					
	1965	1973	1974	1979	1980	1983
Commercial Primary Energy Supply	6,060.84 (100.00)	15,417.89 (100.00)	15,082.26 (100.00)	26,856.26 (100.00)	30,859.37 (100.00)	31,878.04 (100.00)
Indigenous Source	4,009.91 (66.16)	4,327.59 (28.07)	4,486.45 (29.74)	4,617.19 (17.19)	4,201.50 (13.62)	3,944.52 (12.37)
Coal	3,133.79 (51.71)	2,062.80 (13.38)	1,819.33 (12.06)	1,686.28 (6.28)	1,595.47 (5.17)	1,386.36 (4.35)
Oil	18.72 (0.31)	151.29 (0.98)	189.00 (1.25)	207.54 (0.77)	190.26 (0.62)	121.18 (0.38)
Natural Gas	278.73 (4.60)	1,354.86 (8.79)	1,428.03 (9.47)	1,703.97 (6.34)	1,762.65 (5.71)	1,323.71 (4.25)
Hydro Power	578.67 (9.55)	758.63 (4.92)	1,050.09 (6.96)	1,019.40 (3.80)	653.02 (2.12)	1,113.27 (3.49)

Table 3.1: Primary Energy Supply by Sources and Energy Types in ROC 1965–83

(000 MTOE)

	1965	1973	1974	1979	1980	1983
Imported Source	2,050.93 (33.84)	11,090.30 (71.93)	10,596.08 (70.26)	22,239.07 (82.81)	26,657.87 (86.38)	27,933.52 (87.63)
Coal	0 (0.00)	105.42 (0.68)	382.70 (2.54)	1,710.06 (6.37)	3,099.12 (10.04)	4,177.09 (13.10)
Oil	2,050.93 (33.84)	10,984.88 (71.25)	10,213.38 (67.72)	19,116.29 (71.18)	21,728.78 (70.41)	19,537.13 (61.29)
Nuclear Power	0 (0.00)	0 (0.00)	0 (0.00)	1,412.72 (5.26)	1,829.97 (5.93)	4,219.31 (13.24)
Non-Commercial Primary Energy Supply	1,466,00	1,170.50	1,138.10	988.70	961.30	883.53
Primary Energy	7,526.84	16,588.39	16,220.63	27,844.96	31,820.67	31,761.57

Source: Energy Committee, Ministry of Economic Affairs, _Energy Balance in Taiwan, Republic of China_

minimally from 5 per cent in 1965 to 6 per cent in 1979 and then down to 4 per cent in 1983. The share of hydro-power also fell from 10 per cent in 1965 to 3 per cent in 1983. An important new component of commercial primary energy supplies was nuclear energy, which when first utilised in Taiwan in 1979 furnished 5 per cent of commercial primary energy. As indicated in Figure 3.1 it subsequently increased to 13 per cent in 1983.

The changes in the composition of the primary energy supply outlined above were affected by two main factors. In the first place there were changes in the relative prices of energy types. Secondly, the government implemented policies that sought to substitute oil for coal before the oil crises and then to re-substitute coal and nuclear power for oil after the second oil crisis.

The use of non-commercial primary energy sources was already in decline by 1965. Fire-wood and agricultural wastes were widely used in rural areas befores 1965 when the non-commercial primary energy supply was estimated as 1,466 thousand metric tons of oil equivalent. This decreased markedly to 883 thousand MTOE in 1983. The average rate of decline was 2.7 per cent per annum during this period. The exploitation of these non-commercial primary energy sources was reduced after electricity and liquefied petroleum gas became readily available in rural areas as substitutes for fire-wood and agricultural wastes. The extension of electricity was particularly important in this respect. Since the 1970s, the degree of electrification in Taiwan has reached 99 per cent.

The total primary energy supply -- defined as the sum of the commercial primary energy supply plus the non-commercial primary energy supply -- was estimated as 7,527 thousand metric tons of oil equivalent in 1965, of which 80 per cent came from commercial primary energy sources, and the remaining 20 per cent came from non-commercial energy sources. The total primary energy supply increased to 32,762 thousand MTOE in 1983. However, the share of non-commercial energy in the total primary energy supply decreased to 2.7 per cent in 1983. The average growth rate of the total primary energy supply was 10.4 per cent during the period before the first oil crisis (1965-73), 11.4 per cent during the adjustment period (1974-9), and 1.0 per cent during the period following the second oil crisis (1980-3).

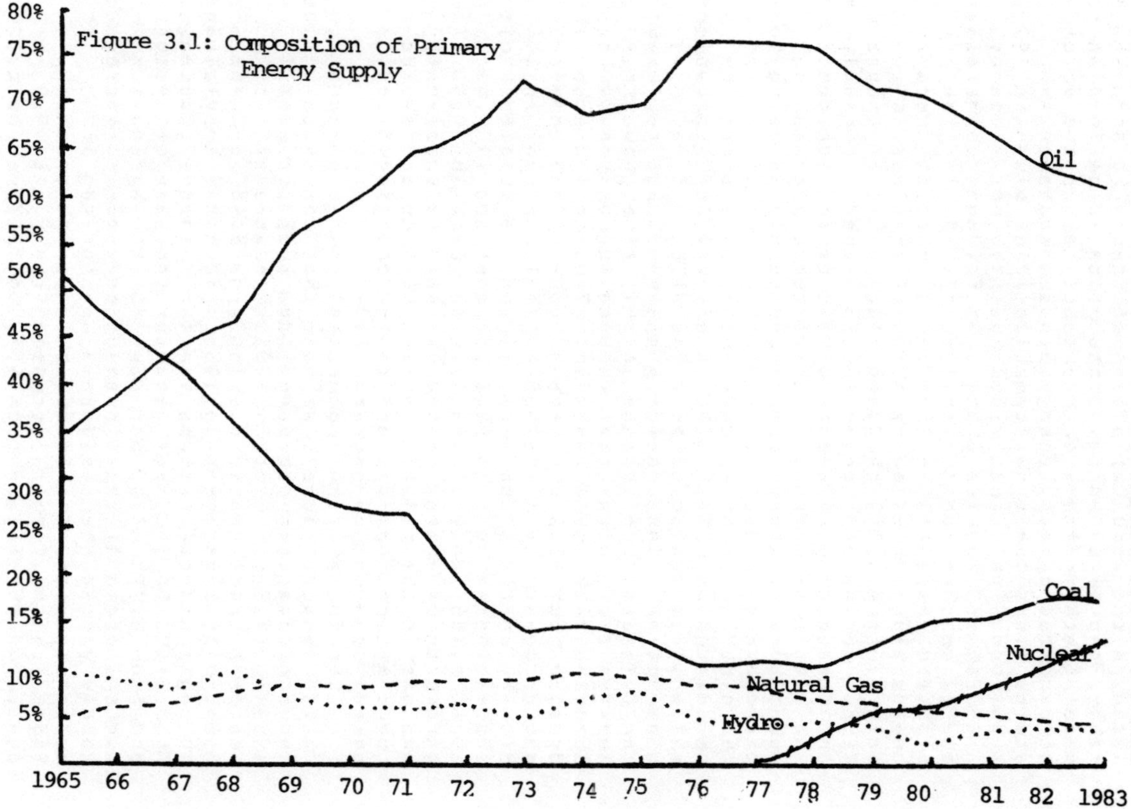

Figure 3.1: Composition of Primary Energy Supply

Changes in Energy Demand

Based on the OECD Definition of Energy Balance Table, the final energy consumption is defined as equal to the primary energy supply minus the volume of exported primary energy minus the change in stocks minus the transformation input plus the transformation output minus loss and net account.

Table 3.2 gives changes in Taiwan's commercial energy consumption during 1965-82. During the past eighteen years (1965-83) final commercial energy consumption increased by almost five times in Taiwan, from 4,243 thousand MTOE to 21,718 thousand MTOE. During the period 1965-83, energy consumption on average grew at a rate of 9.5 period per cent.

It is noted that the difference between quantities of energy demand and supply is owing to the conversion factors used for electricity. Ten to the ninth power of kilowatt-hours of electricity is calculated as 0.2236 MTOE in electricity generation; while it is conversed as 0.086 MTOE in final consumption. Consumption patterns do not represent the full extent of change in this time, however. The types of energy that were being consumed were changing with equal rapidity. Thus coal consumption dropped from 52.7 per cent of total final commercial energy consumption in 1965 to 17.1 per cent in 1983. Picking up the slack were oil and electricity whose shares increased from 30.3 per cent and 11.9 per cent in 1965 to 60.1 and 17.6 per cent in 1983. The structure of energy demand has been responsive to changes in the relative prices between energy types, to government policy, and to the changing trends in energy consumption patterns.(1)

Looking at final commercial energy consumption at the sectoral level, we note that the share of the industrial sector decreased from 58.5 per cent in 1965 to 51.5 per cent in 1983. The transportation sector's share nearly doubled from 8.48 per cent in 1965 to 16.2 per cent in 1983. Both the service and the agricultural sectors saw their shares reduced, from 21.96 to 15.7 per cent for the service sector, and from 5.7 to 3.95 per cent for the agricultural sector. Some of these changes were due to increased energy use in the residential sector and of non-energy uses for feedstock. As indicated in Table 3.3 the former increased from 6.6 to 9.0 per cent, and the latter from 5.33 to 12.7 per cent.

Non-commercial energy types such as fire-wood, charcoal, and agricultural wastes are consumed mainly in the residential sector. Unfortunately, no time-series data are available for this type of

Table 3.2: Commercial Final Energy Consumption by Energy Types

	1965	1973	1974	1979	1980	1983
Total Commercial Final Energy Consumption	4,242.75 (100.00)	10,310.69 (100.00)	10,179.57 (100.00)	19,005.57 (100.00)	20,221.12 (100.00)	11,718.26 (100.00)
Coal	1,236.43 (52.71)	2,099.99 (20.73)	1,845.86 (18.13)	2,027.34 (10.67)	2,254.75 (11.15)	3,710.36 (17.08)
Oil Products	1,283.26 (30.25)	5,474.69 (53.10)	5,511.38 (54.14)	12,211.43 (46.25)	12,969.06 (64.14)	13,066.14 (60.16)
Natural Gas	216.54 (5.10)	1,109.52 (10.76)	1,113.57 (10.94)	1,581.03 (8.32)	1,572.75 (7.78)	1,125.56 (5.18)
Electricity	506.51 (11.94)	1,626.50 (15.77)	1,708.76 (16.79)	3,185.77 (16.76)	3,424.56 (16.94)	3,816.18 (17.57)

Source: Energy Committee, Ministry of Economic Affairs, *Energy Balance in Taiwan, Republic of China*

Table 3.3: Commercial Final Energy Consumption by Sectors 1965–83

(000 MTOE)

	1965	1973	1974	1979	1980	1983
(1) Total Commercial Final Energy Consumption	5,242.75 (100.00)	10,310.69 (100.00)	10.179.57 (100.00)	19,005.57 (100.00)	20,221.12 (100.00)	21,718.26 (100.00)
(2) Agriculture	243.13 (5.73)	528.88 (5.13)	566.05 (5.56)	804.72 (4.24)	802.01 (3.96)	858.60 (3.95)
(3) Mining	131.29 (3.09)	101.39 (0.99)	113.14 (1.11)	139.26 (0.73)	147.61 (0.73)	156.18 (0.72)
(4) = (5)+(6)+(7)	2,350.50 (55.41)	5,770.91 (55.97)	5,540.59 (54.43)	10,209.27 (53.71)	10,813.39 (53.48)	11,035.45 (50.81)
(5) Manufacturing	2,299.87 (54.21)	5,632.94 (54.63)	5,376.58 (52.82)	9,930.85 (52.25)	10,471.71 (52.79)	10,551.24 (48.58)
(6) Construction	15.53 (0.37)	34.74 (0.34)	58.17 (0.57)	97.34 (0.51)	144.68 (0.72)	95.74 (0.44)

Table 3.3: Commercial Final Energy Consumption by Sectors (1965-83)

(000 MTOE)

	1965	1973	1974	1979	1980	1983
(7) Public Utilities	35.10 (0.83)	103.23 (1.00)	105.84 (1.04)	181.08 (0.95)	197.00 (0.97)	388.47 (1.79)
(8) Transportation	359.79 (8.48)	1,270.78 (12.32)	1,372.52 (13.48)	2,783.80 (14.65)	2,997.06 (14.82)	3,508.57 (16.15)
(9) Service	650.04 (15.32)	955.34 (9.27)	836.30 (8.22)	1,158.10 (6.09)	1,219.38 (6.03)	1,445.10 (6.66)
(10) Residential	281.72 (6.64)	771.65 (7.48)	851.57 (8.37)	1,553.73 (8.18)	1,626.85 (8.04)	1,961.42 (9.03)
(11) Nonenergy Uses	226.28 (5.33)	911.73 (8.84)	899.42 (8.84)	2,356.69 (12.40)	2,614.81 (12.93)	2,752.45 (12.68)

Source: Energy Committee, Ministry of Economic Affairs, Energy Balance in Taiwan, Republic of China.

energy consumption in Taiwan. However, the Energy Committee did conduct two surveys aimed at assessing the level of non-commerical energy use in 1960 and in 1982. By interpolating and extrapolating the data found in these surveys, we can approximate non-commercial final energy consumption during 1965-83. We estimate that 1,466 thousand MTOE were consumed in 1965, but consumption shrank to 883 thousand MTOE in 1983. The annual growth rate of non-commercial final energy consumption during these 18 years thus was -2.77 per cent.

Now, by combining the commercial and non-commercial final energy consumption, we estimate that in 1965 total final energy consumption was 5,709 thousand MTOE, which then increased at an annual rate of 7.9 per cent to its 1983 level of 22,602 thousand MTOE. Of this 1963 total, non-commercial final energy consumption was responsible for only 3.9 per cent (down from 25.7 per cent in 1965), and commercial final energy consumption accounted for 96.1 per cent (up from 74.3 per cent in 1965).

IMPACT OF TWO OIL SHOCKS ON THE ECONOMY

Impact on Inflation

Throughout the 1960s and during the opening two years of the 1970s the economy of Taiwan developed rapidly and without the severe fluctuations in prices that have burdened many third world countries. Between 1965 and 1973 inflation, in terms of the Consumer Price Index (CPI), averaged 4.0 per cent per year, and in terms of the Wholesale Price Index (WPI), the figure was even lower at 3.6 per cent. The economy was not so fortunate during the two oil shocks of the 1970s, however. During both crises the inflation rate, whether measured in terms of the CPI or the WPI, reached double-digit proportions.

For many years prior to the first oil shock, which began in October 1973, Taiwan's oil costs had remained inexpensive and basically stable. Between 1965 and 1973, the price of imported Arabian light oil increased from US $1.80 per barrel to US $3.33 per barrel. The domestic oil prices of this period reflected this mild increase, rising by 0.78 per cent annually.

The 1970s witnessed two major surges in imported oil prices with a relatively stable period of adjustment sandwiched inbetween. The first oil shock (1973-4) sent the price of Arabian light oil soaring; by the end of 1974 it had reached US $11.65 per barrel. During these two years the average annual price of imported oil grew by 140 per cent. This contributed heavily to the 31.72 per cent annual rise in the SPI inflation index and to the 27.83 per cent increase in the CPI during these two years. Import prices stabilised during the next three years, and upward domestic price movement was accordingly mild. This period, however, proved to be the calm before the second storm in 1979-80 when the import price of oil averaged a 53.34 per cent annual increase, which helped produce an average WPI inflation rate of 17.69 per cent (14.39 per cent, in terms of the CPI). Inflation during this latter oil crisis, then, was less severe than during the first crisis but was still at the double-digit level.

These sudden, large oil price increases of the 1970s affected domestic prices in two ways. First, both the WPI and the CPI were influenced directly, as higher import bills led to higher domestic prices for oil products. Second, non-energy products also rose in price because many of them required oil products as intermediate inputs. This indirect effect on manufactured products raised the prices of goods intended for both domestic and export markets.

In fact, the Council for Economic Planing and Development estimated in one study that 56.3 per cent of the domestic WPI increase during 1973-1974 was generated by imported inflation, with the balance stemming from wage increases (21.3 per cent), and other factors (22.4 per cent). For the second oil crisis, the study found that fully 66.8 per cent of the WPI growth was the result of imported inflation, with 16.6 per cent coming from wage increases, and 14.6 per cent from other factors.(2) An I/O price model was used to calculate that the oil price hike in 1973-4 directly produced a 13.7 per cent gain in the WPI, and that the oil price increase in 1979-80 directly caused an increase in the WPI of 7.6 per cent. From this we can discern that oil imports alone were responsible for 77 per cent of the imported inflation during the first oil crisis and for 63 per cent of the imported inflation during the second oil crisis period.

Impact on Trade and Balance of Payment

For most of the 1970s, the volume of imports of oil was rising, but the rate of this increase was well behind the pace of the price hikes. The annual volume of oil imported during 1973-4 rose by 21.4 per cent over the 1972 level, but the import bill skyrocketed by 165.5 per cent per year at that time. Thus during the first oil crisis only 13 per cent of the expanded oil bill derived from quantity increases, while the remaining 87 per cent reflected the higher oil price. During the second oil crisis the volume of imported oil actually decreased, by 2.8 per cent per annum compared to the 1978 import figure, but the import bill still grew by 91.5 per cent each year; this increase was thus entirely due to higher oil prices.

The combination of a rising value of imports at ever expanding prices increased oil's share of Taiwan's total imports. Between 1973 and 1980, the value of imported oil doubled, and oil's share in total imports expanded from 7.5 per cent in 1973-4 to 15.6 per cent in 1979-1980.

The two oil shocks both quite obviously affected adversely the trade balance and the balance of payments in Taiwan. In the immediate aftermath of the first oil crisis, the government of the ROC was reluctant to adjust upward the prices of public utilities, which gave Taiwan's export price a relatively downward bias. In 1973, then, Taiwan's exports were very competitive and sales increased at a brisk pace so that by the end of 1973 Taiwan had recorded a trade surplus of US $569 million. This surplus put tremendous pressure on domestic price levels, however, and helped to boost the inflation rate to a dangerously high level, 40.58 per cent in terms of the WPI in 1974.

The export situation in 1974 changed considerably. Calculated in 1976 constant prices, exports declined by 7.4 per cent in 1974 while imports increased substantially, which produced a hefty US $1,121 million trade deficit in that year. This moreover was followed by a further deficit of US $508 million in 1975. Not surprisingly, these shifts in the trade balance affected Taiwan's overall balance of payments. In 1973, Taiwan was able to record a balance of payments surplus of US $90 million, which was already a retreat from the US $569 million recorded in 1972. A deficit of US $54 million appeared in 1974. During the readjustment years, from 1976-8, the situations of both the trade balance and the balance of payments improved markedly. The second oil crisis, however, again rocked the economy by slowing down exports just when the import bill was expanding rapidly. The trade balance in 1979 fell to US $291 million from the previous year's US $1,761 million and was followed by a US $547 million deficit in 1980. Similarly, the balance of payments deteriorated from a surplus of US $1,951 million in 1978 to a surplus of US $96 million in 1979 and then to a deficit in 1980 of US $127 million.

During the 1971-82 period, with the exception of 1974, 1975, and 1980, Taiwan was able to amass a substantial trade surplus and to accumulate US $6.3 billion in foreign reserves during the 12 years. These reserves allowed the economy to face the adverse effects of the two oil shocks without having to resort to foreign loans to finance energy-induced trade deficits.

Impact on Economic Growth Rate

The economy of the ROC is highly open. In 1974 the value of imports and exports comprised 44 per cent and 51 per cent of the GNP respectively. The decrease of export growth rate caused the GNP growth rate to fall. The GNP growth rate averaged 7.4 per cent during the post-oil-shock period, 1974-82. This is significantly lower than that of 11.0 per cent during the pre-oil-shock period, 1965-73. It is worth noting that the annual GNP growth rate slowed to 2.7 per cent during 1974-5 and to 4.5 per cent during 1981-2. If these two subperiods were excluded from the post-oil-shock period, the difference in GNP growth rates between pre-oil-shock and post-oil-shock period is almost negligible.

MACROECONOMIC AND ENERGY CONSERVATION POLICIES AFTER THE FIRST AND SECOND OIL CRISIS.(3)

Macroeconomic Policies Subsequent to the First Oil Crisis

Despite the sharp increase in import prices during the second half of 1973, domestic prices were relatively downward biased throughout the year. Domestic prices were able to remain low because of the government's decision to maintain existing prices and rates for oil products and public utilities; in addition, agricultural subsidies on wheat, soybeans, and other crops were also extended to support the artifically low food prices. Exports in 1973 as a result grew rapidly, and the economy as a whole ended the year with a trade surplus of US $569 million. This surplus added fuel to money supply expansion and combined with the vigorous growth in the export sector, led to substantial wage hikes and to a fundamentally overheated economy. Public inflationary expectations led to the hoarding of certain commodities. All these factors, then, set the stage for the inflation rate to explode in 1974 as prices ended the year at 40.34 per cent higher than at the end of 1973.

The government next moved to curtail domestic effective demand, to attack inflation, and to restore general economic stability in January, 1974 when the 'Economic Stabilisation Programme' was unveiled. The highlights of this programme included a substantial increase in interest rates and a corresponding tightening of credit, an upwardly adjusted price for petroleum products, electricity, transportation sevices, and wine and tobacco, a reduction in the government subsidies for imported soybeans and wheat, and the partial liberalisation of price controls through the replacement of price ceilings with negotiated prices. The programme's effect was almost immediate. Prices jumped in February, but soon stabilised on a higher plateau. Price negotiations were then eliminated in June. In sum, this once-and-for-all price adjustment was successful on two fronts: it eliminated the public psychology of inflation by allowing prices to rise almost overnight to high levels at which they then remained; and it employed contractionary monetary policy to successfully check the growth of demand. Although the double-digit inflation was then stopped, a recession occurred in the wake of the 'Stabilisation Programme'.

In order to offset declining investment in the private sector produced by the stabilisation programme, the government poured funds from its coffers into the Ten Great Projects, which had also been the target of substantial public investment in 1973. As a result, the rate of increase in 1974 for investment in fixed capital formation was 9.2 per cent, about equal to the 1973 level. Import tax rates were also reduced sharply. In 1974 customs duties were brought down by some NT $6.7 billion, equivalent to 25 per cent of the duties actually received during the year, and the figure would expand to NT $16.1 billion if import-tax refunds for exports were included. Finally, although the overall trade balance deteriorated significantly in 1974, the NT/US dollar exchange rate was maintained at the 1973 level of 38:1 to stabilise domestic prices. By contrast, the Korean won was devalued by 18 per cent against the US dollar.

Government policy designed to stabilise prices without plunging the economy into a recession was not to succeed. Depressed global export markets combined with a rising import bill and the anti-inflationary measures adopted at the beginning of 1974 finally brought about a deep recession that persisted until late 1975. In March 1974 Taiwan's foreign trade balance moved into the red, which was a direct result of the import bill rising just when imports were trailing off. In the second quarter, the trade balance plummeted to a deficit of US $570 million, or the equivalent of one-sixth of the quarter's entire GDP.

The recession struck with the greatest impact on small-and medium-sized enterprises, which in growing numbers were forced to lock the gates to their plants. Surrounded by the growing urgency of the problem, the government began taking measures to bail out small businesses and industry and to stimulate exports as early as May, 1974. These measures were carried out selectively so as not to jeopardise economic stability, allowing the easing of credit to strengthen export financing and the lowering of interest rates on loans for the production of goods for export.

The recession was exacerbated in the second half of 1974 when, contrary to the respective gains of 9 per cent and 6.2 per cent registered in the first two quarters of the year, manufacturing output fell by 3.2 per cent in the third quarter. The difficulties encountered by business and industry continued to multiply as a result.

The government next gradually adopted a series of stronger measures between September and December to push the economy out of its recession. The most important actions taken were as follows:

1. Interest rates on bank loans were reduced by 1.25-1.50 percentage points and interest rates on savings deposits were reduced by 1 percentage point in mid-September; both rates were lowered further by one-half of a percentage point in mid-December;

2. Guaranteed reserve requirements for bank deposits were lowered along with the reserve requirements for foreign exchange settlements of imports;

3. The Central Bank of China earmarked NT$5 billion for the refinancing of export loans;

4. There were temporary resumptions of import tax refunds on previously stipulated secondary materials and of wastage allowances.

Interest rates were lowered again in February and then in April of 1975; the rate for export loans dropped to its lowest level ever, 7.5 per cent. Meanwhile, government financing to public and private enterprises was provided in large amounts.

No fundamental macroeconomic policy changes or principles have been adopted since the first oil crisis. The most important measure was the 'Economic Stabilisation Programme,' but this was a short-term rescue operation, not a long-term policy orientation. As mentioned above, the government's initial response to the sudden and swift upward movement in the imported price of oil in 1973 was to try to regulate prices and to continue its subsidization programme, but both these measures raised public fears of further inflation and hence they were soon abandoned. It was at this point that the stabilisation was introduced to allow the prices of petroleum products, electricity, and transportation services to better reflect true costs. In a nutshell, then, the lesson learned by the government of the Republic of China as a result of the first oil crisis was the importance of 'cost-reflecting' pricing in energy policy.

Energy Conservation Programmes After the First Oil Crisis

The first oil price rises indeed came as a shock to policymakers in the Republic of China. Faced with mounting import bills, the Executive Yuan first acted in November of 1973 when it passed an energy conservation programme which solicited the help of the whole nation in saving energy. For example, in December, the Ministry of the Interior extended limitations on the use of neon signs.

Immediately after the oil price hikes, the government promised not to raise public utility prices, but rather announced its intentions to curb petroleum use by 15 per cent and to adopt a stabilisation programme in the future. The stabilisation programme raised utility prices in part to help to curtail demand. Other demand-cutting actions were additionally implemented in January, 1974; for example, progressive tariff rates on electricity were introduced to replace the regressive rates then in use.

Limitations on energy use were rescinded after the oil embargo was over. Demand did not rise rapidly at that time, however, because of the depressed state of the domestic economy.

Energy and Macroeconomic Policies after the Second Oil Crisis

In view of the failure of the price-control policy of 1973, the government of the ROC adjusted the prices of domestic oil products and electricity right after the price increase of imported oil during the second oil crisis period. Meanwhile, macroeconomic policies were deliberately used to deal with the domestic inflation caused by the huge increase in oil price. Policies adopted then included cutting taxes, tightening the money supply, and reducing public expenditure, especially with respect to the capital formation of public enterprises. Such capital formation decreased in 1982, and the government's consumption expenditures only increased by a limited margin.

Since the ROC economy was highly open, the attack on domestic economy brought out by the oil crisis was unavoidably severe. The economic growth rate declined from 13.85 per cent in 1978 to 8.08, 6.60 and 5.04 per cent in the following three years. As a result, the private investment intention stagnated. In the second half of 1981, the Ministry of Finance promulgated an investment tax credit package for those enterprises replacing their old boilers and purchasing new machinery. In June, 1982, the extent of qualification for tax credits was further widened. Meanwhile, customs duty was cut in half for imported machinery. From April of 1982 until the end of 1983, the deduction in customs duty was estimated as costing NT $3.8 billion or US $95 million dollars.

The increase of deposits at banks slowed down immediately after the second oil crisis, due to anticipated inflation. To stimulate bank deposits the interest rates were raised twice in May and August of 1979. At the same time, the Central Bank lowered the reserve ratios for checking accounts, passbook deposits and saving deposits. And it further manipulated open market operations to ease the fund shortages of the commercial banks. As a result, by the second half of 1981, the domestic inflation slowed down. Unfortunately, the private investment did not significantly improve mainly due to the gloomy economy. In August 1981, the bank union started to lower interest rates for both loans and deposits to facilitate investment further. From then until the end of 1982 the interest rates were lowered five times. The exchange rate of the NT dollar was devaluated against the US dollar by 4.63 per cent by the Foreign Exchange Center on 12 August

1981.

During the brief interlude between the 1973-4 and 1979-1980 oil crises, the energy intensity per unit of real GDP increased by 14.95 per cent. This ill-fated increase was partially due to long-term planning favouring the petrochemical and heavy industrial sectors, including the establishment of an integrated steel mill to upgrade the industrial structure. Unfortunately, these industries were both quite energy-intensive and fast-growing. Between 1973 and 1979, the annual growth rate for 18 petrochemical products averaged 27 per cent per annum, while the output of the steel industry grew by 15 per cent per annum.

Why were these energy-intensive sectors being developed at a time when the government actively sought to restrict aggregate energy demand growth in the economy? To understand the economic rationale behind this step, we must take a very brief look back at the industrial structure of the 1950s and 1960s. Even though high growth during these two decades was accompanied by impressive industrial structural change, for the most part simple processing and export operations fueled by the imports of basic materials and intermediates characterised the economic structure. A shortage of basic materials, moreover, was one of the most important factors underlying the inflation that arose after the first oil crisis. To eliminate the problem of inflation-feeding supply shortages, the government undertook to develop indigenous supplies of basic materials and intermediates. This strategy calling for the development of the energy-intensive heavy industrial and petrochemical sectors was most vigorously pursued in the 5-year span between the two oil crises.

Not surprisingly, the second oil shock struck a heavy blow at the domestic economy. As a result, the four-year plan covering 1982-6, (released in 1981), required a number of fundamental policy changes. The expansion of energy-intensive industries -- such as aluminium, zinc, and lead -- was curtailed and incentives were alternatively offered to encourage the development of these industries abroad as part of joint venture projects. The expansion of the steel refining and copper refining industries was specifically tied to the pace of the development of the electrical and non-electrical machinery industries. The development of the petrochemical industry was to continue, but at a pace relative to the supply of the domestic market and the material requirements of the export sector. The plan identified the increased output from low-energy, high-value-added strategic industries in the machinery manufacturing and information sectors as the key priority to be pursued vigorously in the 1980s.

These policies help illuminate the more general approach to energy conservation, now held by economic planners in the Republic of China. The new orientation has evolved from past economic management experience and from the conditions of resource scarcity in the domestic economy and the ever present threat of a third oil crisis. The government is now interested in restricting oil consumption in the followng three ways: by developing a sophisticated energy-saving programme that promotes energy conservation through the use of energy efficient machinery, by improving the industrial structure by expanding the overall output shares of energy-efficient, skill-intensive, and high-value-added industries; and by diversifying energy sources for domestic consumption, particularly in the area of electric power generation. The most recent four-year plan (1982-6) stipulates a target of increased efficiency in energy use of 10.9 per cent during the plan period.

In addition the government in August 1980 moved to shore up the foundations in the fight against energy waste with the passage of the Energy Management Law, which provides the legal basis for energy-saving policies. This law will be discussed in the next section.

PLANNING FOR FUTURE ENERGY SUPPLY AND ENERGY POLICIES

Planning for Future Energy Supply

Following the guide-line of Energy policy for the Taiwan Area ROC, (section 1 and 5), which was promulgated on 5 October 1984, the Energy Committee, Ministry of Economic Affairs, set out a plan for future energy supply from 1984 to 2000. This plan was released in November, 1985.

The total commercial energy supply will increase from 33,644 thousand MTOE in 1984 to 43,835 thousand MTOE in 1990 and 67,589 thousand MTOE in 2000. The average annual growth rate will be 4.5 per cent between 1985-2000.

These estimates were based on the assumption that the real annual economic growth rate will be 6.5 per cent for the same period. Due to the insufficiency of domestic supply, the imported energy as a percentage of total commercial energy supply will increase from 88 per cent in 1984 to 93 per cent in 2000.

However, the imported oil as a percentage of total energy supply will decrease from 59 per cent in 1984 to 45 per cent in 2000. In contrast, the percentages of imported coal and nuclear energy will rise respectively from 14 and 15 per cent to 28 and 17 per cent by the year 2000. Liquefied natural gas, which will be imported after 1990 will account for 2.8 per cent in 2000. The percentage of hydro-power will keep around 2.4 per cent during 1984-2000. New forms of energy, such as geothermal energy, wind power and biomass are planned to play only fairly limited roles in the future. The percentage share of these forms will increase from 0.9 to 2.4 per cent.

In order to cope with the increasing demand for imported energy, the government has worked to diversify the types of energy imported as well as the sources of external supply. Also, the goverment has sought to increase its participation in the exploration and development of crude oil and coal in foreign countries on a joint-venture basis.

The effect of the diversification of energy forms and sources has been quite significant in the past decade. Imported crude oil as a percentage of total energy supply declined from 71 per cent in 1973 to 58 per cent in 1984 through the substitution of nuclear energy and coal. The pattern of foreign supply has been significantly altered. Crude oil imported from Saudi Arabia, Kuwait and neutral zone has been decreased from 85 per cent in 1980 to 69 per cent in 1984. On the other hand, importation from Indonesia, Malaysia, Ecuador and others has been increased from 15 per cent in 1980 to 31 per cent in 1984.

The China Petroleum Company has promoted joint-venture exploration and development of crude oil reserves in the Philippines, Indonesia, Malaysia, Mauritania, Australia and Ra's al Khaymah, United Arab Emirates. The discovery of offshore crude oil reserves in Ra's al Khaymah is one of the most successful results of these efforts. Its daily production is estimated at 12,000 barrels.

Institutions in Energy Planning and Energy Demand Management (4)

Energy planning in the Republic of China was begun in 1968 with the establishment of the Energy

Planning and Development Committee. This committee was initially under the guidance of the Council for International Co-operation and Development of the Executive Yuan, but two years later it was renamed the Energy Policy Committee and transferred to the Ministry of Economic Affairs. In November, 1979, the Energy Policy Committee was reorganised and renamed as the Energy Committee. It was set up under the Ministry of Economic Affairs and was made responsible for the implementation of energy policy and for the enforcement of the Energy Management Law.

The management of national energy demand in the Republic of China is legally based on the Energy Policy for the Taiwan Area, ROC, and the Energy Management Law.

The former was first promulgated by the Executive Yuan on 26 April 1973, while the latter was enacted on 5 October 1984. Several new important articles relating to energy utilisation and conservation, the enactment of the energy law and its execution, and special funding for energy research and development were included in the first version of the policy's revision. The contents of the most recent version of the Energy Policy for the Taiwan Area incorporate five sections relating to the assurance of the stability of energy supply, the rationalisation of energy pricing, the promotion of the effectiveness of energy utilisation, the prevention of energy-related environmental pollution, and the strengthening of energy research and development.

The Energy Policy for the Taiwan Area, ROC, especially features the rationalisation of energy pricing. The policy requires that pricing reflect real costs and should be properly interrelated with factors of energy conservation and export competitiveness. Under this regime the Chinese Petroleum Corporation and Taiwan Power Company are expected to achieve a reasonable rate of return and to generate sufficient funding to support long-term development. The pricing of petroleum products and natural gas is correlated with their respective heating values and the possibilities of mutual substitution; whereas electric rates are to be based upon time-of-use costs in order to encourage off-peak power consumption and higher load factors.

Also, energy policy has focused on effective energy utilisation. Government energy administration is keen to reform the industrial structure and to strengthen factory-level management. While energy-intensive industry is discouraged, there is positive emphasis on industrial electrification in order to support industrial upgrading and automation. Policy focuses on the achievement of energy savings through the development of mass transportation and rapid transit systems and the manufacture and use of energy-saving traffic devices. Energy consumption standards for vehicles have been formulated. Policy also requires the formation and regular review and amendment of energy efficiency standards for new buildings and energy consuming equipment. Government emphasises the dissemination of information on energy conservation in order to achieve maximum overall effectiveness of energy utilisation.

The Energy Management Law, promulgated in 1980, attempts to further long-term efficiency in energy utilisation and management. In addition to the setting up of a special fund for energy research and development, this Law highlighted the following conditions: the establishment of an energy audit system within large energy-consuming enterprise; (5) the stipulation of minimum energy standards for energy-using equipment and appliances; the adoption of new energy conservation standards for motor vehicles and new buildings; the installation of supplementary individual control units for energy consumers who use central air conditioning systems; and the limitation of steam producers.

Government has recognised that energy conservation policy must be integrated with industrial policy as a whole. The necessity of economic sructural change to maintain high growth rates and energy conservation is emphasized within national economic policy. The latter favours the shifting away from energy-intensive industry. In the skill or technology intensive industries such as electronics, machinery, and transportation equipment, electricity consumption amounts to 21.4 kwh per one million NT dollars of gross product or approximately one-third of the average obtained in the manufacturing industry as a whole. Similarly the same sector's oil consumption at 1.2 kilolitres is only about one-eleventh of the average in manufacturing. Given this energy-saving feature the Ten Year Perspective Economic Development Plan for 1979-89, the weight of this sector in manufacturing is to increase from 25 to 35 per cent.

In the co-ordination of supporting fiscal and financial planning, economic planners hope to promote the efficient use of energy in principal industries by means of improving manufacturing processes and installing energy-efficient machinery and equipment. According to the Overseas Assistance Associates, Inc., in its report, 'Towards a New Pattern of Energy and Economic Development for Taiwan, the Republic of China,' installation of new float glass furnaces could reduce the energy consumption of the glass manufacturing industry by nearly 40 per cent. Other potential energy savings that could be realised within a period of ten years through replacement and modernisation of existing facilities are 30 per cent of total energy and 60 per cent of oil in the pulp and paper industry, 14 per cent of electric power in the chlorine and alkali industry, 5 per cent of natuarl gas in urea manufacturing, and 7.5 per cent of total energy in the steel industry.

Economic policy has also placed a priority on participation in joint ventures with oil-producing countries for the manufacture of energy-intensive products. For example, the Taiwan Fertiliser Company has built a urea plant in Saudi Arabia with Saudi equity participation. A portion of the urea production from this plant, which makes use of the abundant supply of local natural gas as raw material, will be shipped to Taiwan, thereby reducing ROC's need for energy imports.

Energy policy was consistently sought to diversify the sources of energy by substituting power and coal for oil. According to United Nation's estimates published in 1978, coal reserves in the world available for economic recovery amount to 660 billion metric tons. At the annual rate of production of 1977, these reserves are good for 250 years. World uranium reserves estimated at 1.65 million metric tons can still last about 58 years. In ROC's Ten Year Perspective Plan, nuclear power will make up 29 per cent of total installed capacity in 1989, up from 17 per cent in 1979. The share of coal-fired thermal power stations is expected to rise from 12 to 32 per cent during the same period.

The successful management of energy demand must be correlated with the expanded economical use of public transportation. The three large transportation and communication systems completed in the 1970s as part of the 'Ten Great Projects' -- the North-South Freeway, the electrifiction of the Western Trunk Railroad, and the North Link Railroad -- are already overtaxed. However, significant funding continues to pour into new transportation projects. The twelve large-scale public projects begun in the late 1970s, include the completion of the round-the-island railroad network, the construction of three new cross-island highways, the improvement of roads in the Southern area from Kaohsiung to Pingtung; and the widening to four lanes of the Pingtung-Oluanpi highway.

There is a wide consensus of support in the government for other public programmes which would improve public railway travel and reduce urban automobile traffic. Items now on the agenda for active consideration include the improvement of the electrified railway system as a more convenient mode of passenger transportation, the expansion of railroad facilities to service commuter traffic to the big cities, as well as the introduction of new and the extension of old mass-transit systems in Taipei and other large cities.

Also in its quest for the improved management of energy demand, the government has not neglected the importance of financial incentives. For example, the 'Measures Governing the Application For Investment to Renovate Boilers by Productive Enterprises', promulgated on the basis of the 'Enforcement Rules of the Statute for the Encouragement of Investment', offers tax deductions in the order of 15 per cent of purchases from domestic suppliers and 10 per cent of purchases from foreign suppliers. In the event that enterprises are not able to offset such deductions against the current fiscal year's taxable income, they have the option of applying it over the following four years. In addtion, government has offered enterprise a series of loans either in foreign currency for the purchase of foreign products or for the purchase of domestic-made machinery in order to either replace oil boilers or to install economisers and heat recovery equipment in order to enhance boiler energy efficiency. Furthermore, the tariff structure has been modified allowing exemptions for the importation of energy conservation equipment for research and experimentation. Investments in energy-saving equipment can be depreciated either on an extended basis or on an accelerated basis within two years.

The programme for the management of energy demand through legal sanction and financial inducement has been backed up in a continuing public relations campaign. Indeed, in trying to popularise the importance of energy management and conservation, the government has employed all of the mass media in the hope of reaching a broad audience.

To back up the mass media campaign, new energy-related teaching materials have been introduced into all elementary and middle schools. Government agencies have promoted the dissemination of energy-conservation materials and the exhibitions of energy-saving devices and equipment all around the island. The government information programme has attempted to facilitate the exchange of technical information between research institutes, energy conservation equipment suppliers, factories, commercial enterprises, and various government agencies. Seminars, conferences, and factory visits have frequently been organised in order to introduce new energy-saving technology to commercial-energy users. Seventeen categories of professional textbooks and journals -- incorporating the latest advancements and research in energy technology, news reports, up-to-data, and case studies--have been published and distributed to the energy management staffs of large energy users. A citation programme has also been in force since 1973, whereby consumers who have made a significant improvement in energy conservation or efficiency are publicly recognised.

Surveys have found that approximately 40 per cent of energy management personnel are graduates of technical or vocational schools. The Energy Committee has, therefore, contracted with a team of researchers from the National Taiwan Normal University to undertake a study of the energy-conservation courses taught in these vocational institutions. The research project has been charged with compiling and publishing new educational materials and with the training of teachers.

In response to the second oil crisis, the Energy Committee of the Ministry of Economic Affairs organised its 'Energy Management Personnel Training Programme' in 1980. The programme was designed to facilitate the training of management personnel of large energy users by members of the Energy Committee. This new training programme trained roughly 2,000 energy managers from the staffs of the large energy consumers and an additional 800 people from companies using large amounts of air-conditioning. This initial training was followed up by a broader range of courses that cover both the general areas of energy management, auditing, and air-conditioning and also more specific spheres of energy use such as in the cement, ceramics, and paper industries. These courses, offered between 1981-3, provided specific training to 4,032 personnel.

In addition to the various energy technical service teams formed by the Chinese Petroleum Corporation, the Taiwan Power Company as well as the newly established Energy Conservation Task Force, the Ministry of Economic Affairs actively assisted industries in energy conservation. In 1983 CPC teams visited 920 energy users and TPC teams visited 2,603 consumers. In the last 18 months, the task force has completed and delivered to individual plants 534 service reports. The total benefits of the recommendations forwarded in these reports are estimated at US $35,750,000, while they call for an investment of US $26,250,000 in energy conservation improvements.

CONCLUSION

Despite very significant domestic energy deficiency and dependence on different forms of external energy supply, the economy of the ROC has performed rather well even in the context of the decade of 'energy crisis'. The effects of the two oil shocks were signficant, but temporary, and the government was able to sustain over the long-term a relatively fast rate of growth, a modestly low rate of inflation and a favourable balance of payments. In reacting to the crisis, the government maintained a cost-reflecting policy towards energy pricing, and economic planning was significantly adjusted in order to achieve energy-savings through effective conservation. The government was also able to diversify both the forms of energy and sources of energy supply in a rational strategy of substitution for expensive oil imports. In response to international crisis and domestic energy deficiency the government of the ROC was able to combine an effective economic strategy with the responsive management of energy demand.

NOTES

1. See Chi-Yuan Liang, Energy Demand Management Technical Assistance Project: Country Report of the Republic of China, Chapter 2, Asian Development Bank, 1985.

2. W. A. Yeh and W. C. Hwang, "An Analysis on the Patterns of Price Fluctuations in Taiwan during the 1970s," Council for Economic Planning and Development, Executive Yuan, the Republic of China,

May 1981.

3. The material used in this section is provided by Professor Kao-Chao Lee and Ms. Shiow-Jiin Chiou of the Council on Economic Planning and Development.

4. See Chi-Yuan Liang, op. cit, Chapters 7-10, for more detailed description.

5. Up to now, some 3,140 energy users, who account for about 42 per cent of total commercial final energy consumption, have been assisted in establishing their own audit systems.

Chapter Four

KOREAN ECONOMIC AND POLITICAL PRIORITIES IN THE MANAGEMENT OF ENERGY LIABILITIES

Thomas Stern

The story of South Korean energy policy is an illustration of turning a necessity into a virtue. It is the tale of an underdeveloped country, in the midst of an unprecedented 25 years of rapid economic growth, facing still another tribulation, namely an energy fuel shortage, and dealing with it in such a way as to not only minimise its impact, but to transform a domestic liability into an international political asset. Undoubtedly, not all the benefits of the country's resource deficiencies were perceived at the beginning of the process. Indeed, Korean policy-makers were at least as disturbed by such world events as oil embargoes as were their counterparts in other oil-dependent countries, and some of the advantages that accrued to Korea in the context of international reactions to the oil crises of 1973-4 and 1978-9 were unplanned and unforeseen. Nevertheless, it is to the Korean policy-makers' credit that they approached the challenges with full confidence in their ability to meet them and that they took advantage of the opportunities presented by some highly adverse circumstances and events. Furthermore, the Korean policy of building close international relations through the procurement of energy fuels is a model that other nations might well study and from which they might profit.

It should be noted at the outset that Korea's energy situation differs from many other countries in two major ways: first, the Korean economy is relatively energy-intensive compared to other countries at a similar level of national income; and second, Korea's energy import dependence is already significant and may well increase to over 90 per cent in the 1990s. Indeed, barring success in offshore petroleum exploration in contiguous waters, it appears almost certain that practically all of

Korea's domestic incremental energy needs will have to be imported at some point in future.

South Korea's present policy emphasises five objectives:

1. To increase the reliability of energy fuel sources by increasing the variety of fuels and by increasing supply sources;
2. By diversifying potential supply sources to increase competition and thereby reduce costs;
3. To use new Korean markets to build closer political ties with the producing countries including those which have been traditionally hostile;
4. By increasing energy fuel supply sources, to increase the demand for Korean goods in the exporting countries;
5. To counter North Korean influence in those countries that are energy fuel exporters.

Even a brief review of available statistics rapidly brings into focus the essential factors of Korea's energy position. The first and foremost fact is the increasing demand and thereby dependency on foreign sources of supply.

The lesson from Table 4.1 is clear and unmistakable. The Republic of Korea (ROK) is subjected, like most other newly industrialising countries, to an inexorably increasing demand for energy stemming from its expanding industrial base and the rapid rise in its standard of living. Governmental efforts to stem the tide have obviously only been partially successful. Had the government not imposed heavy duties on imported oil and oil products, demand would probably have increased at an even faster pace. The future rate of increase is very difficult to predict since Korean industrial production is beginning to veer towards less energy-intensive manufacturing in the high-tech area. Nevertheless, high energy consuming industries will continue to dominate the Korean economy and, therefore, considerable increases in energy consumption can be anticipated for the rest of the century.

One of the problems faced by the Korean government is illustrated by the story that appeared in the Korea Herald (US Edition), on 20 November 1984:

> Energy consumption in the first nine months of the year totaled 36.3 million tons of oil equivalent (TOE), a rise of a whopping 10.6 per cent over the same period the previous year. The year-on-year growth rate forms a striking contrast to the comparable percentage of 5.7 per cent in 1983, minus 1.0 per cent in 1982 and 5.8 per cent in 1981. A ministry [Ministry of Energy and Resources] official said, his ministry had originally projected a 6.2 per cent year-to-year rise in the energy consumption for this year.

Table 4.1: Energy Consumption of the Republic of Korea, 1962-84

Year	Consumption	
	Total Primary Energy (In 1000 TOE)	Per Capita (TOE)
1962	10,346	0.39
1966	13,057	0.44
1970	19,676	0.61
1973	25,642	0.75
1975	26,644	0.76
1979	43,464	1.16
1980	44,115	1.16
1981	46,052	1.19
1982	45,974	1.17
1983	49,700	1.24
1984	51,492	NA

Source: Ministry of Energy and Resources (1984 Yearbook of Statistics)

The hope of maintaining a slow energy growth rate is of course directly connected with Korea's need to import most of its fuels. The only fuels that are produced in Korea are anthracite coal, hydroelectric power and fire-wood.

Table 4.2: Domestic Production of Anthracite, Hydro-electric Power and Fire-wood

Year	Anthracite (1000 MT)	Hydro-electricity (GWH)	Fire-wood (1000 MT)
1962	6,924	702	19,104
1966	11,613	985	16,468
1971	11,699	1,320	14,668
1976	16,782	1,789	11,339
1982	17,931	2,709	8,900
1983	20,595	2,723	8,492

Source: Ministry of Energy and Resources (1984 Yearbook of Statistics)

Table 4.2 reveals two factors in the Korean energy picture: the continuing economic growth which reduced the dependence on fire-wood (not to mention the stern measures adopted by the government to re-forest the denuded hillsides) and the areas of potential growth in energy demand. It seems clear that, given the resources, the Koreans could easily consume greater quantities of hydro-electric power and anthracite. This is noteworthy for North Korea is rich in both. When the Korean Peninsula was divided after World War II, the North inherited most of the natural resources while the South acquired the agricultural lands. The need of both countries for the resources of the other invites speculation as to their future political and economic relations.

Although Table 4.2 demonstrates a continuous rise in the production of limited domestic energy resources, Table 4.3 establishes a steady increase in the ROK's importation of petroleum and coal since 1962.

Table 4.3: The Petroleum and Coal Imports of the Republic of Korea, 1962-83

Year	Oil (1000 bbl)	Coal (1000 mt)
1962	6,684	180
1966	16,579	91
1971	85,431	56
1976	132,407	1,586
1981	195,977	11,823
1983	214,666	10,872

Source: Ministry of Energy and Resources (1984 Yearbook of Statistics)

The increase in coal imports reflects not only Korea's rapidly expanding industrial base, but also the efforts to de-emphasise oil in the national energy mix. In 1962, all oil imports consisted of petroleum products. By 1983, these products were only 20 per cent of total oil imports, reflecting Korea's greatly increased refining capacity.

This high rate of importation is not only a problem from a national security point of view, but from the economic standpoint as well. The cost of the 1983 imports exceeded six billion US dollars, or 23 per cent of the total 1983 import costs of 26.192 billion US dollars.

Although the increase in energy consumption is quite clear, so is the increased efficiency of usage.

In the latter part of this chapter, the history of the ROK's projections for future energy requirements will be discussed with reference to Table 4.4. These increases in efficiency occurred during a period in which Korea greatly expanded its heavy industrial production facility.

Table 4.4: ROK's Energy/GDP Ratio, 1962-83

	1962	1972	1980	1981	1982	1983
TOE/Mil Korean Won	3.40	1.12	1.17	1.14	1.08	1.07
TOE/1000 US $	1.64	0.74	0.77	0.75	0.71	0.70
Index ('80=100)	26.9	95.7	100	97.4	92.3	91.5

Source: Ministry of Energy and Resources (1984 Yearbook of Statistics)

Traditionally, this sector has had a voracious appetite for copious quantities of energy.

Two remaining historical factors are vital to an understanding of Korea's international energy policy. The first is the changing mix of fuels consumed by the Korean economy and the second is the diversification of the external sources of oil supplies.

Table 4.5 confirms the findings of other statistics with respect to the inexorable rise in coal, oil and electric power consumption and the sharp decline in the use of fire-wood. Oil has become the substitute for fire-wood and although its consumption has stabilised (the 1984 increase was less than one per cent), it is still the predominant energy fuel in the Korean consumption pattern.

Not yet clear from the statistics, but prominent in Korean plans, is the prospective role of liquefied natural gas. The government has had under serious consideration the construction of a second LNG storage terminal, partially to increase the supply of this fuel to the Korea Electric Power Corporation which intends to substitute LNG for crude oil in the generation of electricity.(1)

That fact leads to the last cardinal point in the Korean energy equation. The sources of supply for both oil and anthracite coal have shifted over the years as the Republic has attempted to diversify procurement for both political and economic reasons.

The statistics in Table 4.6 raise an interesting set of related questions. Has the pre-eminent role of Saudi Arabia in the provision of oil to ROK been rapidly diminished from 61 per cent

Table 4.5: Proportional Energy Consumption in Oil Equivalent

Year	Coal (1000 TOE)	%	Oil (1000 TOE)	%	Electric Power (1000 TOE)	%	Fire-wood (1000 TOE)	%
1962	3,434	35.1	881	9.0	126	1.3	5,349	54.6
1966	5,469	45.0	1,820	15.0	259	2.1	4,611	37.9
1970	5,592	31.3	7,373	41.2	666	3.7	4,251	23.8
1975	7,566	32.2	11,100	47.2	1,430	6.1	3,240	14.5
1980	12,426	32.9	20,046	53.0	2,815	7.4	2,517	6.7
1982	14,549	37.2	18,853	48.2	3,252	8.3	2,417	6.3
1983	15,321	36.8	20,265	48.7	3,665	8.8	2,378	5.7

Source: Ministry of Energy and Resources (1984 Yearabook of Statistics)

Table 4.6: The ROK's Crude Oil Imports by Country of Origin

Country	1962	1970	1975	1980	1982	1983	1984
Saudi Arabia	--	21,995	51,861	111,855	88,458	58,876	35,773
Kuwait	5,835	24,998	53,637	45,401	21,328	20,749	15,841
Iran	--	22,197	882	15,515	22,899	31,415	39,819
Oman	--	--	--	--	--	17,853	24,094
Ecuador	—	—	—	662	9,123	7,665	11,998
Malaysia	--	--	--	--	1,843	9,488	15,266
Brunei	--	--	--	--	4,696	8,026	5,691
Indonesia	--	--	--	400	15,403	8,788	16,919
Libya	--	--	--	--	5,868	9,033	8,564

Source: Ministry of Energy and Resources (Monthly Energy Statistics)

in 1980 to 18 per cent in 1984 for the sake of diversification, or are the Koreans indicating their concern for late Saudi payments for the projects constructed by Korean firms? Secondly, why has Korea increased so drastically its purchases from Iran, particularly since this action could not have pleased its major ally, the United States? Was this policy related to the provision of arms to Iran from North Korea? Was it related to a market that the Republic was trying to create for Korean goods? Thirdly, were the Libyan procurements related to the Korean bids for construction of major irrigation projects in that country? Or were they to counter the close Libya-North Korea relationships that have been developing over recent years? Questions of this nature could be raised in relation to any of the major historical shifts in the ROK's procurement of energy fuels.

Obviously, South Korean import decisions are not solely governed by economic factors. The competition with North Korea does play a prominent role; the use of energy fuel procurement to cement closer relationships in the Pacific Basin and Southeast Asia is evident; and the judicious use of buying power to develop markets and political ties also appears to have played a vital role. As Lee Hoesung, Vice President, Korea Institute of Energy and Resources (KIER) has said: 'Notwithstanding oil price weakness, Korea will continue to diversify its import sources, away from the Middle East. The energy trade with Pacific countries is expected to grow in the future.'(2)

The trend with respect to the diversification of anthracite imports is not as dramatic as in the case of oil. However, Korean investment policy appears to have focused on Korean firms which have already invested, or are in the process of providing capital for the further exploitation of coal resources in Indonesia as well as the United States, and for the development of coal ports.

Finally, in this area of fuel diversification, nuclear power has been assigned the leading role in a major drive toward electrification. Not only is this a significant step for a country in the economic development stage of Korea, but some significance must also be attributed to the Korean selection of sources. Five contracts have been signed with American firms, two with Canadian and two with French concerns. Although it may be true, as the Korean government insists, that these decisions were essentially economic, all the vendors regardless of nationality were convinced during the bidding stage that the policies of their governments were a vital factor in the decision-making. It has been rumoured in fact that some vendors were active in attempting to reorient their government's policies and laws in directions more palatable to the Korean government.

The Korean Response to the Oil Shocks of the 1970s

The Korean response to the oil shocks of 1973-4 and 1978-9 especially helps to elucidate the government's general reaction to interrelated factors of domestic economic development and energy deficiency. According to the analysis of the Korea Economic Institute, the second of these shocks had a greater impact on the Korean economy and precipitated a more comprehensive policy response in economic planning.(3)

In the crisis year of 1974, the percentage of petroleum imports as against total imports rose from 7 to 15 per cent, and, even though there was little change in the volume of these imports over 1973, their value climbed a staggering 245 per cent. Korean planning, nevertheless, focused on continued economic expansion, and the GNP registered an 8 per cent increase in 1974 and 7.1 per cent increase in 1975. Over these years inflation climbed to 25 per cent, but then dropped in 1976 and 1977 to the pre-1973 rate of 10 to 15 per cent. The 1974 trade deficit quadrupled to two billion US dollars, but the balance of trade began a recovery in 1975 due to 'mildly restrictive demand management policies' and a significant expansion of exports to the Middle East which by 1977 resulted, in a modest, but historically unprecedented, surplus in the national current account balance.

The Korean government managed to cope with the first shock, but as the following analysis by the Korea Economic Institute suggests the second shock of 1978-9 had more extensive implications and repercussions:

> Although the 1979 oil price escalation was proportionally milder, the volume of petroleum imports increased by an average of 9.5 per cent in 1979 and 1980. The import bill for petroleum rose 42 per cent in 1979 and 82 per cent in 1980. Even though Korea's total trade was three to four times higher in 1979-80 than in 1974, the share of oil imports in total imports jumped from around 15 per cent to 25

per cent.

The 1979 oil shock also hit harder because the government had begun to slow economic growth and contain inflation in late 1978. The strongly expansionary years of 1976-8 had led to misplaced investment, structural imbalances, wage increases above gains in productivity and a deteriorating international competitive position. In addition, weather badly hurt the harvest in 1980. The combined consequences were a 5.7 per cent decline in GNP in 1980, a 20 per cent inflation rate and a widening of the current account deficit to about $5.5 billion.(4)

It is interesting to note the differences in policy approach among the governments of Japan, Taiwan and Korea. Although all three were subject to severe inflationary pressures in 1973, Japan and Taiwan deliberately engendered brief recessions to offset the inflationary effect of higher oil prices. The Korean government took an entirely different approach. It in fact ignored the first oil shock; it took no action to counter the rising cost of oil, but passed the increases on to the consumer. The dampening effect of higher prices on economic activity was ameliorated in part by passing part of the price increase on to foreign purchasers of Korean wares.(5)

The consequences of the second oil shock are still being debated. Some observers suggest that Korea changed its approach to some extent by reducing the inflationary impact of price increases, although without damaging the basic goal of economic growth. These observers admit that there was a drop in GNP in 1980, but they point to the strong rebound in 1981-4 suggesting that the consequences of the second oil shock were rather minimal.(6) Others have taken the position that the second oil shock dealt a severe blow to the Korean economy. The oil bill absorbed 30 per cent of foreign exchange earnings. The economic downturn in the industrialised countries reduced the demand for Korean goods, thereby further exacerbating the balance-of-payment problems. The won depreciated rapidly, even further increasing the cost of oil and petroleum products which were dollar denominated. Since Korea's economy had been overheating even before the oil shock, the government decided to impose tight monetary and fiscal policies. The result was that real GNP fell over six per cent, and the ROK suffered its severest recession in 20 years.(7) The second oil shock also forced the Korean government to borrow heavily abroad, despite the rise of international interest rates to unprecedented levels.

It was only after the second oil shock that Korea began to examine seriously its energy position and policies. The first oil shock had been absorbed too easily and had hardly brought home any lessons. By 1980, Korea better understood its precarious position. The government thereafter entered vigorously into the era of diversification, both in terms of fuels and in terms of sources. The Koreans effectively linked these two diversifications in order to assure supplies, and by expanding trade relationships achieved in most instances, closer international political ties.

Five-Year Planning and Energy Policy

The definition of policy and economic objectives in response to international economic crisis and domestic energy deficiency took place within the familiar contextual framework of bureaucratic change and inertia. The five-year plans were initiated in the early 1960s as a way to steer the country's economic efforts toward a few selected goals. The degree of detail of the five-year plans did vary from administration to administration depending in large measure on the philosophical bent of the ministers and staffs responsible for economic development. Each plan contained a section on energy policy.

However, many observers believe that during the years when oil was relatively inexpensive, the government did not have much of an energy policy. As a matter of fact, until after the first oil shock, there was no Ministry of Energy and Resources (MER). Energy issues were handled by the Ministry of Commerce and Industry (MCI), and were looked upon as matters of secondary importance.(8)

The advent of the MER did not translate immediately into a five-year energy action plan. According to Kwang-Jo Shur, Senior Research Fellow at the Korea International Economic Institute, MER 'understood the gravity of [the first] oil crisis only incompletely' paying inadequate attention to the statistics which clearly indicated a growing consumption of oil and a growing dependence on foreign imports. The second oil shock however could not be ignored in the same manner. High prices and the prospect of faltering economic growth would not permit further evasion; hence the MER produced the first energy five-year plan (1982-6) based on its projected energy requirements as set out in Table 4.7.(9)

Table 4.7: ROK's Long-term Energy Profile

	1982-6	1987-91	1992-6	1997-2001
GNP Growth (annual %)	7.5	7.1	6.7	6.7
Energy Consumption Increase (annual %)	5.2	6.1	5.2	4.9
Dependence on Imported Energy (%)	79.0	84.7	88.0	91.5

Source: Business Korea, April, 1984.

These statistics will be discussed in the latter part of this chapter. At this point,attention should be drawn to the estimated dependence on imports, which will become an increasingly important national security issue. Solutions can only come from skillful international political manoeuvring as well as economic diplomacy. The complexity of the Korean dilemma was summed up by Anthony Geber, as follows:

> Energy planning is complex and uncertain. Several factors make it more difficult in Korea. The strong dependence on imports of primary energy make security of supply important. At the same time, Korea's objectives of high growth, continued export orientation and structural reorientation of industry, put a high premium on energy efficiency and flexibility.(10)

While all economic projections are subject to uncertainty, energy projections in particular are prone to a high degree of uncertainty. Consider, for example, how quickly the following MER assumption has become dated in the context of slumping international oil prices:

> [The World price of crude oil] ... will be constant until 1984 and then increase by seven to eight per cent annually after 1984 ... Mostly because of successful efforts to conserve energy, Korea's energy consumption projections have been lowered considerably from those of the original plan. The revised plan calls for diversification of energy sources to reduce Korea's dependency on crude oil. To achieve diversification, the ROK hopes to utilise bituminous coal, nuclear power and gas and to stabilise procurement of oil through long-term supply contracts, stockpiling oil and development of oil and other energy sources overseas through joint ventures or other cooperative arrangement to assure future supplies.(11)

Although the assumption concerning 'constant' oil pricing may seem dubious in light of the oil 'glut' and the weakening of the dollar, Korea's strategy has not changed. Diversification in fuel as well as supply sources are still the policy of the day.

THE POLITICAL COSTS AND BENEFITS OF ENERGY DEPENDENCE

The over-riding advisability of diversifying both fuels and sources presented the Republic of Korea with a number of foreign policy dilemmas. The ROK was historically a staunch ally of Israel. The South Koreans admired Israel's successful management of its relationships with the US. It was only after vigorous debate that they began to distance themselves from Israel in response to the oil embargoes. The Israelis finally closed their Embassy in Seoul and managed their bilateral issues with Korea through their Ambassador in Japan. Repeated negotiations to re-establish residential Embassies came to naught as those Korean policy-makers concerned with the reactions of the Arab oil producers were repeatedly able to blunt the arguments of the pro-Israeli lobby.

Dependence on a few sources of supply was not desirable either in economic or in political terms. However, Korea faces obvious and unique challenges which have imposed constraints on the development of foreign policy options. In his recent analysis Joseph Yager reviewed the implication of Korea's 'bitter struggle with strong domestic Communist adversaries [North Korea]' and concluded:

> The merits and feasibility of many of the possible international movements, including some in energy, may depend on how they affect this domestic political struggle ... Some of the energy-related activities of South Korea and Taiwan are designed to counter actual or anticipated moves of their Communist national rivals as well as to increase the reliability of energy supplies.(12)

Yager's analysis also compares the responses of Northeast Asian countries in the following way:

> The heavy import dependence of Northeast Asian countries has inevitably affected their foreign policies. Japan and, to a lesser extent, South Korea and Taiwan have made extensive efforts to increase their reliability of energy imports by investing in efforts to find and develop energy resources in other countries. Other investments in energy-exporting countries--some of them energy related--have been designed to solidify relations with those countries.(13)

Indeed, as the Korean energy record is examined, the temptation arises to suggest that the oil shocks were welcomed for they opened up whole new vistas for Korea's foreign policy. This is of course not the case, but the oil embargoes did have the following consequences: the penetration of Korean enterprises primarily through construction projects and oil purchases in markets which had been monopolised by North Korea (for example those of Libya, Iran); the expansion of Korean economic interests through investments (for example with Mexico, Ecuador); the consolidation of relationships with Pacific and Southeast Asian countries through energy fuel purchases (for example, from Australia, Malaysia, Brunei) and the expansion of relationships with African countries through uranium prospecting (for example in Sudan, Gabon); and tentative contacts with adversaries through coal purchases (for example, from the PRC, North Korea). Such contacts with North Korea and the PRC have been shrouded in secrecy. Public data has not been available since in all cases a middle-man was used for the transaction. Nevertheless, rumours persist that such trade has been undertaken in the past and that it may still be alive today.

The significant factor in this impressive list of reactions to the oil shocks is that the Republic of Korea took advantage of a necessity and turned it into a virtue. The history of Korea's energy diplomacy suggests the utilisation of both economic assets and liabilities to gain political advantage. The potential for international energy co-operation is briefly detailed below in a country-by-country survey.

Korea and Japan

The relationship between Korea and Japan is of primary importance. This relationship is especially relevant to the universal desideratum to find oil within or near national boundaries. In the mid-1970s, the waters west and south of the Peninsula were subdivided into nine blocks. Almost all were involved in international legal disputes because ownership of parts of the blocks were claimed by the PRC and Japan. The issues with the PRC have not been resolved, but issues between the ROK and Japan have been settled by treaty. While the initial high hopes and enthusiasms have been seriously dampened in the past ten years by a succession of dry holes, the drilling process continues. One MER official, with characteristic Korean enthusiasm, declared: 'We will continue the oil prospecting work on the continental shelf with a never-say-die spirit'.(14)

The enthusiasm and hopes that Korea has shown for these drilling ventures has become obvious in the headlines of the Korea Herald throughout 1984-5. (15) The common thread among all the stories is the expression of disappointment with previous efforts and of high hopes for future developments. The evidence to date would suggest that considerable caution must be exercised with respect to the possible development of economically viable offshore oil wells; however, a sufficient number of foreign firms continue to invest in exploration which suggests that some potential may still exist.

Korea and Australia

High on Korea's energy agenda is the expansion of sources of coal. Australia is blessed with ample fields of bituminous coal which became highly desirable to those Korean companies that converted from oil to coal.

The ever rising importance of bituminous coal is illustrated by the fact that consumption increased 33 per cent from 1983 to 1984 following an increase of 13 per cent in the previous year. Since essentially all the bituminous coal must be imported, the importance of this commodity in the general import program of Korea can be easily discerned.

Korea's preferred approach to acquisition of Australian coal is through investment, particularly in the mines of South Wales. These investments have been joint partnerships not only with indigenous concerns but in consortia with Italian, Japanese and German concerns. The four major Korean concerns involved in Australian coal development are Lucky-Goldstar, Pohang Iron and Steel, Hyundai and Daesung Consolidated Mining Co.(16)

Korea and the PRC

The Korean hunt for coal has even brought them to the Chinese shores. From the late 1970s to 1982, coal moved directly from the PRC to Korean ports, although the arrangements were made through brokers in Hong Kong. In response to complaints from North Korea, shipments were allegedly suspended in 1982.(17) Since the official statistics never suggested that there were any imports from the PRC, it is impossible to determine the extent of such trade. It seems quite clear that it did take place; it is not similarly clear that it has ceased. In fact, there are many incentives for a continuation of such trade, primarily economic on the PRC's side and principally political on the part of South Korea. A friendly, or at least a neutral PRC, would act as a stabilising force on the Peninsula, and would constitute the ultimate vindication of Korea's policy of establishing relationships with those countries that have close ties with North Korea.

Korea and Iran and Libya

Among the countries that maintain close ties to North Korea are Iran and Libya. This situation has confronted Korea with a number of difficult policy choices, reflecting its antagonism towards the North and its need for close relationships with the United States as well as its wish to establish linkages with Israel.

In the cases of Iran and Libya, Korea chose to highlight its competitive position with North Korea and entered into commercial relationships with both countries even though the United States had branded both as international outlaws. Not all the trade conducted with these countries has found United States' approval. In the case of energy fuels, the United States has not raised any major objections and the ROK has increased its oil imports from both Iran and Libya. In the latter case, the Koreans were rewarded with a major construction contract which will more than compensate for the foreign exchange costs of its oil purchases. There have also been purchases of Korean goods and construction contracts by Iran, although the amounts are not publicly available.

In any case, Korean purchases of oil from Iran and Libya have permitted the Republic to compete with North Korea for the political support of both Islamic countries.

Korea and Indonesia

Among Korea's most successful explorations must be listed the oil finds in Indonesia. In a joint venture with Pertamina, the KODECO Energy Company of Korea found oil and gas in the Madura block just off Java. Korea was the first developing country to hit oil or gas in Indonesia and is indeed proud of this achievement. It took the joint venture over two years to find and exploit an economically viable oil well, which culminated in a delivery of 428,000 barrels of crude oil to Korea in August, 1984. Oil imports from Indonesia almost doubled in 1984 from the previous year suggesting that this source will become increasingly more important, even though the Madura wells will never be a major producer. Of some significance is the fact that the Cities Service Company, although recognizing the availability of oil in the Madura block, refused to develop it since it was not sure of the size of the reserves. The Koreans applied improved oil-exploration equipment and sunk four test wells, which gave sufficient assurance of the economic viability of the find. The Madura find was not only a major technological advance for Korea, but also further cemented the ties between the Republic and Indonesia.(18)

Korea and Latin America

For a number of years, Korea has been trying to increase its penetration of Latin American markets. Language barriers and cultural differences have proven to be major impediments. However, the need to diversify oil sources presented golden opportunities which the Koreans quickly grasped.

Imports from Ecuador increased over 50 per cent in 1984 compared to the prior year. With the addition of Mexico as an oil supplier, Korean imports from Latin America doubled in the first five months of 1985 as compared to the same period in 1984. The imports were over 11 million barrels and accounted for almost 13 per cent of total oil imports for the period. (19)

Korea and United States

The energy relationships between these two nations are complex. The level of mutual satisfaction varies from fuel to fuel. The United States does not provide any oil or petroleum products to Korea, although it has publicly committed itself to provide such commodities in a crisis. The United States' ban on the export of any domestically produced oil has eliminated any possibility of such trade, even though it would be mutually economically beneficial and would have a major impact on the bilateral balance of trade which is currently in Korea's favor.

On the other hand, Korea has been interested in American natural gas and coal. Korean companies have invested in both Alaskan and Pennsylvanian coal fields and are consuming fuels from those regions. Korean firms have also invested in the development of related coal port facilities in order to facilitate the shipment of these fuels to Korea.

Negotiations have been ongoing to permit a Korean consortium to join the US Federal government and the Alaskan State government in the construction of a liquid natural gas pipeline linking Prudhoe Bay to the southern port of Kanai.

The major American contribution to Korea's energy production has been through the construction of six nuclear power plants. Two have been completed and are operational and the other four are under construction. The competition for the awarding of these contracts has always been bitter and acute with American, German, French, Swiss and British firms deeply involved in attempting to obtain multi-million dollar contracts. All the concerned Embassies in Seoul were marshalled to support the bids of their respective nationals; rumours of political pressure ran rampant. Ambassadors and staffs watched each other's moves and reported fully on all activities related to the awarding of the nuclear power plant construction and equipment acquisition contracts. When the United States lost the bid for two plants to the French, many assumed that this was an indication of Korean dissatisfaction particulary with the restrictive aspects of US nuclear export legislation. On the other hand, it was rumoured that the award was made to a French concern in exchange for the French Government's continuation of its policy of non-recognition of North Korea. The attribution of awards to political factors was one more piece of evidence of the close linkage between energy economics and international relations.

Just one month after US Treasury Secretary W. Michael Blumenthal made a strong pitch for American contractors during President Carter's trip to Seoul in 1979, the Korean Government awarded the work for nuclear power plants 7 and 8 to American firms. A flurry of controversy surrounded the subsequent round of contractual bidding relating to Units 9 and 10. The following analysis by Business Korea suggests that the French attempted to undercut the US bidding for a nuclear supply system by emphasising their readiness to help Korea gain greater access to the PRC:

> The awarding of the contracts for Units 9 and 10 to French firms stirred up some of the most heated speculation of behind-the-scene politicking. As early as March 1980, the Korean press speculated that the nuclear supply system contract had been guaranteed to Framatone for diplomatic reasons. In April that year, a team of 34 French businessmen ....visited top Korean officials. Persistently denying rumors that the project had been pledged to France, the government invited bids in a process that has been characterized as a charade. Framatone got the US $483 million job in November 1980, and the French firm Coyena the US $483 million contract to supply enriched uranium. The French foreign trade minister then stated that France will more actively assist Korea in boosting trade to mainland China.(20)

The French were also accused of playing the 'North Korea' card. Business Korea tapped diplomatic sources which reportedly charged that the French had not only attempted to exploit their continued support of the ROK in international forums such as the UN, but they also raised the issue of French recognition of Pyongyang with great, but unexpected effect. Within 24 hours of the Korean

Electric Company's warning to French contractors as to the imminent re-evaluation of projects concerning Units 9 and 10, Paris assured Seoul that there would be no re-evaluation of French policy on the recognition question. It is of course easy to confuse cause and effect. However, it is clear that the use of energy fuels for political purposes is a two-way street for both the buyer and the seller.

THE POLITICAL AND ECONOMIC DIMENSIONS OF THE ROK'S ENERGY FUTURE

Long Range Projections.

In December 1983, The Korea Institute of Energy and Resources (KIER) published a study of Korea's energy requirements through the year 2000 which was part of a larger 'Year 2000' analysis commissioned by the Government. The KIER Energy Outlook closely follows the assumptions and methodology of the OECD/IEA World Energy Outlook (1982). It forecasts that total energy consumption in Korea will grow at 5.6 per cent per annum during the 1980s and 5.1 per cent per annum during the 1990s to 130 million tons of oil equivalent by the year 2001, assuming a 7.5 per cent growth in GNP during the 1980s and a 6.7 per cent growth during the 1990s. The energy-intensity index of the Korean economy (expressed in TOE/GNP) is projected to decline by about 1.5 per cent. Oil consumption is projected to grow at 2.4 per cent during the 1980s and 3.1 per cent during the 1990s. Consequently, the share of oil in total primary energy use is projected to decline from 58 to 46 per cent in 1991 and 38 per cent in 2001. Some observers have questioned the optimistic nature of these forecasts, raising doubts about Korean capability of achieving such GNP growth rates and the requisite declines in energy intensity.(21) Time will tell, but past skeptics of Korean capabilities have been repeatedly surprised.

The projections in Table 4.10 clearly reflect the quantitative assumptions underlying future Korean energy policies. They appear to represent a continuation and acceleration of present directions and are embued with a familiar spirit of optimism and confidence. In addition to the total growth of demand stimulated by a rapidly expanding economy,

Table 4.8: Energy Demand Forecast

	Actual	Projected	
	1981	1991	2001
Energy Demand (MTOE)	46.1	79.6	130.4
TOE/GNP (1981=100)	100	86	73
Oil Dependency (% of energy)	57.3	42.2	35.1

Source: Ministry of Energy and Resources: Korea's Energy and Resources, Staff Report, 29-30 August 1984.

Table 4.9: Projected Energy Demand by Sector (%)

	1981	1991	2001
Industry	44.0	43.9	45.2
Transportation	14.5	20.4	21.8
Residential and Commercial	36.9	31.5	28.9
Public and Others	4.6	4.2	4.1
TOTAL ENERGY DEMAND ('000 TOE)	46,052	79,608	130,358

Source: Ministry of Energy Resources: Korea's Energy and Resources, Staff Report, 29-30 August 1984.

Table 4.10: Projected Energy Demand by Fuel

	1981		1991		2001	
	No.	%	No.	%	No.	%
Oil	182,252	(58.4)	260,912	(46.4)	356,731	(38.1)
Coal	28,847	(33.1)	44,196	(31.4)	72,731	(38.1)
Hydro Power	2,709	(1.5)	3,484	(1.1)	4,420	(0.8)
Nuclear Power	2,897	(1.6)	48,484	(15.1)	106,181	(20.4)
LNG	---	---	2,000	(3.3)	5,000	(5.0)
Other	2,492	(5.4)	2,211	(2.8)	2,211	(1.7)

Quantities are expressed in '000 bbls for oil, '000 tons for coal and LNG, TOE tons for other, and in GWH tons for hydro-electric and nuclear power.

Source: Ministry of Energy Resources: Korea's Energy and Resources, Staff Report, 29-30 August 1984.

these projections suggest:

1. The further drive toward fuel diversification as indicated by the sizable growth of nuclear power and the introduction of LNG as a significant energy resource; the continued dependence on oil, even though a decrease in the share of total consumption is predicted;
2. A declining rate of increase in energy consumption from 52 per cent in 1982-6 to 4.9 per cent in 1997-2001 in the context of a growing dependence on imported energy which will account for 91.5 per cent of Korea's energy requirements in the year 2001;
3. A relatively minor shift in the contribution that coal and hydro are expected to make.

The third point suggests the absence of political judgements in the KIER projections.

Increasing Energy Dependence

Korea's energy import-dependence is already very large and is likely to increase to over 90 per cent by the end of the century. Although this would be a challenge to any nation, it is particulary important to the Republic whose economy is relatively energy-intensive compared to other countries at a similar level of income. To date, of course, import-dependence *per se* has not hampered economic performance in comparison to resource-rich countries. It is not entirely profitable to speculate on the exact nature of Korea's energy requirements; under any assumption, Korea will clearly have to continue its large import programme.

This central fact perhaps eases some of the dilemma for Korean policy-makers for, unlike their counterparts in other countries, they need not worry about energy independence and they can concentrate on the development of policies which will insure an adequate supply of fuels at reasonable costs. This essentially will require the continuation of present directions adapted from time to time to changing world circumstances. The central theme of assuring supplies through cementing political alliances will undoubtedly endure and may well in fact receive increasing attention. The counterpoint to this theme--cementing political alliances through procurement of energy fuels--may also become more prevalent as opportunities arise. The interplay of politics and economics has guided Korea in the increasing diversification of energy sources and forms, whenever possible. This trend should continue as Korea attempts to reduce the relative significance of oil in the energy sector, even though in gross terms, the amount of imported oil will increase.

The Nuclear Power Option

The importance of nuclear power in the future development of Korea's energy programme is illustrated in Table 4.11 which summarizes the Korea Electric Company Investment Plan as of 1984.

In the late 1970s, some Korean projections called for the construction of 44 nuclear power plants by the end of the century. Over a period of time, the impracticality of such an ambitious scheme reduced the requirement to approximately 25 stations. Nevertheless, even the revised plan is ambitious and expensive and has ramifications which range beyond the questions of economic feasibility.

Table 4.11: Projection of Installed Electric Capacity (MW)

	Nuclear	Coal	Oil	Oil/LNG	Other	Total
1984	1,916	1,620	6,151	---	3,006	12,737
1986	3,816	2,540	3,651	2,500	4,090	16,597
1991	7,616	4,040	3,641	2,500	4,534	22,331
1996	11,216	10,840	2,856	2,250	7,181	34,343
2001	16,616	18,940	710	2,000	9,436	47,702

Source: Korea Electric Company Electric Plan

Countries with nuclear power plants can purchase fuel ready for use as is currently the situation in Korea, or they can establish their own nuclear fuel fabrication plants. Korea is proceeding with plans to develop a processing capability, although it insists it has no plans to produce enriched uranium domestically.(22) Enriched uranium is a well-known potential source of fuel for military weapons. Any nation's capability to produce enriched uranium generates considerable concern in the United States and other nations opposed to nuclear proliferation. In the mid-1970s, when it was rumoured that Korea was interested in acquiring capability and when it appeared that it might receive assistance from a European country, the United States exerted considerable pressure on both nations to force a reconsideration of the programme, which was eventually cancelled. The spectre of Korean interest in acquiring nuclear capabilities beyond power generation will continue to haunt Korean relationships with other nations and will require considerable skill on the part of the Korean political leadership to allay the anxieties of its allies and friends. A test of this skill will surely come as the issue of the disposal of nuclear waste becomes more acute. One of the options is obviously reprocessing in Korea, but that will stimulate American concerns once again.

New Sources of Supply

None of the analyses to date seem to have considered two other political eventualities, namely, closer ROK ties to the PRC and rapprochement with North Korea. In both cases, energy is likely to play a vital role. In the case of the PRC, past trade based on coal exports to Korea is likely to continue and even increase. In the case of North Korea, if the current negotiations on opening trade relations between the two parts of the Peninsula are successful, the obvious imports by the South will be coal and hydro-electric power, both of which appear to be plentiful in the North.

CONCLUSIONS

Yager, in his analysis of potential energy developments in Korea after 1991, predicts some slowing in the rate of economic development, although this is not regarded as inevitable, even given some of the problems that might retard that economic expansion. He concludes: '...there are no compelling reasons for believing that a slowdown in Korea's economic growth will markedly reduce the rate of expansion in its total energy requirements.' On the question of the energy intensity of the economy, Yager sees a number of factors both positive and negative which will tend to cancel each other out, so that the growth of energy requirements in the 1990s will be comparable to that experienced in the preceding decade. In the final analysis, Korea's dependence on oil will increase during the 1990's, suggesting that Korean resource diplomacy may, therefore, become even more active as the country seeks to diversify further the geographical sources of oil imports.(23)

This resource diplomacy will create both challenges and opportunities for Korea. In the first place, political ties between Korea and some energy fuel suppliers will be strengthened. That is particularly true for those suppliers which present opportunities in other fields. For example, the Latin American producers are a potential fertile field for Korean exports. In addition the ROK can be expected to resort to various methods including the manipulation of oil purchases to limit North Korean diplomatic penetration of the area.

On the other hand, linkages to Gulf oil

producers are likely to diminish as imports from that region are reduced. This might give Korea greater flexibility in its Israeli policy, although this issue affects Korean relationships with all Islamic countries. In that latter group are Iran and Libya, with which the Koreans can be expected to maintain resource relationships both to earn foreign exchange through construction projects and commodity sales. In the short run, the ROK desires to limit and roll back, if possible, North Korean penetration into the Arab world.

Some analysts have noted that a pattern of energy trade is developing which gives support to the concept of a Pacific Basin community. As Korea's dependence on Gulf Oil decreases, its investment in Indonesia's oil increases. There have been increases in Korean investment in US coal and Alaskan LNG, as well as in the purchase of uranium enrichment services from the United States. In general, Korea's energy fuel imports from Pacific Basin countries are increasing dramatically, leading to the obvious speculation that such activities may eventually lead to a Pacific Basin energy community. In fact, this view is supported by the following recommendation of the ROK's Ministry of Energy and Resources: '...a device for a common conference of Asian developing countries energy organization like the IEA of the advanced countries.'(24)

The desirability of closer co-operation and political linkages among Pacific Basin countries will grow particulary as issues relating to nuclear power development are addressed. Regional approaches to waste management, reprocessing and fuel enrichment are attractive alternatives to single country solutions as they avoid many economic and political pitfalls.

Analysts have been noticeably delinquent in taking into consideration the political dimensions of energy issues. Korea can be expected to continue its skillful management of its resource diplomacy, exploiting the necessity for imports to build political alliances, expanding its influence and opening new markets. Those who aspire to counsel the government of the Republic of Korea on its energy policy should remember the political benefits that Korea expects to achieve through its energy policy. Considerations based exclusively on economic factors are unlikely to be heeded; those which support political objectives will be given greater attention.

In that connection, careful attention must be

given to the potential effects of closer political relationships with the PRC and North Korea on ROK's energy policy. Should a period of detente develop in Northeast Asia, it could be anticipated that South Korea's dependence on coal from both the PRC and North Korea will increase as well as the new use of hydro power imported from the North. Korea's energy requirements may well become one of the key factors in bringing greater stability to Northeast Asia.

NOTES

1. Korea Herald, 2 December 1984.
2. Hoesung Lee, 'Oil Pricing, Trade and Taxation: the Korean Viewpoint', Paper presented at the 1984 International Pacific Basin Congress, Melbourne, Australia.
3. See Anthony Geber's analysis in Korea's Economy vol. 1, no. 4.
4. Ibid.
5. Joseph Yager, The Energy Balance in Northeast Asia (The Brookings Institution, Washington, D.C., 1984), p. 60.
6. Ibid., p. 224.
7. Hoesung Lee, 'Oil Pricing, Trade and Taxation: the Korean Viewpoint', paragraph 1.2.
8. Business Korea, April, 1984.
9. Business Korea, April, 1994.
10. Geber, Korea's Economy, vol. 1, no. 1.
11. Cable Report, American Embassy, Seoul, Korea, 8 February 1984.
12. Yager, The Energy Balance, p. 73.
13. Ibid, p. 75.
14. As quoted in the Korea Herald, 11 November 1985.
15. For example, refer to the following headlines: 'French Oil Firm Plans to Participate in 7th Mining Block Development Projects', 6 May 1984; 'Korea Embarks on 11th Challenge at Continental Shelf', 15 May 1984; 'Surveys Positive for 6th block. Six U.S. Firms Consider Teaming with PEDCO', 9 August 1984; 'Oil Fever Has Big Firms on International Search', 23 November 1984; 'Korea, Japan to drill 7th Bloc in '85', 13 February 1985. Shelf Oil Ventures Under Way', 24 May 1985
16. Business Korea, April, 1985.
17. Yager The Energy Balance, p. 66.
18. Business Korea, August, 1983 and November, 1984.

19. Korea Herald, 2 July 1985.
20. Business Korea, April, 1984.
21. Yager, The Energy Balance, pp. 201-10.
22. Yager, Korea Herald, 20 July 1984.
23. Yager, The Energy Balance, pp. 207-10.
24. Republic of Korea, Ministry of Energy and Resources, Korea's Energy and Resources (Staff Briefing Paper), 29-30 August 1984, p. 19.

Chapter 5

JAPAN'S RESOURCE DIPLOMACY

F. Quei Quo

Among the industrial powers which require a large quantity of energy supply for their survival and growth, Japan is the most vulnerable.* For a country which consumes approximately 11 per cent of the energy produced in the world, only 18 per cent of her energy needs are met by domestic supply. For the remaining 82 per cent, Japan relies on imports from overseas.(1) These figures from 1983, nevertheless, represent a considerable improvement compared to an 86 per cent dependence on imported energies in 1978.

Needless to say the 1973 and 1979 'oil shocks' were compelling learning experiences which required that the Japanese immediately come to terms with the obvious vulnerability of Japan's energy deficient economy. This chapter will examine this vulnerability from the broader perspective of national security and will focus on the government's energy policy especially as it relates to the Japanese exercise of resource diplomacy.

JAPANESE VULNERABILITY

In addition to the fact that Japan is endowed with very limited natural resources, she is dependent on international trade for her economic survival. Japan's international trade which consists mainly of industrial products accounts for 16 per cent of its GNP in 1983. Japan's post-war industrial growth began to take its shape in early 1950s with emphasis on heavy industries such as steel and shipbuilding, which are highly energy-intensive. Furthermore, due to the difficulties of domestic coal supply and the

---

* The research grant from the SSHRC of Canada for the author's standing project on Japanese politics from which this Chapter is derived is hereby acknowledged with appreciation.

cheap cost of oil in the early 1960s, most Japanese industries, including electric plants, converted to the use of oil. In 1962 oil for the first time in history surpassed coal to become the major source of energy in Japan. Oil and coal respectively accounted for 46 per cent and 36 per cent of national energy consumption. The relative reliance on oil has become increasingly significant. By 1978 oil constituted 75 per cent of Japan's energy supply and 54 per cent of this oil was committed to industrial uses.(2) In 1983, 99.7 per cent of Japan's oil supply was from overseas. Japanese vulnerability, therefore, can be summed up in the over-dependence on oil in industry and the over-dependence on trade for economic survival and growth.

The close relationship between the Japanese economy and the international market has raised interesting debates on the impact of the 'Reverse Oil Shock' in 1983 when there was a slump in oil price.(3) Superficially, a decrease in oil price must be beneficial to Japanese economy as it means less cost for industrial products and also less flow of dollars to the oil producing countries. The 1973 oil-price increase caused the Japanese GNP to register a negative growth of 1.3 per cent for the first time in the post-war period. However, some Japanese argued that a decrease in oil price would have a negative impact on Japanese economy. For by now Japanese sales to the oil-rich countries have increased and any decrease in producer buying power would mean less purchases from Japan. Japanese exports to the Middle East countries now account for 12 per cent of total annual exports. Furthermore, Japanese loans to oil-producing countries like Indonesia and Mexico could face problems of repayment if their income from sales of oil decreased. Some have even argued that lower oil prices would deter the development of expensive substitute energies which are technology-intensive. The debate, itself, is an indication of the vicious circle caused by Japan's vulnerability in energy issues.

Japanese vulnerability goes beyond the price issue. As a matter of fact price, itself, is not that hard for the Japanese to adjust to, nor do the Japanese deem it the main problem. Geographically Japan is distant and isolated from the major producers of oil, coal, and gas in North America, the Middle East, South America, and the USSR. Japan may attempt to diversify its overseas sources of supply in a bid to contend with an historical dependence on Middle Eastern oil, but Japan must still cope with the geopolitical uncertainties of transportation and sea-lane security. Associated with these geographical factors, are problems relating to the selection of site for stock-piling coal and oil, the specifications of earthquake-proof nuclear reactors and the apparently obvious limitations of energy resources.

A more serious problem for Japan is the variety of petro-chemical industries dependent upon the use of petro-byproducts such as fertiliser, polyethylene, plastics, and the sales of related plants and technology to the newly industrialising countries (NICs) and other developing nations. Between 1970 and 1976 Japan's export of chemical products grew at an average of 20 per cent per annum. In 1970 chemical and textile products constituted 18.6 per cent of the nation's exports. This figure, subsequently dropped to 7.5 per cent in 1982. Other than mining, Japan's overseas investments in the NICs are mainly concentrated in the chemical and textile industries. The latter accounted for 19.1 per cent of the accumulated overseas investments as of 1976. By the end of the 1970s Japan's chemical industries were 49.5 per cent petro-chemical and the capital investment made in the early 1960s far exceeded that in any other industries.(4)

The ultimate vulnerability, however, lies in the latent conflict between Japan's resource diplomacy and her alliance with the US for military security. In other words, it appears difficult for Japan to pursue its resource diplomacy without giving proper consideration to the American global strategy. The Japanese purchase of extra oil from Iran in 1979 and the American criticism of Japan's failure to back up US policy against Iran illustrates this point. For the US, the Middle Eastern situation should be judged and responded to in accordance with the strategic requirements of the East-West balance of power. For Japan, however, economic concerns relating to the supply of oil, may override power politics. The historical Japanese emphasis on the 'separation between politics and economics' should be related to contemporary resource diplomacy. As will be discussed later, the Japanese are hard to convince that their independent foreign policy does not exempt them from international political responsibility.(5) Japan's involvement in the joint projects with the USSR for the Siberian and Far Eastern resource development must be reviewed in a similar vein in order that proper consideration is given to possible American reactions. On the other hand, like in the case of Japanese-South Africa relations, Japan has at times had to ignore internationally sensitive political and moral issues in order to achieve greater security of energy supplies. The Japanese government has been reluctant to jeopardise the South African supply of energy resources, particularly with respect to the import of South African uranium since 1978.

THE JAPANESE RESPONSE

Japanese response to energy problems has encompassed energy conservation, the maximum utilisation of domestic sources, the development of energy substitutes for oil as well as emphases on efficient and effective energy installations, energy research, close co-operation with energy-exporting countries, and the stockpiling of energy resources. However, the Report On Strategy For Comprehensive National Security (Sogo Anzen Hosho Senryaku) submitted to the Prime Minister in 1980 admitted that measures such as increased stockpiling, development of new resources and effective control over domestic distribution would make only a very limited contribution to solving the nation's energy problems. As shown in Table 5.1 the immediate goal is to decrease the heavy reliance on petroleum and rapidly to increase the percentage shares of nuclear energy and LNG.

Table 5.1: Components of Japan's Energy Sources

	1975	1983	1990 (est.)	1995 (est.)
Petroleum	73(%)	62(%)	53(%)	48(%)
Coal	16	18	18	18
Hydro Power	6	5	5	5
Nuclear Power	2	7	11	14
LNG	2	8	12	12
Others	1	1	2	5

Source: Mainichi Shimbun, 31 May 1985.
Total (%) exceeds 100 due to rounding of fractions.

Presently, Japan accounts for approximately 50 per cent of the world's LNG trade. The LNG comes mainly from Alaska, Brunei, Abudabi, and Indonesia. More than three-quarters of the LNG imports are used in power plants. Through the last half of the 1980s the amount of imported LNG is expected to double the current figure. Japan also consumes approximately 12 million tons of LPG which constitutes 3 per cent of national energy consumption. The major providers are Saudi Arabia, Kuwait, and Australia. This is the only kind of energy where domestic use exceeds that of industry (49 per cent and 26 per cent, respectively). Although efforts are being made in the development of thermopower, solar energy, wind power etc., the outlook for their share in the nation's total energy supply is rather dim. According to the Government plan, these alternative energies might be able to substitute for 40 million kilolitres of oil or 5 per cent of the national energy supply by 1990. Unless there is a significant technological breakthrough and domestically available resources are converted into energy production, Japan's vulnerability will continue. Conversion from oil to coal, more reliance on LNG, LPG, or nuclear energy, will still mean a dependence on foreign countries even given future changes in the sources of energy supply and the domestic energy mix.

The Report, therefore, recommends two major approaches: collective measures with other oil-importing nations and development of close bilateral relations with the resource-rich nations. The latter approach had already been suggested and practiced by the government and industries long before the Report. The route of collective measures with other nations, however, was not really the one which the Japanese government and industries would have preferred to follow. The Report may have anticipated the international pressure which in fact was brought to bear against Japan at the 1980 Tokyo Summit where the joint efforts among the major industrial powers were discussed. Although Japan is a member of the IEA most Japanese politicians, bureaucrats and industrialists have little faith in the international agency's ability to cope with a prolonged energy crisis. Japan is the most vulnerable among the industrial powers; therefore, any collective response to producer cutbacks is likely to have a more severe impact on Japanese industries in international markets. Some even argued that this is a zero-sum game in which collective measures are beneficial only to the strongest.

Several facts stand out to convince the Japanese that they will stand alone when the real crisis comes. During the second oil crisis the major oil companies unilaterally cut off their supply to Japan. In 1979, Canada, on whom Japan relies for 70 per cent of her domestic uranium supply, imposed an embargo due to the illegal Indian nuclear-test. The American refusal to sell Alaskan oil to Japan exemplifies further that nations are self-centered in this game. Even if the US maintains its current rate of oil imports and Japan succeeds in reducing its reliance on oil to less than 50 per cent of her energy needs, it is expected that by 1990 the two nations will be searching for about the same quantity of oil supplies in international markets. Although Japan was in the end quite happy with the generous allocation allowed her at the 1980 Tokyo Summit, she also knows that nations like the United States and the UK who have considerable domestic supplies, are in a comparatively advantageous postion. So far, Japan's genuine interest in collective measures remains in the field of energy research. Previous ministers and Prime Ministers all appealed for closer joint efforts in energy research in their speeches delivered in the US. For example, Prime Minister Fukuda's speech in New York on 4 May 1978 emphasised joint research in oil-sand and oil-shale projects.(6)

Japan has given the greatest emphasis to developing good bilateral relations with the resource-rich countries. Even before the oil crisis of 1973 both the Japanese government and industries were already engaged in overseas investment and economic co-operation in oil-producing countries. The Japan Arabian Oil Company established in 1958, had early success in drilling. The North Sumatra Petroleum Development Company, established in 1960, laid the foundation for Japan's oil supply from Indonesia. In 1971 the Mitsui Group went for a 50/50 joint development with the Iranian National Petroleum Corporation and formed the ill-fated Iran-Japan Petroleum Corporation (IJPC). Construction of the petro-chemical complex started in 1973 but was never completed due to the revolution in Iran first and the Iran-Iraq War later. The Japanese Government not only assigns priority to oil producing countries in her disbursement of overseas development assistance

(ODAS), it also provides tax concession to Japanese corporations for their investment in overseas resource development. Indonesia has always been the major recipient of Japan's ODA. Although the Middle East region was of little concern to the Japanese for many years, between 1969 and 1983 the region's share of cummulative ODA and non-government assistance from Japan now comes to 20.6 per cent. In 1978 Fukuda was the first Japanese Prime Minister ever to visit the Middle East countries. Since 1978 energy diplomacy has become a major part of the Government's international activities. Foreign Affairs Minister Sonoda visited Mexico in 1979 and successfully extracted a guaranteed oil supply from that country.

The most serious effort by Japanese government and industries, therefore, lies in the multiplication and diversification of supplies overseas. This is in addition to the efforts made in developing any new energy-intensive industries close to energy-supply centers overseas rather than in Japan. Aluminium projects were, for example, developed in Indonesia and Brazil, whereas copper projects were located in Canada, Zaire and Zambia. This type of offshore diversification applies to all kinds of resource supplies, and the rule of thumb is not to exceed one-third of the total import from any single country. Because of the unfortunate experience earlier, 40 per cent of Japan's uranium imports now originate with South Africa as compared to 37 per cent from Canada, 10 per cent from the UK and Australia and 8 per cent from France and its former colonies.

As shown in Table 5.2 there have been considerable shifts in the sources of Japan's oil supply in recent years. The Middle East countries used to provide roughly 80 per cent of Japan's oil supply in the 1970s, and this figure has since 1980 declined to 70 per cent. Within that region the importance of Iran as supplier has also declined for obvious reasons. Saudi Arabia, the single most important supplier to Japan has increased its share from 30 to 35 per cent. The United Arab Emirates has also increased its share from 10 to 15 per cent. Mexico and the PRC stand out as two new and important suppliers. During the 1970s Venezuela was the only country in Latin America that exported oil to Japan, and these exports only accounted for 0.1 per cent of total exports. Beginning in 1980 the Mexican supply to Japan doubled every year and now provides 4 per cent of Japan's imported oil.

Table 5.2: Japan's Oil Suppliers

	1977	1978	1979	1980	1981	1982	1983
<u>Latin America</u>							
Venezuela	0.1	0.1	0.2	0.8	1.1	0.7	0.6
Mexico	-	-	-	0.6	1.8	2.6	3.8
<u>Middle East</u>							
Saudi Arabia	30.6	28.6	28.4	31.6	34.3	35.4	28.1
Iran	17.1	16.8	9.9	6.1	3.5	6.2	11.0
Iraq	3.1	3.4	5.4	7.4	1.5	1.8	0.3
Kuwait	7.9	7.9	9.1	3.1	4.0	1.5	1.6
Neutral Zone	3.6	4.9	6.5	5.3	4.3	5.2	5.7
United Arab Emirates	11.2	10.3	10.1	13.7	13.6	13.4	15.1
Qater	1.0	2.3	3.0	2.9	3.7	3.6	3.7
Oman	3.5	3.6	3.9	3.1	4.1	3.5	5.0
<u>Africa</u>							
Algeria	0.1	1.1	0.1	0.6	1.2	1.0	0.8
Libya	0.4	0.8	0.2	0.5	0.5	0.1	-
Nigeria - Angola	0	0	0	0.4	0.7	0.2	0.5
<u>S.E. Asia</u> & <u>Oceania</u>							
Indonesia	13.6	12.8	14.4	14.3	15.8	15.2	14.0
Brunei-Malaysia	4.9	5.2	3.4	3.2	2.2	2.3	2.3
Australia	0.1	0.8	0				
Australia-Burma				-	2.1	2.0	1.8
<u>Socialist Countries</u>							
USSR	0	0	0	0	0	0	0.1
PRC	2.8	3.2	3.1	3.6	4.6	4.8	5.3

Source: Statistics are derived from the Ministry of Foreign Affairs, <u>Annual Blue Books 1976 - 1984</u>.

Table 5.2 also reveals a surprising fact that the often-talked about Soviet-Japanese co-operation in the development of Siberia and the Russian Far Eastern oil and gas has so far born little result. Instead, the Sino-Japanese co-operation has been growing rather rapidly especially in China's supply of coal and oil to Japan. The contrast is no accident. Behind the difference is the history of international politics of the 1970s and the early 1980s. Japanese energy policy has responded to the escalation of East-West tensions, the trade and investment opportunities in China's new 'open door policy' and the political instability of the Middle East.

JAPAN'S RESOURCE DIPLOMACY

As of 1967 the Japanese Goverment required that at least 30 per cent of its oil supply should come from its own development ventures overseas. Until then the Japanese had thought of overseas supplies only in terms of purchases instead of joint ventures in developing new sources. In 1966, for example, when the first Japan-Soviet Business Co-operation Committee met in Tokyo, it was the Russian delegation that mentioned the possibility of a joint venture in the development of Siberia and the Russian Far East petroleum, natural gas, pipe-line and forestry industries.(7) However, the Japanese delegation was then more interested in selling plants, getting construction contracts and sending lumberjacks abroad. The Soviets offered to sell to the Japanese 20 to 24 billion cubic metres of natural gas per annum in return for Japanese capital and mechanical supplies for development of the Sakhalin oilfield. However, by the time the Japanese began to show a serious interest in 1970, the Soviets announced that the estimated quantity had been overly optimistic and export to Japan might have to wait for new exploration.

The Soviet-Japanese co-operation in the development of Siberian natural resources had its highest hope in 1973 when PM Tanaka visited Secretary General Brezhnev in Moscow. In the joint communique, however, it was especially pointed out that the proposed co-operation should not exclude the participation of a third nation. Clearly, the third nation was the United States of America. The progressive deterioration in detente during the 1970s however affected the prospects of greater Japanese involvement in Soviet economic development. Indeed, there were many technical as well as administrative problems that had hindered the growth of Soviet-Japanese co-operation. But, most of all, it was the political distance between the two nations that prevented any closer economic co-operation between the two.

The prospects for Soviet-Japanese co-operation

had dimmed considerably by the late 1970s; however, the People's Republic of China, which was then coming out of a decade of political fantasy and economic isolation offered an exciting alternative. Japanese interest in China's petroleum development began as soon as the Chinese government decided to welcome foreign assistance in a new national drive to promote resource exploration.(8) The new policy was prompted not merely by the more open and liberal attitude of the new regime. Declining energy production figures were also a cause for worry on the part of the government which proposed to modernise the nation and quadruple its GNP by the end of the century. As shown in Table 5.3 the Chinese were producing only slightly more than what they were consuming domestically.

Table 5.3: China's Energy Production and Consumption

	Year	Production	Domestic Consumption
Coal	1979	635.6 mt	585.2 mt
	1980	672.4 mt	594.0 mt
Oil	1979	161.5 mt	89.3 mt
	1980	159.1 mt	88.4 mt
Natural Gas	1979	14.5 bill.cm	
	1980	13.8 bill.cm	
Hydro Electricity	1979	50.1 bill. kwh	
	1980	56.8 bill. kwh	

Source: Sino-Japanese Economic Council, 1982.

In the past, Chinese export of oil and coal was mainly for the purpose of earning foreign currencies. It accounted for 10 per cent of the Chinese income from exports. By the end of the 1970s, it had become evident that even for its own development needs, China had to find new sources of energy supplies.

Negotiation between China and Japan began in 1978 and materialised in an agreement for a joint venture in 1980. The project involved the Bohai-West and Bohai-South offshore drilling. The Sino-Japanese Petroleum Development Company and the Chengbei Petroleum Development Company were established in April, 1980, with 47 Japanese firms holding 40 per cent interest and the Japan Kodan sharing the remainder. The first company would be responsible for the Bohai project while the second one would be involved in the Chengbei project where the Chinese had already found oil. The Japanese were responsible for all the exploration capital, but their costs were to be paid back with any oil recovered. At the development stage, the Japanese would provide 49 per cent and the Chinese 51 per cent of the capital needed. When it reached the production stage, both the capital and the management would become Chinese responsibility. For a period of 15 years, Japan would get 42.5 per cent of the product, including sales for the recovery of capital cost. By 1983, all of the three wells drilled were successful. It was expected that by the end of 1985, these wells would start production and the estimates run as high as 100 million kilolitres.

Other than the Bohai Project, the Japanese then took very little interest in the South China Sea survey and exploration which did involve most of the major international firms. Obviously, Japan's objective in the overseas oil project is to secure supplies rather than to generate profits. The geographical proximity of northern China is also an advantage as it will shorten the transportation route by more than a half. Also Japanese companies fared well in the acquisition of the 16/06 contract block in the Pearl River Mouth Basin during the final stage of the first round of bidding in November, 1985.

A new problem in the Sino-Japanese energy trade is the Chinese pressure for increases in Japanese oil imports in order to balance out China's trade deficit with Japan. The Japanese are, however, reluctant to do so due to the more relaxed conditions of the international oil market.

The latest report on negotiations concerning the Five Year Agreement 1986-91 indicates that Japanese industries see little need for increases in oil and coal imports from China beyond the current annual figures of 8 million tons and 4 million tons respectively.(9) For the Chinese, from a long-range perspective of trade relations between the two nations, unless the Japanese agree to increase their imports in coal and oil from China, they will not be able to meet the payments for imports from Japan. For the Japanese, the issue is multilateral, not bilateral, as they are facing similar demands on the part of the Australians and others. Evidently, Japanese needs for coal and oil are not expected to increase significantly due to the decline of the steel industry and a shift to nuclear energy. Thus, the picture seems to be changing, though slowly, from a seller's to a buyer's market.

The foregoing discussion of Soviet-Japanese and Sino-Japanese relations suggests that neither the Japanese government nor Japanese business and industry have complete freedom in the choice of resource policies. First of all, the issue is public and national in nature. More and more government intervention, whether in the form of administrative guidance or regulative measures will be required. Secondly, the issue is multilateral for Japan even though others may tend to see it from a bilateral perspective. Thirdly, the issue is often linked to other international bilateral or multilateral issues; for example, the linkage between Japan's energy diplomacy and the US strategy in the Middle East. Overall, however, it is Japan's concerns for American approval that dominate the final decision in Japan's resource diplomacy. In other words, Japan will continue to pursue whatever independent policy she deems necessary as long as it does not cause violent American resentment. At the same time the Japanese have also become aware of the inevitability of linkage between economic success and political responsibility. Thus Japanese policy towards the Middle Eastern countries has not only encompassed economic and cultural ties, but also more positive political ties. The offer of their good offices in the Iran-Iraq conflict is a case in point.

Current Japanese strategy has focused on reducing Japan's vulnerability as opposed to increasing energy supplies. With the shift to the age of high-technology Japan will become, in the long run, the base for sophisticated technological production. Energy-intensive production will be relocated offshore wherever the energy supply is cheaper and easily accessible. In this regard Japan will become a large investor overseas. As modernisation in China progresses, there will be more Japanese investment and joint ventures in that country. The more Sino-Japanese co-operation develops the greater possibility for Japan to survive, in terms of energy and raw material suplies, as a regional power. Ultimately, however, the U.S. market and nuclear umbrella are the most powerful influence on Japan's choice of policies.

JAPAN'S ENERGY FUTURE

The future can be projected only from the record achieved so far, and the Japanese record in meeting the challenge stands as brilliant. This evaluation, however, does not meet the approval of most Japanese energy critics as they have on the contrary tended to be overly pessimistic. For example, most Japanese reviewers would consider Japan's efforts in overseas petroleum development a total failure, as these did not succeed in achieving the projected supply of 30 per cent of Japan's oil needs by 1985 nor have they proved to be especially profitable. Even the present scaled down target of 20 per cent of total supply by 1990, is doubtful. What must be kept in mind is the fact that Japan is a late investor in the international market of oil industries. Therefore, Japanese overseas oil investment has suffered from many disadvantages such as paying higher royalties and giving better financial incentives to the resource countries. While Japanese investors have had to carry higher costs, they have often had to tolerate a less impressive rate of return. However, the 30 per cent target was not reached mainly because of the high sulphur content of the oil produced and the absence of production-distribution chains in Japan. Thus, as shown in Table 5.4 the absolute figure for Japanese oil production overseas has in fact increased, although its relative weight in the total imports has not necessarily progressed accordingly.

Emphasis on exploration and development of new oilfields, however, passed its peak ofter 1976. With the advice of the IEA and later the second oil crisis caused by the 1978 revolution in Iran, Japan's energy policy shifted to emphasise development of substitutes for oil. Review, for example, the budgetary figures in Table 5.5. The Sunshine Plan which was initiated in 1974 to search for 'clean' energies became the main instrument in the accelerated search for substitute resources. With the introduction of new tax revenue designated for the specific purpose of energy development, the fund available for research grew ten-fold after 1980. Still the emphases on liquefaction and gasification of coal and projects in this category

Table 5.4: Japan's Overseas Oil Production

(unit=1000 kl)

Year	(A) JIPO Imports	(B) Total Imports	A/B Rate(%)
1961	1,545	39,163	3.9
1962	4,94a3	47,261	10.5
1963	8,943	62,399	14.3
1964	10,321	74,160	13.9
1965	11,290	87,626	12.9
1966	14,787	104,199	14.2
1967	15,915	125,137	12.7
1968	17,978	146,848	12.2
1969	18,037	174,563	10.3
1970	20,114	204,872	9.8
1971	19,466	224,379	8.7
1972	20,910	253,037	8.3
1973	24,589	288,606	8.5
1974	27,517	275,887	10.0
1975	23,277	262,786	8.9
1976	23,997	275,826	8.7
1977	23,671	277,478	8.5
1978	29,532	275,359	10.7
1979	24,689	277,143	8.9

Source: Sekiyu Sangyo no Genjo, (1980).
JIPO oil is oil imported from Japanese overseas investment projects.

claim approximately one-half of the budget. Under the 1979 revised version of the Sunshine Plan, the coal liquefaction will assume 48.5 per cent of the estimated 57 million kilolitres of new energy supply in 1995. It is worthwhile noting that the plan also calls for development of three liquefaction plants overseas, each capable of producing 290 thousand barrels per day, by 1990.

Enthusiasm for technological breakthroughs, especially in coal liquefaction, however, has to be realistically scaled down. For example, the SRC II Project had to be stopped because of the 240 per cent increase in plant construction costs and also because the estimated production cost of U.S. $48.80 a barrel far exceeds the market value of oil. Similarly, in 1982 the projected energy needs for 1990 were scaled down 15 per cent and the expected supply of new energy was cut down one-third. It is now estimated that the development of substitute energy will be delayed for about ten years.

Table 5.5: Budget for New Energy Development

	1980	1981	1982	1983	1984
			(100 million yen)		
Technological development in Oil-substitution	39	204	343	384	390
Coal Resource Development	43	66	86	62	44
Thermo Resource Development	75	79	56	52	68
Grants-in-Aid	24	179	26	26	26
Coal Subsidies	271	288	246	235	230
Alcohol etc.	-	-	76	179	204
	452	816	833	938	962

Source: Compiled by Suzuki Shigeru in his Nihon no enerugi kaihatsu Seisaku, Mineruva, Kyoto, 1984, p. 234.

According to Japanese studies, unless there is an annual growth of more than 3 per cent in the oil price, accompanied by non-growth in the cost of substitute materials such as coal, no production of new energy on a commercial basis is possible before the next century.(10) The solar power experiment station developed in Kagawa Prefecture was also stopped in March, 1983 due to economic inefficiency. The Japanese conclusion is that it can be utilised in remote areas on a small-scale basis, but that it is rather impractical as an important substitute source of energy at the national level.

In both overseas oil exploration and the domestic search for substitute energy, it is the Japanese government, not the private sector, that plays the key role in terms of the provision of loans, grants, loan guarantees for loans, tax advantages, most of all, the necessary co-ordination of efforts. In spite of all of these efforts the Japanese appear to have concluded that the very little that can be done to alter the overall picture of energy deficiency. As a report presented at the Conference on Energy Problems sponsored by the Japanaese Academy of Science put it, the 'time' and 'quantity' factors simply render the efforts insignificant from the overall perspective, even though these efforts might be successful ones. Surely, any new oil development takes time and any success in the experiment of substitute energy can relieve only so much pressure on the current heavy reliance on oil. What has become evident is the complexity of the problem intertwined with so many other problems such as environmental control, technological development, finance and monetary policy. Ultimately it is tied to the economic survival of the nation. Most important is the growing Japanese realisation that energy resources can become political, instead of purely commerical commodities.

The latest move on the part of the US to allow sales of Alaskan oil to Japan can be seen as an exchange for Japanese willingness to increase its defense expenditures over the 1 per cent ceiling of GNP. It is anticipated that the increased budget will be spent mostly for purchase of AWACS, P3-C and other anti-submarine weapons. American linkage politics pressures the Japanese to bear more responsibility for the security of Asia. The US welcomes Japanese concentration on the security of 1000 miles of vital sea-lanes running in and out of the Japanese home islands. About 80 per cent of Japan's oil supply passes through the Malacca Strait and the sea-lane traffic of oil-tankers only gets heavier and heavier as Japan pushes for the goal of Strategic Petroleum Reserve of 30 million kilolitres by 1988.(11) Thus, superficially the more realistic the Japanese become the clearer they may see a convergence of interest between their energy policy and the national security issue.

The key point, however, is the real intention of the American pressure. Were the American intention to pressure the Japanese into a closer military alliance, presumably against the USSR as a potential enemy, a slight increase in the Japanese defence budget alone would not satisfy the situation. In that case the US should be prepared to guarantee the Japanese supply of energy needs which, of course, seems impossible. For Japan, therefore, an independent resource diplomacy remains important; it not only assures the continuous supply of raw materials, but also means that the resource rich nations may well become increasingly important markets for Japanese goods in the long run.

In conclusion, Japan is still 82 per cent dependent on imported energies, and in light of the tremendous degree of vulnerability, detailed above, the diversification of sources of supply and of the domestic energy mix and pattern of consumption can only been seen as a palliative rather than as a comprehensive solution to continuing dependence. The Japanese response to the latter condition, given the funding and timing limitation of energy substitution and new technological development, will not allow for a quick made-in Japan solution. Japan's resource diplomacy has had, therefore, to be innovative in the context of new and complicated economic and geopolitical relationships between states. The management of dependence has led to new trading and investment opportunities. Japan's resource diplomacy has had to master an increasingly varied set of international variables, and as such diplomacy has reflected foreign policy choices which have not always been consistent with US strategic positions. Japan's resource diplomacy is in part informed by a skepticism as to the future effectiveness of collective measures on the part of the major industrial powers. It may stretch the elasticity of Japan's traditional strategic relationship with the US, but it is not inspired by a consciously systematic challenge to the overall structure of the Japanese-American security relationship.

NOTES

1. Compare the 1983 Japanese figure of energy export dependence to France at 63 per cent, West Germany at 50.5 per cent, the US at 12.7 per cent and the UK at 20 per cent.

2. A comparison of oil consumption in 1978 by various economic sectors reads as follows: In Japanese Industry (54 per cent), Transportation (22 per cent), Household (10 per cent); In US Industry (12 per cent), Transportation (60 per cent) Household (23 per cent); In West Germany Industry (26 per cent), Transportation (28 per cent), Household (40 per cent).

3. For such arguments see Chudo Yukimasa,

"Omen of the Post-Oilshock Era Posto Oilshok Jidai no Yocho in Gikkan Pen, pp. 57-61.

4. For an analysis of Japan's petro-chemical industry see Watanage Tokuji and Saeki Koji, Tenki ni tatsu Sekiyu-kogyo (Petro-chemical industry at crossroads), (Iwanami: Tokyo, 1984).

5. For example, see Ronald A. Morse's criticism of Japan's energy policy, Nihon no enerugi Anzen hosho seisaku o tsuku in Chuo Koron, September, 1981, pp. 122-37.

6. See the annual Blue Books on Diplomacy especially the volume for 1979, Ministry of Foreign Affairs, the Government of Japan.

7. See Suzuki Keisuke, Niso Keizai Kyoryoku: Siberia Kaihatsu kyoryoku to Nippon (Soviet-Japanese economic co-operation: the Siberia development co-operation and Japan), (Nippon Kokusai Mondai Kenskyusho: Tokyo, 1974).

8. For details of Japanese involvement in the petroleum development in China see Nichyu Keizai Kyokai, Chugoku no Sekiyu kaihatsu to sho-gaikoku no kyoryoku (Chinese petroleum development and foreign corporations), (Sino-Japanese Economic Council: Tokyo, 1982).

9. For the latest report see, Yomiuri Shimbun, 5 September 1985.

10. Nippon Keizai Chosa Kyogikai, Sekiyu Daitai Enerugi no Sogo Hyoka to Teigen (Overall Evaluation and Suggestions on Oil-Substituting Energy), 1982.

11. Nippon Kagakusha Kaigi, Nihon no Enerugi Mondai (Japan's Energy Problems), Tokyo, 1980.

12. Hotta Toshihiko, Enerugi Seisaku no Genjo to Kongo no Tembo ni tsuite -- Sekiyu bichiku o chushin toshite (On energy policy and its outlook - with emphasis on petroleum reserves), Tokyo, 1983.

Chapter Six

VIETNAM'S ECONOMY AND ENERGY PROBLEMS: TERRITORIAL AND STRATEGIC IMPLICATIONS

Justus M. van der Kroef

Modern Vietnam has known little of the ways of peace. Her economy has been skewed, not just by the impact of the French colonial experience, but by three decades of struggle for independence and national consolidation under Communist leadership. Even during the period between 1975 and 1978 a newly unified Vietnam quickly was drawn into ever sharper conflict with the government of Pol Pot's Democratic Kampuchea. After 1978 Vietnam again has been on a continuous war footing, fighting both in Cambodia and confronting a hostile People's Republic of China.

The following pages seek to focus on Vietnam's energy problem primarily in the context of her international political imperatives. First, consideration will be given to the condition of Vietnam's economy today and of the place of her energy potential and production in it. Subsequent sections will deal with the Cambodian conflict and its strategic and economic implications for Hanoi, and, because of their possible role in future oil production, with the territorial disputes between China and Vietnam in the South China Sea.

THE STATE OF VIETNAM'S ECONOMY

In its 1984 annual 'overview' report The Conference Board in New York dubs the condition of Vietnam's economy as 'catastrophic'. Indeed, this is the case notwithstanding some notable impulses of growth in some sectors, such as agriculture. Comparisons with a few of Hanoi's neighbours in Southeast Asia quickly tell the story. In 1983 Thailand, with a population of 50.7 million had a Gross Domestic Product (GDP) of US $40.3 billion, and an estimated _per capita_ income per annum of about US $760;

Malaysia and her population of 15.8 million, had a GDP of US $29.07 billion, and an estimated US $720 *per capita* income; and even the Philippines, not exactly the most trouble-free economy of the region, managed with a population of 53.4 million, to have a GDP of US $34.2 billion and an estimated *per capita* income of US $775. But as for the Socialist Republic of Vietnam (SRV), and its 58.8 million people, authoritative current Gross National Product estimates range from only US $6 to 16 billion, usually settling at US $12 billion as a commonly acceptable figure. *Per capita* income estimates for the SRV, though varying, usually hover around US $150 (1983), down from US $275 in 1979.(1)

Vietnam also suffers from 'galloping inflation', estimated by Western diplomatic sources to be running at a rate of between 70 and 90 per cent. Hanoi Radio has admitted that the limited quantity of and breakdown in the distribution of goods has led 'quite a few cadres, party members and state personnel' to become 'depraved'. Complaints about corrupt and overbearing party officials are common, especially in South Vietnam.(2) Though declaring that 'some progress' had been made, an editorial in Hanoi's principal daily, nevertheless, complained in mid-1984 that abuse of authority, misappropriation of funds, and other 'cases of corruption, lavish feasting and bribery' were still manifest in the food production and distribution co-operatives and collectives.(3)

For the long term, Vietnam's economic problems seem even more disquieting. Toward the close of 1984, Hanoi's hard currency reserves amounted to only US $16 million, while her foreign debt totalled over US $6 billion. Some US $4 billion of the latter is owed to the Soviet Union and East European countries, and the rest to non-Communist institutional creditors. Most of the latter are West European and Japanese banks. To be sure, according to an assessment of the Vietnamese economy made early in 1984 by the International Monetary Fund, there has been significant growth recently in the SRV's export economy. Export values rose from US $475 million in 1982 to an estimated US $743 million in 1984, a little over a third of the latter being in much needed convertible currencies. But the payments due on its foreign debt alone in the next few years will swallow up virtually all of Vietnam's hard currency earnings.(4)

Hanoi's emissaries for the past two years have been busily attempting to rearrange the large amounts owed to Japan, France, Libya and other creditors. But more will be needed than wizardry in debt rescheduling to balance the SRV's economy. Shut off from access to many of the world's major financial markets and commercial opportunities, Hanoi's foreign trade has become ever more one-sided. In 1984 about 58 per cent of Vietnam's imports came from the USSR, and 52 per cent of all her exports went there. Inability to modernise plant equipment, along with persistent shortages of raw materials, continue to plague the SRV's export economy. The situation is made worse by a lack of management expertise and by the shoddy quality of goods produced, particularly in the food processing, textiles and light machine building industries. The SRV's government press, while noting a growth in diversity and volume of exports, also keeps complaining about decreasing quality of goods, transporation delays, and even the failure of raw materials produced to meet the uniform standards needed to make reprocessing possible.(5)

To be sure, the destruction and dislocating effects of the decades-long struggle for unification of the country are responsible in a major way for the country's presently retarded development as compared to other Southeast Asian states. No other country of the region experienced anything near the length, duration, and extent of the ravages of war in the post-World War II era as did Vietnam. Yet, and to a growing degree, much of the SRV's economic predicament today seems a self-inflicted wound, stemming domestically from uncertain and vacillating public policies, and, in foreign relations, from a costly involvement in Cambodia and its negative international consequences.

Hardly a year after Communist forces victoriously entered Saigon (now named Ho Chi Minh City), the grand concepts of a massive development effort in the Second Five Year Plan (1976-80) had become illusory. There were growing tension and border disputes with the Beijing-backed regime of Democratic Kampuchea (DK), headed by Premier Pol Pot. A deepening political conflict with the People's Republic of China also ignited periodic frontier clashes and, eventually, in 1979 there was a brief 'punitive' Chinese invasion of the SRV. These developments tended to limit systematic and broadly based national development. By September, 1979, at the sixth plenary meeting of the Vietnam Communist Party (VCP), and again at the close of March, 1982, when the party's Fifth National

Congress was held, pragmatic survival rather than purity of ideological doctrine had become the lodestar of Vietnamese economic policy.(6) As the VCP's Central Committee already had put it in its report to the Fifth Congress in March, 1982:

> We failed to fully realise the difficulties and complexities of the advance to socialism from a primarily small production economy, as well as the difficulties resulting from 'prolonged war', management deficiencies, and 'unfavourable' international developments.(7)

The hybrid economy which has been developing in Vietnam since then has witnessed, among other phenomena, the growth and obvious productivity of a contract system in agriculture (which allows peasant producers to keep and dispose freely of what they produce once a set quota has been delivered to the government), a system of capitalist style incentives in industrial production, including bonuses, wages paid by piecework, and decentralisation of and considerable autonomy in plant management. But all these function alongside agricultural co-operatives, state farm 'collectives', and centralised control over allocation of energy, major communication facilities, and the mining of coal (the SRV's principal mineral export), phosphates and iron. The distributing trade in particular presents a bewildering mixture of state-controlled retail outlets in some areas, state-supervised co-operative stores, and especially in South Vietnam, individually owned small shops, crafts, and restaurants in others.

The concessions to private incentive, particularly in agriculture, have not come easy to the more ideologically committed leaders of the VCP. There are frequent exhortations to the nation to keep the ideal of a truly collectivised economy in mind at all times.

The ambiguity in the thinking of VCP's leadership in matters of economic public policy is apparent, for example, from the following passages in an address by Party Secretary General Le Duan to the plenary meeting of the VCP Central Committee, 3 July 1984:

> In order to master the market, eliminate capitalist trade, and transform small merchants, it is decisive that we must strive to develop socialist trade, enlarge its

> battleground, enhance the quality of state-run trade, and pay utmost attention to the organisation and development of marketing co-operatives, considering the marketing co-operatives as the effective supporting forces of state-run trade.
>
> In the present economic situation we advocate the policy of maintaining the free market in a given area of the countryside and cities as places to trade and barter staple products between producers and consumers without the intermediary transactions of speculators.
>
> All the activities of small merchants --including their services--should be tightly organised and controlled and be gradually replaced by socialist trade.(8)

'Tight organisation' of the private small business community has meant regularly and steeply rising taxes, as well as pressure on the small business person to join a state-run retail trade co-operative or merge with a state-owned store.(9) Yet the steady 'socialisation' of the distributing sector of the economy continues to be accompanied by widespread shortages of basic consumer goods and extensive black marketeering--both vigorously denounced in party pronouncements. Meanwhile there is also a tendency to blame nature for production shortfalls. On 26 December 1984, Vo Van Kiet, Vice-Chairman of the SRV Council of Ministers blamed a 1984 food production increase of only 300,000 tons over the previous year on 'the greatest natural disasters' since 1975, as well as on the 'intensified plots' by the state's enemies. A relentless self-examination of the premises of economic public policy, as occurred in Deng Xiaoping's China, apparently is not contemplated. Other party directives, meanwhile, urge cadres and government officials to recognise that in the SRV today 'the family economy (i.e. private production) has become part of the socialist economy' and has a 'positive impact', and at the same time urges bureaucrats 'to simultaneously develop the collective economy and the economy of co-operative members' families'.(10)

It is but one of the dilemmas of the present SRV economic system that the desired upsurge in agricultural productivity, following the introduction of the privately oriented contract system, has put more money in the pockets of some (by no means all) of the peasantry. But the SRV's economy is unable to supply the consumer goods on which the farmer is ready to spend this increased income.(11) The result has been an added stimulus not only to an already rampant inflation but also to the extensive black market. One major conduit that feeds the Vietnamese, Laotian, and Cambodian black markets is the porous frontier between Thailand and Cambodia. In Laos and Cambodia combined, not just 140,000 Vietnamese troops, but additional thousands of Vietnamese civilian 'technicians', party officials, and peasant settlers are located. The participation of these Vietnamese in this black-market channel periodically prompts official but largely ineffective, denunciations and show trials of 'economic saboteurs'. The SRV's southern coast, easily accessible to Thai and Cambodian smugglers operating in the Gulf of Thailand, and who are said to be in league with ethnic Chinese entrepreneurs in several Southeast Asia countries, also affords entrepots for the thriving Vietnamese underground economy.

As 'contract' farming produces black market-oriented 'hot money', which the SRV government, with little success thus far, has been trying to sop up by persuading peasants to buy long-term government bonds, other and large segments of Vietnamese society, ten years after the Communist victory, still eke out a meager existence. Given the ambiguities of her economic policy and her sluggishly expanding production base, Vietnam's economic problems today are aggravated yet further by a virtually uncontrolled expansion of her population. During the past five years, the SRV's population growth rate averaged 2.6 per cent per annum. The economic consequences have been predictable. In mid-March, 1984, a commentary over Radio Hanoi declared that 'The number of jobless workers has increased every day in recent years', and that 'in the cities alone' there were 'hundreds of thousands', particularly 'youths reaching work age', as well as discharged members of the armed forces and 'graduates from the general education schools and various training courses', who were out of work. Special public work projects, ranging from processing wool fibers, to 'crocheting and embroidery' and 'chicken raising' had been established by the government for the unemployed. But the same commentary went on to note that though local authorities had arranged for hundreds of thousands of jobs, they had failed to obtain 'necessary capital and materials' to expand employment opportunities. Hence the huge national jobless problem was only being 'inconsistently and slowly resolved'.(12)

VIETNAM'S ENERGY POTENTIAL

Where and how fast to get the 'necessary capital and materials' is the spectre that haunts the Vietnamese economy today. The need for redevelopment of the country's energy resources is but one dimension of the problem. Hanoi, for the time being, has pinned its long-term hopes for meeting its energy needs on three sources: coal, thermal and hydro-electric power, and oil. Only the first has reached any degree of significant productive exploitation today, but in this area too there is stagnation. Since 1981 annual coal (anthracite) production has fluctuated between 6.3 and 6.1 million short tons.(13) The SRV's proven, recoverable coal reserves currently are estimated to be about 130 million tons. Over 5 million tons of annual production is used domestically. Most of the remainder is shipped either to Japan and Singapore, or via these countries to other non-Communist states, often in flag-of-convenience vessels. In 1982 Vietnam's coal exports earned her government about 40 million US dollars, or nearly 10 per cent of the value of all the country's exports that year.(14) With regular Soviet assistance the modernisation of Vietnamese mines in the Vang Danh and Mao regions is proceeding, if slowly. For example, in May, 1984 the new Uong Bi coal sorting plant, with a planned output of 1.8 million metric tons, was opened.(15)

At present the contribution of hydro-electric power to Vietnam's energy economy is negligible. Harnessing the potential of the SRV's major rivers, for example the Mekong in the south and the Yuan and Bo in the north, has barely begun. Any significant role of hydro-electric power in future development could only be expected if there were to be both sizable capital infusions and drafting of a realistic and integrated national industrial planning policy. Vietnamese spokesmen appear optimistic about current projects in this energy category. VCP Central Committee Secretary Hoang Tung, toward the close of 1984, claimed that though 'for the time being ... we still have a weak power industry', the Pha Lai thermal electric power plant, with a 600 megawatt capacity, was now beginning to come on line, supplying industrial projects in Hanoi and environs. According to Tung the Hoa Binh hydro-electric plant on the Song Da River is also under 'rapid construction'. When finished it will be Southeast Asia's largest hydropower facility, with a 2,000 megawatt capacity. The building of a hydropower plant at Tri An in South Vietnam is also going forward, aided further by Soviet grants provided under a new long-term 'technical co-operation' agreement signed on 18 April 1984 in Moscow. According to other sources the Hoa Binh project costs nearly US $2.5 billion. But Soviet aid for it thus far has reached only 1.3 billion US dollars. The project will not be finished until 1990, although some generators will come on line by 1987. This will bring production changes for North Vietnamese factories which presently use coal. About 3 million tons of coal will presumably become available for export once the Hoa Binh project is in full production.(16) In January, 1978, the SRV, along with its Laotian ally and Thailand, formed an 'Interim Committee for Co-ordination and Investigation of the Lower Mekong Basin'. Since the early 1970s United Nations agencies have been interested in developing the Mekong's hydro-electric potential. The Interim Committee has kept on meeting, despite frequent upsurges in political tensions between Thailand and Laos, and Thailand and the SRV. There is no prospect, however, that Vietnam will benefit any time soon from proposed Mekong River power grids.

Significant benefits from oil production also still lie in the future. All of the SRV's current petroleum needs must be met by imports. The imports for 1982 are detailed in Table 6.1. Such oil exploration as is taking place is located primarily offshore, and, in the case of the potential resources in the South China Sea, is the centre of an intensive international territorial conflict to be discussed below. Thus Vietnam is importing well over ten million barrels per annum. If her industrial development is to take flight and at the same time her present military power is to be maintained, this amount will quickly treble. Given the diffusion of sourcing and marketing in the international oil trade today, particularly when it involves a country like the SRV which must operate under a US trade embargo, no exact information as to the Vietnamese oil imports is publicly available.

The USSR and Romania are believed to be the chief suppliers.

Table 6.1: Imports of Oil Products into the SRV in 1982 (bblls per day)

gasoline	6,000
kerosene	3,000
distillate	9,000
residuals	8,000
all other	500

Source: US Department of Energy, Information Service

At present the only significant Vietnamese area of active exploration and potential production is located some 100 kilometres offshore in an arc stretching southwards from the Vung Tau Peninsula. Already in 1974, the then South Vietnamese government of President Nguyen Van Thieu granted offshore exploration rights in southern waters, well north of the Natuna Islands which are claimed by Indonesia. Even so, the Thieu concession ignited a relatively low-key territorial dispute between Vietnam and Indonesia which, in effect, has continued until this day.(17) Successful test wells drilled by Royal Dutch Shell and Mobil in 1975 in this region eventually turned out to be unrewarding. The political implications following the collapse of the Saigon government and the subsequent imposition of the US embargo has also made exploration less attractive. Initially, the new SRV government granted search and exploratory rights in the same area to three other non-Communist oil corporations, Italy's Agip, the German Federal Republic's Deminex, and Canada's Bow Valley. The first two withdrew in early 1981 after disagreement with the SRV's own state oil corporation, Petrovietnam. Bow Valley, citing equipment problems, has remained inactive though it has not formally withdrawn.

However, already in July, 1980, the USSR signed an agreement with Hanoi to explore offshore oil and gas resources.(18) Exploration reportedly having been favourable, on 19 June 1981, a SRV-Soviet protocol was signed establishing a joint enterprise called Vietsovpetro to regulate production in Vietnamese waters. Public pronouncements on the success of this enterprise are few and often have been contradictory. For example, on 28 May 1984, Tass reported from Ho Chi Minh City that 'the first oil' had been struck by a Vietsovpetro drilling vessel two days earlier. Yet a few days before, in its 24 May 1984 issue, the authoritative Far Eastern Economic Review quoted SRV deputy premier Tran Phuong as saying that 'despite the hundreds of millions of rubles' invested in Vietnam's search for oil there were 'no concrete results' as yet. Tran Phuong chided the 'boastful' claims of 'our experts', though he hoped that Vietnam would be able to begin meeting its own oil needs by 1990.

In the oil business one can never underestimate the sudden gushes of success. Still, it is a virtual certainty that for the better part of the next decade the SRV will continue to have to rely on imports to meet her needs in petroleum products. Moreover, there are no indications, certainly not in the non-Communist world, that any other country or oil company is interested in emulating the Vietsovpetro example. Apart from the relative uncertainty over profitable returns on further offshore exploration in Vietnam, a major reason for the present disinterest on the part of the international oil producing community is political. Specifically, that disinterest stems from: the international embroglio in which Hanoi has found herself since 1979 because of her Cambodian venture, and because of her increased strategic dependence on the USSR; and the Sino-Vietnamese territorial conflict, which in so far as it involves contending claims to areas of the South China Sea and adjacent waters, directly impacts also on the scope of future offshore oil exploration rights.

In its 15 April 1985 issue, the authoritative Oil and Gas Journal reported that Vietnam was prepared to drill as many as 32 wells from two platforms in the oil development project underway with Soviet help, 75 miles off the Vietnamese port of Vung Tau. Other sources report that actual production of oil in Vietnam may begin by the end of 1985, and that since the total offshore find is estimated to be one billion tons, a crude production rate of 15 million tons per year can be reached very shortly.

CAMBODIA AND THE SOVIET FACTOR

In the closing weeks of 1978, after more than three years of border clashes with the forces of the government of 'Democratic Kampuchea' (DK) headed by Premier Pol Pot and President Khieu Sampan, units of the SRV armed forces, ultimately aggregating about 180,000, invaded Cambodia in force. On 7 January 1979, a new Hanoi-backed government, called the People's Republic of Kampuchea (PRK), was proclaimed in Cambodia's capital Phnom Penh. Heng Samrin, one-time political commissar and divisional commander in the Khmer Rouge, became the PRK's head of government. The DK, with an armed force of about 50,000 still intact, escaped toward the Thai border, whence it has been carrying on a persistent guerrilla struggle ever since. The full revelation of the genocidal brutality of the Pol Pot regime, the refugee and famine problems, and the controversy surrounding the legitimacy (or lack thereof) and long-term strategic implications of the Vietnamese invasion and occupation, were to focus renewed international attention on Cambodia in the following years.

This is not the place to review the complex pattern of diplomatic gambits in and out of the United Nations and in other international forums designed to force Hanoi to withdraw its forces from Cambodia and create conditions for a democratically elected regime there.(19) Suffice it to note that in this struggle to persuade the Vietnamese to leave Cambodian soil it was the SRV's neighbours in the Association of Southeast Asian Nations (ASEAN), a group formed in 1967 and now comprising Brunei, Indonesia, Malaysia, the Philippines, Singapore and Thailand, that has played a leading role. Largely because of ASEAN's patient persistence, anti-Vietnamese and anti-PRK groups joined at a meeting in Kuala Lumpur, Malaysia on 22 June 1982 in the formation of the 'Coalition Government of Democratic Kampuchea' (CGDK).

This CGDK alliance comprises not only the original underground DK government, but also the 18,000-man 'Kampuchean People's National Liberation Front' (KPNLF) headed by former Cambodian Premier Son Sann, and the 1,000-man 'Army of National Sihanoukists' (ANS) led by the CGDK's President, Prince Norodom Sihanouk, who was until 1970 Cambodia's principal leader.

Despite serious internal policy divisions within ASEAN and within the CGDK, both of them (through the support they have been able to generate) have contributed significantly to the creation of an international climate in which Vietnam has become something of a pariah. Western financial aid to the SRV, and, with the limited exception of France, investment interest as well, came virtually to an end after 1979 and the Vietnamese occupation of Cambodia.(20) In early 1982 Hanoi accused the Asian Development Bank and other international lending institutions of forcing her into various debt repayment problems and of denying needed loans. These loans, according to Le Hoang, deputy director of the SRV State Bank, 'should have been granted to us' in accordance with standard procedures.(21) Meanwhile, annual resolutions in the UN General Assembly demanding Vietnamese withdrawal from Cambodia and reaffirming the DK as the legitimate occupant of Cambodia's UN seat, kept winning ever larger margins of support. All this appeared to leave Vietnam's strategic survival, and such economic development impulses as it might muster, increasingly at the mercy of the USSR and its bloc supporters. Future exploitation of Vietnam's energy resources similarly seemed to fall hostage not just to the Cambodian embroglio, but also to the Sino-Soviet rivalry for allies among the newly independent Communist Indochinese states.

The latter factor should be analysed briefly, along with the growing Vietnamese dependence on the Soviet bloc, because of both the impact on the present state and the near prospects of the SRV's energy economy. Even before Pol Pot's Khmer Rouge forces seized the Cambodian capital of Phnom Penh on 17 April 1975, the People's Republic of China had been supplying them, as meanwhile Soviet-Khmer Rouge and Vietnamese-Khmer Rouge relations began to cool rapidly. One reason was that both Beijing and Moscow increasingly were jockeying for influence among the Vietnamese, Cambodians and Laotians as Communist victory throughout Indochina neared.(22)

There was also conflict between Khmer Rouge and the Vietnamese--an expression as much of their respective nationalisms fanned by the memory of ancient ethnic and dynastic conflicts, as by Khmer Rouge resentment over the subordinate role assigned them by their Vietnamese allies in the struggle for Communist victory, and fear of future Vietnamese dominance over all of Indochina once that victory had been achieved. Boundary disputes between Vietnam and Pol Pot's new DK government heightened the tensions still further. In June and July, 1975, it came to sharp military clashes between Khmer Rouge and Vietnamese Communist forces in the 'Parrot's Beak' area of Cambodia's Stay Rieng Province and on the then Cambodian-held island of

Poulo Wai and adjacent islands in the Gulf of Thailand.(23)

The second half of 1975 saw the accelerated intrusion of the decades-old Sino-Soviet conflict into the newly Communised Indochina area, as the DK and SRV rapidly moved toward their own confrontation. In October, 1975, during the visit to Moscow of Vietnam's Communist Party Secretary General Le Duan, the Soviets agreed to provide a US $500 million aid package for the SRV's industrial development. Le Duan, in a Kremlin speech on 28 October 1975, declared that the two signatories shared a 'full identity of views'. The VCP Secretary General also praised the USSR for having been 'the first to have opened the road to Socialism' and for now 'paving the way to the most splendid dream of mankind, Communism'.

The Chinese meanwhile, though more circumspectly, were not to be outdone in strengthening their Cambodian ally, Pol Pot's DK. By May, 1976, Thai sources reported that at least 1,000 Chinese technicians and advisers were in Phnom Penh and other Cambodian towns. Chinese vessels were regularly unloading ammunition, rice, and other commodities at the Cambodian port of Kompong Som.(24) At the close of November, 1975, China already had strained its relations with the Vietnamese by formally announcing that the Spratly Islands, located in the South China Sea and claimed by Vietnam, were part of China. Earlier, in January 1974, the Beijing government, despite the protests of the then Republic of South Vietnam (South Vietnam), had sent forces to occupy some and lay claim to all of the Paracel Islands, north of the Spratlys.

During the following years, Chinese and Soviets each strongly voiced support for their respective DK-Vietnamese allies in what was rapidly becoming a new chapter in the seemingly endless Indochina wars. Wearying of repeated DK raids on SRV territory, the Vietnamese, early in December 1977, committed some 58,000 troops to a counter-offensive and a twenty-mile deep penetration of DK territory before their withdrawal. China alternately threatened Hanoi and proclaimed its adhesion to the DK, praising its army for 'defending and helping to build the Motherland'. Moscow, in turn, charged Beijing with having provoked the DK-Vietnamese fighting.(25)

The final SRV offensive on 26 December 1978 against the DK forces, and the swift occupation of most of Kampuchea, therefore, came as the culmination of a conflict in which the longstanding Sino-Soviet dispute, through respective proxies in Indochina, had progressively become intertwined with Vietnam's own policies toward her Cambodian neighbour. Because of this Sino-Soviet entanglement, neither a solution to the present conflict in Cambodia, nor to the problems of long-term stabilisation of Vietnam's economy and of her energy needs seems probable without explicit concurrence by the Soviets and Chinese.

The brief Chinese 'punitive' invasion of the SRV in February, 1979, was meant as a retribution and warning to Hanoi because of its Cambodian conquest. The invasion, together with the development of aid, credit, and trade connect barriers erected against the SRV by virtually all Western nations, soon had the practical effect of turning Vietnam into an economic and strategic satrapy of Moscow. One might add, just as the Lao People's Democratic Republic (LPDR) and Heng Samrin's People's Republic of Kampuchea (PRK) today are satrapies of Hanoi.

Already by September, 1981, one seasoned observer of Indochinese events, William Shawcross, after a Hanoi visit, declared that 'the Soviets provide almost all of Vietnam's fuel', as well as up to a million tons of wheat a year.(26) In addition, Moscow provides 6,000 advisers, and 'at least 10,000 Vietnamese go to Moscow for training of different sorts every year'. According to Shawcross the cost to Moscow of its military aid to Vietnam is about 2 billion US dollars a year. Other non-Communist estimates of the Soviet commitment are lower, but still significant. In 1983, for example, the US Department of Defense, in its published analysis of Soviet military power and its deployment in the world, puts the total of Russian military aid to all of Indochina at only 'over US $2 billion' since 1979, the total of economic aid since 1976 at 'approximately $5 billion', and the number of Soviet economic advisers at 3,750. This 1983 analysis concludes: 'Soviet aid programs currently surpass the peak war years and provide Moscow with leverage over Vietnamese policies'.(27)

The strategic trade-off for this aid is extensive Soviet use of Vietnamese military bases at Danang and Cam Ranh Bay. In September, 1984, a detailed assessment of the new Soviet strategic impact on the South China Sea area was provided by a top official of Thailand's National Security

Council, Prasong Sunsiri. According to Sunsiri, the USSR now deploys a 'regular fleet' of twelve to fifteen surface ships in South China Sea waters and between the South China Sea and the Indian Ocean.(28) The fleet includes aircraft carriers, for example the 37,500-ton Minsk, as well as destroyers and nuclear and conventional submarines. Improvements made by the Soviets at Cam Ranh enable this base to be used by high performance aircraft, including Soviet TU-95D and TU-142F. These planes are flying electronic reconnaissance and anti-submarine patrols. A squadron of nine Soviet 'Badger' type bombers, according to Sunsiri, also has been based at Cam Ranh since the beginning of 1984. In an interview published on 1 January 1985, Sunsiri disclosed that the USSR had stationed 14 MiG-23 fighter-interceptor planes at Cam Ranh, the first such advanced aircraft to be stationed in the region. Sunsiri expressed concern that the planes might be used in Vietnam's military campaign in Cambodia which had become unusually intense around the turn of the year.

From their Vietnamese bases the Soviets are now able to project their power much more quickly and for a longer period of time in the waters off the Asian littoral rim. Western analysts have noted, for example, that previously the 150 vessels of the Soviet Pacific fleet based at Siberia's Kamchatka Peninsula could stay at sea only for 40 days. But the new Cam Ranh facility allows the Soviet vessels to remain 45 days in the Indian Ocean alone. Soviet strategic power can be directed also at the choke points and narrow water passages around Southeast Asia, for example the Malacca, Sunda and Lombok Straits 'through which 50 per cent of the West's oil and 80 per cent of its other strategic material passes'.(29)

To be sure, how successful the Soviets in the long run will be in integrating Vietnam, along with its Laotian and Cambodian allies, into Moscow's own global security system remains very much to be seen. Vietnamese nationalism, always an important dynamic in its Communist movement, likely chafes today under so much *de facto* dominance by the USSR. As early as 1981 Shawcross noted the lack of popularity, at least among South Vietnamese, of the Soviet presence: 'The one phrase a Westerner needs to know is "Khong Phai Lien So"--"I am not a Soviet"'.(30) Yet Hanoi's own strategic interests, including her long-term energy needs, require the Soviet balancing factor. If SRV offshore oil claims, for example in the Tonkin Gulf and around the islands of the South China Sea, are to be pursued to any meaningful degree in the future, a collision with Beijing is inevitable and Soviet naval and air power at Cam Ranh may well be indispensible.

In turn, well before the January 1977 Moscow visit of SRV Defense Minister Vo Nguyen Giap, during which the Soviets agreed to a long-term modernisation and build-up of the SRV armed forces' combat capability, Soviet leaders perceived the possibility of Vietnam serving as 'a new East Germany and a new Cuba', for example as a 'guardian' or 'sentry state', situated at the perimeters of Soviet bloc influence and power, and jutting out into strategically hostile territory.(31) Indeed, the preamble of the Friendship Treaty between the SRV and the German Democratic Republic of 5 December 1977, refers to the 'special responsibility that the two countries are carrying out due to their respective location at the borders of the socialist camp.(32) Having already conceded this much, Vietnam may well find it just as difficult to disengage herself eventually from the Soviet embrace as Poland, Czechoslovakia and other East European states have found it to be.

In the meantime, Soviet analysts keep on recording the benefits Hanoi is receiving from her co-operation with the USSR and her allies. In June, 1978, Vietnam joined the Moscow-led Council for Mutual Economic Assistance and on 4 November 1978 Hanoi and Moscow signed a Treaty of Friendship and Co-operation. This Treaty provides the legal basis for the present strategic and economic relationship between the two countries. Even before and certainly since then, Soviet analysts lead one to believe that the scope of Russian assistance to and trade with the SRV have become indispensible to the latter. Acording to M. Petrov, the inventory of such extensive assistance is inclusive of the following:(33)

1. Twenty-five per cent of Vietnam's electric power is generated by enterprises built with Soviet help, as are 89 per cent of Vietnam's coal production, and 100 per cent of SRV output of tin, phosphates and sulfuric acid;

2. Projects in Vietnam currently under development with Soviet aid range from house-building combines in Hanoi and

Xuanmay, cement plants at Himson with an output per annum of 1.2 million tons; a tractor plant with a production capacity of 20,000 tractors a year, and a 50,000 hectare natural rubber production and processing complex in South Vietnam's Songbe province;

3. Already at the close of the SRV's second Five Year Plan (1976-80), 62,000 Vietnamese technicians had been trained with Soviet assistance, 11,000 of them in the Soviet Union itself;

4. The USSR supplies Vietnam with 'up to 100 per cent of the imports of oil products', the same amount in cotton, 'more than 90 per cent of food imports', and essential percentages in chemical fertilisers, machinery, and rolled stock.

How the SRV can repay its Soviet and East European debts of 4 billion US dollars is unclear. At this point neither debtor nor creditors are pressing the issue. Controversy surrounds some alleged methods of repayment, however. Since the early 1980s the Vietnamese 'guest worker' program in the USSR has gone into high gear. According to the US State Department, as many as half a million Vietnamese might have been working in the USSR by 1983, allegedly in 'harsh--and in some cases, involuntary--conditions', and with a 'substantial portion' of their wages being held back and used to pay off the SRV's debts to Moscow. Even so, many Vietnamese appear to be eager to work in the Soviet Union, and according to Hanoi, in the middle of 1984 alone there were more than 60,000 SRV nationals employed in the USSR, the GDR, Bulgaria, and Czechoslovakia.(34)

In mid-March 1984 it was reported by a former Vietnamese Politburo member and by a US scholar on Vietnam, that since 1982 the SRV had embarked on a program of opium production in the northern provinces of Ha Tuyen, Lai Chau, Cao Bang and others in order to raise 'badly needed foreign currency'.(35) In 1983 the Vietnamese government ordered farmers in Ha Tuyen, for example, to supply one kilogram each to the government per year. Similar quotas were set for farmers in adjacent provinces. Hanoi has repudiated this report, but Thai intelligence and Vietnamese refugee sources insist on its veracity.

Whatever the case may be, there is little question about Vietnam's current economic predicament, and the USSR itself is well aware of the long-term implications of its own burden in relation to Vietnam. By the end of 1983, as one specialist has noted, there was 'a distinct effort' by the Russians to ease that burden, and today 'Soviet trade officials scour Vietnam looking for any sort of exportable goods. Unfortunately poverty-ridden Vietnam has little to offer'.(36) Moreover, to their Vietnamese burden, the Soviets must also add the cost of other Indochina aid commitments. Since the installation of the PRK regime in Phnom Penh, total Soviet non-military aid to Cambodia has been estimated at 450 million US dollars.(37) Meanwhile, aid to Cambodia from non-Communist governments has dropped from 218 million US dollars in 1980 to a mere 2 million US dollars in 1983.

In the SRV Politburo as well, there is dissension over the preponderant Soviet role and development methodology in Vietnam's future. The pro-Moscow faction is led by Premier Pham Van Dong, while chief party theoretician Truong Chinh, an early admirer of Mao, urges less dependence on the USSR. It is difficult to see, however, how Hanoi's economic problems and dependence on the Soviet Union, particularly in terms of energy resource development, could lessen in the future, unless the Vietnamese could find an accommodation with Beijing. Such a turn likely would be wrenching for SRV relations with Moscow and, in any event, almost certainly would be contingent as well on a solution to the Cambodian problem.

SINO-VIETNAMESE TERRITORIAL CONFLICTS

The brief, 'punitive' Chinese invasion of Vietnam on 16 February 1979 came after nearly four years of rising Chinese concern over Hanoi's Cambodian policies.(38) This concern pivoted on grave apprehensions in Beijing over the long-term role that might be played in the region by a Soviet-backed, territorially ambitious, Vietnamese regime that threatened China's own security. A contributing factor undoubtedly was Beijing's anger over the alleged 'ostracising and persecuting' of ethnic Chinese in the SRV, leading eventually to an expulsion of some 200,000 of them in the months following April, 1977.(39) The Hanoi government explained that treatment of the ethnic Chinese was no different from that of other 'bourgeois' elements in the SRV and was part of the planned, broader, socio-economic transformation of the country in keeping with Socialist principles. But this explanation was quickly negated by Beijing as but a mask for the growing official Vietnamese mistrust of and hostility toward all Chinese and China in the context of the mutually strained relations that were developing over Cambodia and over territorial issues. Undoubtedly, the February 1979 Chinese 'punitive' lesson also had behind it Chinese animus against Hanoi over these territorial disputes between the two countries.

One part of the dispute concerns the land boundary between northern Vietnam and the People's Republic of China and the interpretation to be given to the earlier territorial agreements made between the former French colonial government in Indochina and the Chinese. Frontier clashes are common and on 31 December 1984, in a year-end review, Radio Hanoi accused the Chinese of 'dozens of landgrabbing attacks' on Vietnam's northern border. But this aspect of the matter only peripherally involves the exploitation of Vietnam's energy resources, and so need not be considered here. More important for the energy question are the Sino-Vietnamese disputes in the South China Sea area, specifically in the Tonkin Gulf (officially called the Gulf of Bac Bo by the SRV and the Beibu Gulf by the PRC), and two archipelagoes, the Paracel Islands (called Hoang Sa by the Vietnamese and Xisha by the Chinese), and the Spratly (Spratley) Islands (called Truong Sa by the SRV and Nansha by the PRC).

Presently these Sino-Vietnamese disputes in the South China Sea, and their implications for energy development will be examined. But first, it is well to note that even before World War II, and particularly during the last four decades, conflicting territorial claims in the Sea and its adjacent rim waters and straits, and the islands, rocks, reefs, and shoals they all contain, have involved various powers, among them the People's Republic of China, the Republic of China (Taiwan), Vietnam, Cambodia, the Philippines, Indonesia, Malaysia, and Thailand.(40) Confrontation has been common. Early in June, 1983, for example, Malaysia sent troops to the small coral atoll of Terumbu Layang Layang, a part of the Spratlys. The force was sent for fear that the Vietnamese, who systematically have been occupying other islands of

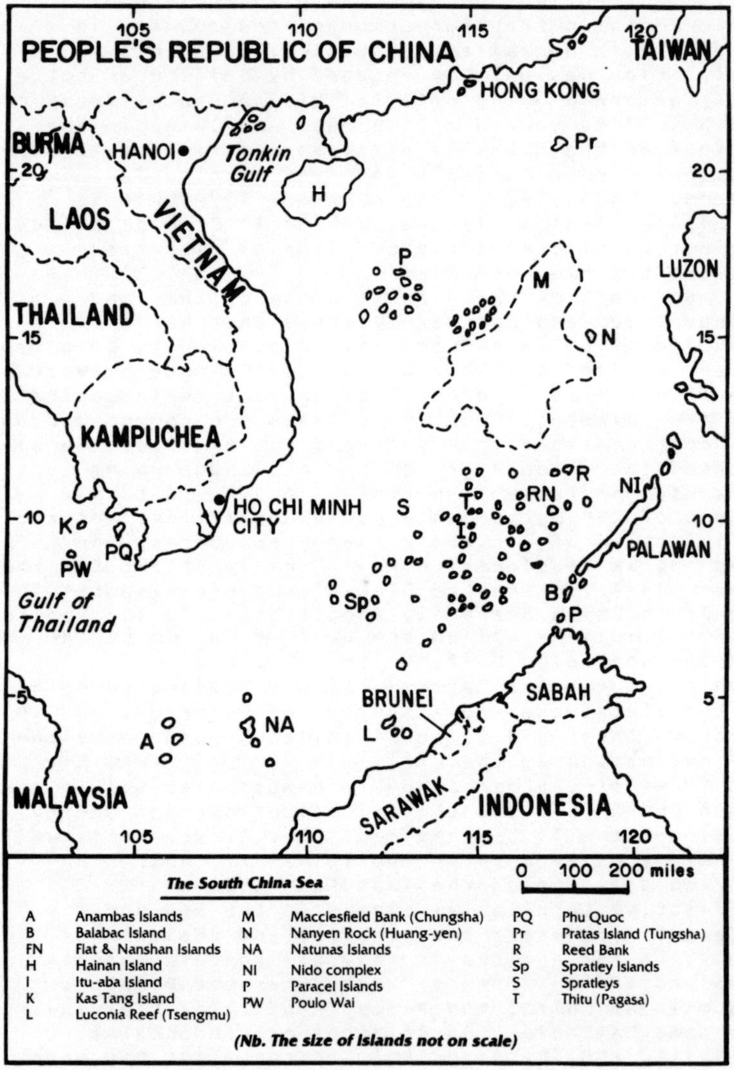

Figure 6.1: Disputed Areas of the South China Sea

the Spratlys, would also seize Terumbu. The Vietnamese had already occupied Amboyna Cay, located 64 kilometres northwest of Terumbu. Amboyna, as the Kuala Lumpur government has emphasised, also belongs to Malaysia.(41)

Not surprisingly, the People's Republic of China, which had repeatedly asserted its claim of ownership over all the Spratly Islands, also protested Malaysia's occupation of Terumbu. But Malaysia, in turn, declared that though it had 'accepted and recognised Vietnam's claim to the Spratlys', the 'greed and arrogance of power' with which Hanoi had occupied Amboyna Cay had been too much.(42) About the same distance from Terumbu, but in a northwesterly direction, lies the Commodore Reef, claimed by the Philippines. The reef lies halfway across to the rim waters off the Philippine island of Palawan. Malaysia's interest in Terumbu becomes understandable when it is understood that Palawan's offshore oil complexes at Nido, Cadlao and Matinloc in July, 1984 were reported by the Philippine Ministry of Energy to have produced 22 million barrels since commercial production started in 1979.(43)

To offer yet another example of the complexity of international claims on the resources of the South China Sea area, one might note that under Thai government auspices, and with the aid of Texas Pacific Oil and Union Oil companies, a 350-mile long underwater gas line currently is being constructed, leading from the southern Thai coast into the Thai Gulf. The Thai Gulf's offshore natural gas reserves here are estimated to be about 12 trillion cubic feet.(44) Already in March 1982, the Heng Samrin regime in Phnom Penh denounced the 'illegal activities' of 'Thailand and Thai Companies' directed against 'the sovereignty and territorial integrity' of the Cambodian government in the Gulf of Thailand.(45) The fact that the USSR, having sent a 'large group' of its Caspian Sea oil and gas exploration experts to assist Vietnamese oil resource development,(46) is now the <u>only</u> partner that both Hanoi and its PRK ally in Cambodia have in the development of their respective offshore oil and gas reserves in the South China Sea and contiguous waters, underscores the significance of the present strategic lineup in the area.

The origin of the Sino-Vietnamese dispute in the Tonkin Gulf lies in the interpretation to be given to the 1887 and 1895 treaties between the Qing dynasty court in Peking and the French colonial government in Indochina. Encouraged by the USSR, the then Democratic Republic of Vietnam (i.e. North Vietnam) in Hanoi, joined subsequently by technical assistance from the Italian ENI state petroleum company, began exploring for oil in the Tonkin Gulf as early as 1971.(47) This aroused Chinese concern and a call for mutual deliberation. In 1973, well before the Communist Vietnamese victory and unification of the country, Hanoi formally adopted and sought vainly to persuade the PRC of the original French interpretation of the 1887 and 1895 treaties.

The SRV interpretation designated the 108th meridian as the basic line of demarcation between Vietnamese and Chinese controlled zones in the Tonkin Gulf. The Chinese maintained, however, that this interpretation which they originally had accepted (perhaps only because of prevailing force majeure and their political weakness at the time) in fact was erroneous. Chinese reasoning was that the 1887 agreement only addressed the issue of the ownership of islands in the Tonkin Gulf, and not of the waters of the Gulf as such. Furthermore, the Chinese government has argued that at the time the two treaties were signed concepts of sovereignty in international law were as yet not sufficiently developed so as to take proper consideration of the implications of exploitation of underwater minerological resources.(48)

Not surprisingly the Vietnamese declined to accept this Chinese view. By early 1974 Hanoi seemed to be prepared formally to incorporate two-thirds of the Tonkin Gulf as part of Vietnam's territorial waters. Such Vietnamese pressure on a staunch ally of its long war against the French and the Americans may have been 'an unfriendly and greedy act',(49) but it was not wanting in legal justification.

As the foundation of Beijing's own interpretation of the 1887 and 1895 treaties one has to look no farther than consistent and longheld Chinese dynastic views of territoriality. Hanoi's (and France's) interpretation of the two treaties indeed would have cost China the far greater slice of Gulf waters. In Chinese tradition, however, Pratas Island (called Tungsha by Beijing), and currently controlled by the Republic of China (Taiwan), marks the northern boundary of Chinese authority in the South China Sea; Nanyen Rock (also called Huang-yen Island) near Macclesfield Bank and some 150 miles off the western coast of the

Philippines' Luzon Island is viewed as the eastern rim of China's territorial waters; and Luconia Reef (also called Tsengmu), just off the coast of Malaysia's Sarawak state, traditionally has been viewed as 'the southernmost tip of China'.(50) The PRC's insistence on restoring traditional Chinese territories is well known. Because of this, as much as because of China's need to develop her own energy potential, and not least because of strategic concerns for her southern flank, Beijing was unlikely to acquiesce in Hanoi's claims to the Tonkin Gulf.

During 1975-9, as Sino-Vietnamese relations rapidly deteriorated, each side kept its claims on the Gulf alive by announcements of continuing exploration efforts or cartographic authority. ENI announced in 1977 that its seismic investigation in the Gulf was still proceeding, while the official new map of People's Republic of China published in the same year indicated all of the 'Beibu Gulf' to be very much part of PRC territory.(51) In October, 1977, comprehensive Sino-Vietnamese discussions began on the outstanding territorial disputes between the two countries. Nothing was accomplished, however, and in August, 1978, talks were broken off, the Chinese laying all the blame on Hanoi. Vietnam, Beijing asserted, now claimed that it was 'too busy with other matters'.(52) It seemed unlikely, in any case, that the SRV would deviate from its formal statement of 12 May 1977, dealing with its territorial waters. This statement again asserted the 1887 Sino-French boundary agreement to be the basis of the SRV's claim to most of the Tonkin Gulf.

The subsequent full-scale Vietnamese invasion and occupation of Kampuchea, and the 16 February 1979 Chinese intervention in northern Vietnam, however, marked a turning point; de facto Hanoi conceded the Tonkin Gulf to China, although the Vietnamese never de jure abandoned their claim. But henceforth, amidst its growing international isolation and forced reliance on the USSR, the SRV was to concentrate its oil exploration efforts in the relatively non-controversial waters off Vung Tau. The PRC, meanwhile, in the period after it had administered its 'punitive lesson' to its Vietnamese neighbour, took to opening up to foreign interests its various oil reserves in and around the Gulf and Yellow Sea in a big way. Forty-three tracts, with a total area of 150,000 square kilometres, were opened to bidding by foreign oil concerns by the China

National Offshore Oil Corporation (CNOOC) in August, 1982. Nine of these were in the Tonkin Gulf.(53)

In and around Hainan, in the Gulf, contract areas were awarded to ARCO, the BP group and Total (Cie Francaise des Petroles' Total Chine) by mid-1983. In July, 1984, the CNOOC announced that the first Gulf offshore oil field was expected to start trial production in the first half of 1986. This field, comprising about 10,200 square kilometres, is a joint undertaking of CNOOC and Total, and is located about 180 kilometres south of the Guangxi province coastal city of Beihai in the Gulf.(54) The concessional and contract area now extended by China to foreign corporations leaves Vietnam with an offshore arc of from 100 to 200 kilometres of Gulf waters. Any concession granted by Hanoi under these conditions would almost certainly be far too close for comfort for most foreign oil companies. Beijing, meanwhile, is determined to push ahead with new concessional offerings: a 'second round' of bidding which included South China Sea and Tonkin Gulf tracts, was announced by the Chinese on 22 November 1984.(55)

On 12 November 1982, Hanoi reiterated its above, cited 12 May 1977, statement on its territorial waters, warning China and foreign oil companies that they would have to bear the consequences of their actions. Beijing rejected these assertions which, the Chinese said, merely reflected 'the expansionist slant' of the SRV.(56) Further protests to Beijing by Vietnam, repeatedly made in the course of 1983-4, objecting that contract areas offered by the CNOOC in the Tonkin Gulf waters surrounding Hainan Island violated Vietnamese sovereignty, were dismissed as 'slanderous' by the PRC.(57) In its periodic publication of alleged PRC 'war crimes', Hanoi includes not only thousands of alleged Chinese 'armed provocations' and violations of Vietnamese airspace at the border, but also Chinese actions in the Tonkin Gulf. As one typical Vietnamese communique on alleged Chinese 'war crimes' put it in February, 1984:

> In the Tonkin Gulf China tried to erase the border line which has been clearly delineated in the documents signed by the French Government and the Qing Dynasty of China. It broke the Sino-Vietnamese negotiation on the Tonkin Gulf, and taking advantage of this situation to openly carry out illegal

> prospecting for oil and gas in the Gulf, including many areas belonging to Vietnam's territorial waters. (58)

The Paracels and Spratlys also remain a continuous source of dispute. On 3 March 1982, for example, two Vietnamese gunboats shelled eleven Chinese vessels (said by Beijing to have been fishing boats) setting them ablaze, and allegedly killing and capturing some of the Chinese crews. The next day Beijing announced that Chinese military units in the Paracels had captured a 'Vietnamese reconnaissance vessel' (probably also a fishing boat), which was said to have unlawfully entered China's territorial waters near the Paracels. Hanoi, in its original version of the clash, asserted that some forty armed Chinese vessels had been sent to spy in Vietnamese waters, and that 'militiamen' on board nearby 'Vietnamese fishing vessels' had 'firmly resisted' the Chinese intruders.(59) In May 1984, a 'small Chinese naval squadron' reportedly moved into the Spratly Islands.(60) It included frigates, a landing craft, and an oil supply ship, and the squadron, at least superficially, seemed intent on reasserting Chinese claims of sovereignty to these islands by force if necessary. No new clashes with the Vietnamese or any other nationals were reported, however.

It would appear that none of the claimant powers in the Paracels, Spratlys, and other adjacent islands in the South China Sea really seem anxious to drive territorial claims to an ultimate confrontation. For example, Spratly Island, the largest and most important island in the Spratly archipelago, remains occupied by the Vietnamese. China, despite her periodic 'show the flag' exercises, does not now appear to be ready to try and dislodge them.

And neither Hanoi nor Beijing have been willing to mount a campaign to push the Philippines from Thitu (also known as Pagasa), Flat, and Nanshan Islands in the northern Spratlys and other adjacent small holdings, collectively designated by the Manila government as the Kalayaan (Freedom) Islands. The Kalayaans, in fact, were strengthened in 1983 by naval fortifications and surveillance facilities in the face of the ongoing verbal barrage of claims and counterclaims on the whole area by Beijing and Hanoi.(61)

Nor, again, have the Vietnamese been willing to risk an armed clash with Malaysia because of the

Layang in the southeastern Spratlys. The weather and surveillance station of the Republic of China (Taiwan) of the island of Itu Aba on the western rim of the Spratlys similarly has not been disturbed, though Taipei's claim to the island formally has been contested by Beijing. South of the Spratlys there has been a long-standing, low-key, Vietnamese-Indonesian conflict over offshore Indonesian oil and natural gas production around the Indonesian-held Natuna Islands.(62) And Philippine interest in the Reed Bank area off the Spratlys, adjacent to the Nido complex of oil fields, thus far also has not provoked a hostile reaction from others.

The reasons for such relative restraint are not hard to find. All the powers claiming sovereign rights to the whole or part of the Spratlys and Paracels, or to adjacent islands, recognise the obvious logistical problem of trying to enforce such rights over scores of small (from 0.5 to 1 square mile) bits of land and reef located hundreds of miles from home base. The strategic value of holding some or all of this real estate is not in question. But thus far serious exploration for, let alone production of, oil or other mineral deposits in or around these islands has not even begun. It is in the rim waters of the South China Sea, for example off Palawan in the Philippines, Vung Tau in Vietnam, or the Beihai Gulf in China, that oil production is soon likely to become a reality.(63)

Undaunted, however, Hanoi and Beijing persist in their conflicting territorial claims to the whole of Paracels and Spratlys. Government 'white books', notably two published by Vietnam in September, 1979, and in January, 1982, and another 'white book' issued by the People's Republic of China in January, 1980, base themselves on early maps, court chronicles and histories of explorations. Thus, the January, 1982 SRV 'white book' asserts that Vietnamese geographies published in the days of the Nguyen court in the seventeenth century demonstrate not only that, 'Long ago the Vietnamese discovered the archipelagoes of Hoang Sa and Truong Sa, but also that the 'Vietnamese state' has occupied them and exercised its sovereignty over them ever since'.(64) To attempt to validate national boundaries of contemporary Asian states on the basis of traditional court lore is hazardous indeed. But the fact is that contemporary nationalist aspirations, whether in the PRC, the SRV, or elsewhere in Southeast Asia, make use of such dynastic traditions and a popularly felt sense of historical reality to buttress the economic and strategic claims and interests of the present.

That tradition also actuates the reciprocal Sino-Vietnamese barrage of verbal crossfire over the Spratlys and the Paracels. Current Vietnamese charges that China keeps on 'nibbling' at 'Vietnam's islands', and that China's alleged plan to 'annex' the two archipelagoes and make them part of its 'Hainan administrative region' constitutes a 'gross violation of international law' and a 'serious challenge to the Vietnamese people', are also and with obvious approval echoed in the Soviet press.(65) Beijing, meanwhile, retorts that its sovereignty over the islands 'is not to be violated by any country, under any pretext or in any way'.(66)

To be sure, there is and will remain in the future the occasional skirmish between 'fishing vessels' and opposing landing parties. Yet, there is no indication that the Sino-Vietnamese dispute over the South China Sea islands will, of its own, plunge the two nations into escalated hostilities any time soon, though undoubtedly, the dispute aggravates the existing tensions between them. Hanoi, as is evident from its caution in the Tonkin Gulf, seems careful not to provoke Beijing. The Chinese, in turn, appear to realise that the USSR would have little choice but to back her Vietnamese ally and dependent in the event Beijing would wish to teach the SRV a second 'punitive' lesson. This would seriously jeopardise Beijing's 'Moscow card', namely the current improvement in Sino-Soviet relations exemplified by the new December 1984 trade and technical agreement between the two countries.

It is just as well, since an appeal to 'international law', as Hanoi has referred to it above, at this stage scarcely is likely to offer a way out of the South China Sea territorial dispute. For example, the new 1982 'Law of the Sea', as finally drafted by the Third Conference on the Law of the Sea, though accepted by the disputant nations around the South China Sea, is filled with provisions that are open to conflicting interpretation. The 200 nautical mile limit set for 'exclusive economic zones' of nation states, and the inevitable overlapping of such zones, or the problem of what exactly is a 'natural prolongation' of a nation's territory when measuring the jurisdictional limit over the continental shelf, all invite differing interpretation and further dispute.(67)

Fortunately, none of the disputants of territory in and around the South China Sea, at least for the moment, has the appetite to add such likely legal wrangling to the already existing level of contention among them.

VIETNAM'S ENERGY FUTURE

A Kampuchean settlement is key to Vietnam's energy future, indeed to the course and speed of the SRV's whole economic development. Whatever the promise of her coal production and hydro-electric capacity, Hanoi's current energy potential is exemplified by Vietsovpetro: the necessity of dependence on the USSR for an indefinite time. Even if Vietsovpetro's offshore rig starts producing in the next two years, the SRV's industrial modernisation will require rising annual oil imports, certainly beyond the ten million barrels currently being imported each year.

The political context of meeting the SRV's future energy needs must include not just Chinese agreement to a Kampuchean settlement. By implication it also must involve a Soviet acceptance of a broadened Vietnamese outreach to the international money markets, and concessions to the world's corporate oil producers. Whether Moscow would be prepared to loosen its strategic and economic hold on its Vietnamese ally, even if it accepts a possibly new 'Finlandized' Kampuchean regime, remains very much to be seen.(68)

A Kampuchean settlement, however, and the emergence of a new regime in Phnom Penh acceptable to the superpowers would not necessarily end the territorial quarrels between Cambodia and the SRV over resources in the Gulf of Thailand. In June and July 1975, it may be recalled (cf. note 23 supra) Khmer Rouge and Vietnamese Communist forces engaged in sharp 'border rectification' clashes and Vietnam drove the Cambodians off the island of Poulo Wai. Other islands near Poulo Wai, for example in the Kas Tang group, were occupied as well by Vietnamese troops, and Hanoi also strengthened its garrison on Phu Quoc Island. On 7 July 1982, Hanoi and its PRK ally, the Heng Samrin regime, signed a new, rather ambiguous border agreement which suggested that Poulo Wai would revert to Cambodia's 'historical waters' and that Phu Quoc would remain Vietnamese. But the same agreement also declares that 'negotiations to delimit the maritime frontier' in the 'historical waters' of the two countries are to be held 'at a suitable time' in the future.(69) Thus far that 'suitable time' appears not as yet to have arrived.

Again, the spectre of ancient and contradictory cartographies haunts contemporary national frontier disputes in Asia: it is difficult to think of a mutually satisfactory Cambodian-Vietnamese land and offshore boundary agreement in which one or the other of the signatories eventually will not feel that it must reclaim its irredenta. It needs no emphasising that the problem of a Cambodian-Vietnamese boundary dispute in the Thai Gulf is likely to be aggravated the more the offshore waters and the bed of the Thai Gulf reveal their energy resources, particularly now that these Thai Gulf riches already are under exploitation (cf. note 44 supra).

In the beginning of 1985 Hanoi seemed to give every indication of being determined to crush militarily all oposition to her dominance in Kampuchea. As a result, even as her dependence on the USSR increases, Vietnam's energy use and development will be affected in the immediate future by her chosen military posture. Hanoi never seems to weary of accusing Beijing of 'intensifying' acts of sabotage and espionage in preparation for another imminent Chinese attack on the SRV.(70) Such accusations, which find their corollary in China's repeated announcements that she will support the anti-Vietnamese resistance in Cambodia 'as long as Hanoi maintains troops there',(71) are used to justify the SRV's extensive war machine. Vietnam today maintains, as it has for more than a decade, the third largest standing army (about 1 million) in the world, an army exceeded only by China's (3.6 million), and the USSR's (1.8 million).(72)

The expense of such a war machine has been controversial. It has been argued for example that the cost to Hanoi of maintaining her 180,000 troops in Cambodia is relatively light, because troop pay is low because maintaining such a force absorbs thousands who otherwise would 'swell the army of the unemployed' in the SRV.(73) Such a view ignores much of the rest of the logistical cost. Year after year the Vietnamese-PRK dry season offensive against anti-Vietnamese groups seems to escalate in severity. Vietnam's tanks, planes and artillery vehicles do not run on water. The constant, large diversion of oil to war needs strains the entire Vietnamese energy base. Regrettably, there seems no end in sight to the fighting; indeed, the 1984-5 Vietnamese dry season offensive against the CGDK makes clear that Hanoi means to 'dig in' for the long haul all along the Thai-Kampuchean border.

From the perspective of economic development and planning, Vietnam's energy problem seems equally intractable. There continues to be uncertainty in the Vietnam Communist Party over the desired character of the country's economy, an uncertainty that is punctuated by persistently sharp, intra-party dissent over planning tactics. The new pragmatism of the mixed economy, formally endorsed by the 1982 Vietnam Party Congress, has no clear focus on Vietnam's future energy needs. Critics in the VCP have charged that the greater autonomy accorded state factories, even as production targets must be met, encourages competitive bidding by managements for the raw materials available in the 'free market'. The problem appears particularly acute in the food processing and textile fields of the economy. This, in turn, is said to be stimulating 'capitalistic tendencies' generally, as state factory managements increasingly sell excess productivity direct to consumers on the free market in order to cover their rising costs.(74)

In the interstices of the national economy between the state factories and farm 'collectives' on the one hand, and the officially limited 'free market' of merchants and small holders on the other, a thriving middleman economy of private traders and, according to the party, even of speculators continue to grow. By September, 1984, Deputy Premier To Huu, a critic of the mixed economic policy, declared that some 50 per cent of the nation's wholesale and retail trade was taking place in the non-controlled market. Subsequent attempts to effect more controls over a number of semi-autonomous import-export companies established originally in order to promote foreign trade, led to widespread evasion, including contraband trade and black market activity, especially in the larger cities. There also appears to be continuing, if scattered, resistance to agricultural collectivisation. In many areas the peasant 'production teams', used as official criteria in noting the advance of collectivisation, exist, by the SRV government's own admission, in name only.(75)

Meanwhile, the dispute within the VCP, the Cabinet and the State Planning Commission between the 'purists' (e.g. To Huu and State Council Chairman Truong Ching) and the 'pragmatists' (like Deputy Premier for Planning Vo Van Kiet) over the shape of the SRV's economy rages on. So long as this dispute continues, and the functional parts of Vietnam's economy are made to fit so poorly together, there can be no rational projection of the country's energy needs and resource development. Today 'unplanned' competition for petroleum allocations between the private and state-contolled sectors of the economy impedes the development of both. Yet neither the central nor local planning agencies appear to be able to assess the relationship between future energy needs and local manufacturing production. In any case, being riveted to the USSR strategically, and in much of its day-to-day economic life as well, leaves Hanoi with few choices. A Vietnamese dependency on Moscow in turn is clearly to the latter's interest, at least for the time being.

A look at Vietnam's trade statistics quickly demonstrates that dependency. The value of Vietnam's exports (mainly coal, processed food, including soya sauce, condiments and rice, and textiles and jute products) rose only from 309 million in 1977 to 498.73 million US dollars in 1983. About half of these exports went to the USSR alone. Most of the remainder was scattered among Japan, Singapore, Hong Kong, and a wide variety of other IMF member countries. In that same period, however, the value of imports into Vietnam rose from 1044.10 million to 1678.92 million US dollars, with some 55 per cent coming from the Soviet Union, and the remainder from Japan, India, Singapore and various IMF member states. Imports today from such various Socialist bloc countries, among them the German Democratic Republic, Czechoslovakia, Poland and others, run about 150 million US dollars alone, while exports to these countries are described as 'negligible'.(76) Together, the USSR and the Eastern bloc account for about two-thirds of the value of all Vietnam's imports.

A diversification of this one-sided trade pattern, particularly of Vietnam's petroleum imports, is known to be among the major policy changes desired by most of Hanoi's present leadership. It is unlikely, however, that the USSR would tolerate such change easily. After all, the 'Brezhnev doctrine' has been applied to other members of the Moscow-directed Council of Mutual Economic Assistance. Also, the concessions Hanoi might have to make in a solution to the Cambodian problem would be too wrenching, even if thereby she would win a lifting of her pariah status in the major Western investment credit and development aid markets. Yet, in the currently depressed international oil market the SRV would quickly find other suppliers. Among the SRV's ASEAN neighbours, for example Thailand and Malaysia, several are on the verge of significant expansion in offshore exploration and drilling in the next few years.(77) Indonesia, despite its embroglio with the SRV over the Natunas, has been particularly interested in reaching a modus vivendi with the SRV over the Kampuchean embroglio. As one of the world's major oil producers, Indonesia would be likely to offer Hanoi attractive terms in the context of a Cambodian settlement.

But for the time being all this must remain speculation. Vietnam's economy and exploration of her offshore petroleum resources essentially seem to be marking time. Any realistic prospect for the country's energy development clearly awaits achievement of a political agreement with her Asian neighbours.

NOTES

1. GDP, GNP, and demographic data are derived from International Institute for Strategic Studies, The Military Balance 1984-1985 (London, IISS, 1984), pp. 104, 107, 110-111. Per capita income data are International Monetary Fund estimates. See also Josef Adamek, Centrally Planned Economies. Economic Overview 1984 (The Conference Board, New York, 1984), Report no. 857, p. 51.

2. Nayan Chanda, 'Vietnam in 1983. Keeping Ideology Alive', Asian Survey, vol. XXIV, no. 1 (January 1984), p. 30, and David Jenkins, 'A Country Adrift ...', Far Eastern Economic Review, 8 November 1984, p. 30.

3. Editorial, Nhan Dan (Hanoi), 18 August 1984, in Foreign Broadcast Information Service, (hereafter FBIS), IV, 27 August 1984.

4. David Jenkins, 'Looking For A Formula', Far Eastern Economic Review, 15 November 1984, p. 127.

5. Editorial, Nhan Dan, 20 August 1984 in FBIS, IV, 24 August 1984.

6. Carlyle A. Thayer, 'Vietnam's New Pragmatism', Current History, vol. 82, no. 483 (April 1983), pp. 158-161, and 'A Change of Course', Asiaweek, 9 April 1982, pp. 22-7.

7. FBIS, IV, 9 April 1982 (Supplement).

8. Radio Hanoi, domestic service, 15 August 1984 in FBIS, IV, 20 August 1984.

1984 in FBIS, IV, 20 August 1984.

9. David Jenkins, 'A Country Adrift', pp. 30-1.

10. Radio Hanoi, domestic service, 27 January 1984 in FBIS, IV, 3 February 1984.

11. David Jenkins, 'A Glint of Greed', Far Eastern Economic Review, 15 November 1984, p. 134.

12. Radio Hanoi, domestic service, 15 March 1984 in FBIS, IV, 20 March 1984.

13. The author is grateful to Mr. John Moens of the US Department of Energy's Information Service, Washington, D.C., for providing these and other data on Vietnamese mining production.

14. David Jenkins, 'Looking For A Formula', pp. 127, 128.

15. Radio Hanoi, domestic service, 19 May 1984 in FBIS, IV, 24 May 1984.

16. Hoang Tung, 'In the Name of Peace and Prosperity', World Marxist Review, no. 18, October, 1984, p. 33; VNA despatch Hanoi, 18 April 1984 in FBIS, IV, 19 April 1984; John Spragens, 'Vietnam and the Soviets: A Tighter Alliance', Indochina Issues (Washington, D.C.), no. 51, November, 1984, p. 3.

17. Hasjim Djalal, 'Conflicting Territorial and Jurisdictional Claims in the South China Sea', The Indonesian Quarterly (Djakarta), July, 1979, p. 45, and Asia Research Bulletin, 30 April 1980, p. 674.

18. Oil and Gas Journal, 2 August 1984, p. 84; The Wall Street Journal, 2 December 1981, and Arthur S. Banks, ed., Economic Handbook of the World 1982 (McGraw Hill Book Company, New York, 1982), p. 583.

19. See, for example, Justus M. van der Kroef, 'Kampuchea: The Diplomatic Labyrinth', Asian Survey, vol. XXII, no. 10 (October 1982), pp. 1009-31, and 'Kampuchea--Protracted Conflict, Suspended Compromise', Asian Survey, vol. XXIV, no. 3 (March 1984), pp. 314-34.

20. David Jenkins, 'Looking For A Formula', p. 127.

21. The Asia Record, June, 1982, p. 7.

22. On Soviet policy toward Vietnam and Kampuchea see Allan W. Cameron, 'The Soviet Union and Vietnam: Origins of Involvement', in W. Raymond Duncan, ed., Soviet Policy in Developing Countries (Ginn-Blaisdell Publishers, Waltham, Mass., 1970), pp. 160-205, and Leif Rosenberger, 'The Soviet-Vietnamese Alliance and Kampuchea', Survey, Autumn-Winter, 1983, pp. 207-31. On Chinese attitudes see Pao-min Chang, 'The Sino-Vietnamese Conflict Over Kampuchea', Survey, Autumn-Winter, 1983, pp. 175-206, and Gareth Porter, 'Hanoi's

Strategic Perspective and the Sino-Vietnamese Conflict', *Pacific Affairs*, vol. 57, no. 1 (Spring, 1984), pp. 7-25.

23. *New York Times*, 14, 20, 22, 25 June 1975.

24. *Bangkok Post*, 5 May 1975.

25. See, for example, *Renmin ribao* (Beijing), 16 January 1978 and Dennis Bloodworth, 'Why Bit Powers Won't Intervene in Indochina War', *The Straits Times*, 14 January 1978.

26. William Shawcross, 'Vietnam--Peace With Dark Shadows', *Far Eastern Economic Review*, 4 September 1981, p. 20.

27. US Department of Defense, *Soviet Military Power, 1983* (US Department of Defense, Washington, D.C., 1982, 2nd edition), p. 97.

28. *The Bangkok Post*, 4 September 1984 and Radio Bangkok, 'Voice of Free Asia', 12 September 1984 in FBIS, 5, 13 September 1984; *New York Times*, 2 January 1985.

29. *The Straits Times* Singapore, 10 November 1983. See also *The New York Times*, 30 January 1984, and W.T. Tow, 'Nuclear Security Problems in the Far East', *Asia Pacific Community*, no. 19 (Winter, 1983), pp. 55-7.

30. Shawcross, 'Vietnam--Peace With Dark Shadows', pp. 20-3.

31. Bao Quoc, 'The Cam Ranh Syndrome. The Threat of Sovietnamisation', *ASEAN Forecast* (Singapore), June, 1984, p. 105.

32. Ibid.

33. M. Petrov, 'Vietnam's Co-operation in the CMEA Framework', *Far Eastern Affairs* (Moscow), no. 1, 1983, pp. 168-79.

34. John Spragens, 'Vietnam and the Soviets: A Tighter Alliance', *Indochina Issues* (Washington, D.C.), November, 1984, pp. 4-5.

35. *Nation Review* (Bangkok), 14 March 1984, FBIS 13 March 1984, and *Wall Street Journal*, 8 March 1984.

36. Douglas Pike, 'Vietnam', in Robert Wisson, ed., *1983 Yearbook on International Communist Affairs* (Hoover Institution Press, Standford, 1984), p. 226.

37. *The Nation Review*, 19 March 1984 in FBIS, IV, 19 March 1984.

38. Pao-min Chang, 'The Sino-Vietnamese Conflict Over Kampuchea', pp. 175-206.

39. See, for example, *On Vietnam's Expulsion of Chinese Residents* (Foreign Languages Press, Beijing, 1978), p. 1, and Pao-min Chang, 'The Sino-Vietnamese Dispute Over the Ethnic Chinese', *China Quarterly*,

40. William R. Feeney, 'Dispute Settlement, The Emerging Law of the Sea and East Asian Maritime Boundaries', Asian Profile, December, 1980, pp. 583-8; Lim Joo-Jock, Geo-Strategy and the South China Sea Basin: Regional Balance, Maritime Issues, Future Patterns (Signapore University Press, 1979), and Justus M. van der Kroef, 'The South China Sea: Competing Claims and Strategic Conflicts', International Security Review, Fall, 1982, pp. 305-29.

41. Far Eastern Economic Review, 29 September 1983, p. 40, and The Straits Times, 10 September 1983.

42. Radio Kuala Lumpur, international service, 14 September 1983, FBIS, IV, 16 September 1983.

43. Bulletin Today (Manila), 5 July 1984. According to other sources oil production off Palawan is declining rapidly, for example, at Nido per day output was reported down to 1500 bblls, as compared to 14,000 in 1979. ASEAN Forecast (Singapore), June, 1984, p. 95.

44. Oil and Gas Journal, 14 December 1981, pp. 132-3.

45. Radio Phnom Penh, 29 March 1982, FBIS, IV, 29 March 1982.

46. Oil and Gas Journal, 2 August, 1982, p. 84.

47. Marwyn S. Samuels, Contest For the South China Sea (Methuen, New York and London, 1982), p. 159.

48. Far Eastern Economic Review, 28 September 1979, pp. 19-21; Asia Research Bulletin, 30 April 1980, pp. 672-3.

49. Chang Pao-min, 'The Sino-Vietnamese Territorial Dispute', Asia Pacific Community, no. 8 (Spring, 1984), p. 38.

50. Hungdah Chiu, 'South China Sea Islands: Implications for Delimiting the Seabed and future Shipping Routes', China Quarterly, no. 72 (December 1977), p. 762, and Far Eastern Economic Review, 25 February 1974, p. 25.

51. Petroleum News Southeast Asia, July, 1977, p. 9, and Zhonghua remnin gonghoguo ditu (Dutuchupanshe, Beijing, 1977).

52. 'Facts About Sino-Vietnamese Relations', China and the World, Beijing Review Foreign Relations Series, no. 1 Beijing Review Beijing, 1981),p. 108.

53. Far Eastern Economic Review, 25 August 1983, p. 61.

54. South China Morning Post, Hongkong, 19 July 1984.

1984.

55. Beijing Review, No. 49, 3 December 1984, p. 11.

56. Asia Research Bulletin, 31 March 1983, pp. 1025-6.

57. Oil and Gas Journal, 21 May 1983, p. 56.

58. VNA despatch, Hanoi, 24 February 1984 in FBIS, IV, 24 February 1984.

59. The Straits Times, 5 March 1982; New York Times, 12 March 1982.

60. New York Times, 13 May 1984.

61. Far Eastern Economic Review, 28 April 1983, p. 38.

62. Hasjim Djalal, 'Conflicting Territorial and Jurisdictional Claims in the South China Sea', p. 45; Oil and Gas Journal, 14 December 1981, pp. 99, 107-8; The Straits Times, 25 December 1981.

63. Corazon M. Siddayo, The Offshore Petroleum Resources of Southeast Asia: Potential Conflict Situations and Related Economic Considerations (Oxford University Press, Kuala Lumpur, 1978) offers a preliminary assessment.

64. The Hoang Sa and Truong Sa Archipelagoes: Vietnamese Territories (Ministry of Foreign Affairs, Socialist Republic of Vietnam, Hanoi, 1982), translated in FBIS, IV, 18 January 1982.

65. Quan Doi Nhan Dan (Hanoi), 21 February 1984; Nhan Dan (Hanoi), 30 May 1984; Izvestia (Moscow), 25 January 1984 (all in FBIS, IV, 23 February 1984; 31 May 1984; and 26 January 1984, respectively.

66. Beijing Review, 26 September 1984, p. 8.

67. Phipat Tangsubkul and Frances Lai Fung-wai, 'The New Law of the Sea and Development in Southeast Asia', Asian Survey, vol. XXIII, no. 7 (July 1983), pp. 858-78. See also Lee Yong Leng, Southeast Asia and the Law of the Sea (Singapore University press, 1980).

68. A 'Finlandization' process and other political solutions to the Cambodian conflict are discussed in my 'Kampuchea: Toward "Finlandization"', Asian Profile, July, 1985 (forthcoming).

69. Radio Hanoi, VNA despatch, 8 July 1982, FBIS, IV, 9 July 1982.

70. Nhan Dan, 25 July 1983, also cited in Sarawak Tribune (Kuching), 26 July 1983.

71. Reuter's despatch, Bangkok, 30 July 1983; Sarawak Tribune, 1 August 1983.

72. International Institute for Strategic Studies, The Military Balance 1984-1985, pp. 18, 92,

111.

73. Nayan Chanda, 'Vietnam's Economy: "Bad But Not Worse"', Indochina Issues, no. 41, October, 1983, p. 4. "Vietnam-Army Sustains the Economy", Comecon Reports, vol. 4, 1985, no. 1, pp. 44-6.

74. Asia 1984 Yearbook (Far Eastern Economic Review, Hong Kong, 1984), p. 286.

75. Ibid.

76. Above data from Indochina Chronology (University of California, Berkeley), July-September, 1984, p. 28.

77. ASEAN Forecast (Singapore), February, 1985, p. 1.

Chapter Seven

THE LAW OF THE SEA AND THE DELIMITATION OF MARITIME BOUNDARIES IN THE EAST CHINA SEA

Hungdah Chiu

In recent years technological developments have accelerated exploration and exploitation of seabed resources in Asia, primarily in the search for oil. In response to this situation a new principle of international law emerged in the 1950s which allowed a country to exercise sovereign rights on the continental shelf--so far as exploring and exploiting natural resources are concerned--beyond the limits of its territorial sea and up to at least 200 metres depth of the seabed.(1) The ramifications of this principle bring an important question of what is to be done in regard to the resulting overlapping continental shelf claims of countries in the area--a situation which is further complicated by the emerging international law principle of a 200 mile exclusive economic zone in the 1970s.(2) This chapter attempts to analyse this problem in the East China Sea area in the context of the 1982 United Nations Convention on the Law of the Sea (hereinafter referred to as LOS Convention) and other relevant principles of international law. This study will concentrate primarily on four East Asian countries, namely, the People's Republic of China (PRC), the Republic of China (ROC), Japan, and the Republic of Korea (ROK). It will begin with a survey of the maritime claims, and exploration and exploitation activities in the area.

MARITIME CLAIMS, EXPLORATION AND EXPLOITATION ACTIVITIES AND CONCESSION AREAS IN THE EAST CHINA SEA

The maritime claims of the four countries in the East China Sea are as follows:(3)

Table 7.1: Maritime Claims in the East China Sea

Country	Territorial Sea (mi)	Economic Zone (mi)	Fishing Zone (mi)
People's Republic of China	12 (1958)		
Republic of China	12 (1979)	200 (1979)	
Japan	12 (1977)		200 (1977)
Republic of Korea	12 (1978)		

In the early 1970s, studies conducted by a United Nations team revealed the possibility of the existence of oil reservoirs in the seabed of East China sea.(4) This prompted the Republic of China (ROC), Japan, and the Republic of Korea (ROK) to grant oil concession zones to foreign oil companies. Some of their concession zones overlap each other. In the late 1970s, the People's Republic of China (PRC) also began to grant oil concession zones to foreign oil companies and conducted exploratory activities in the area very close to a concession granted by the Republic of Korea.(5) These overlapping concession zones or blocks are indicated in Figure 7.1.

The situation is not, however, as serious as it appears to be despite the existence of several overlapping concession zones. First, the ROC's concession zones, except those near the island of Taiwan, are now practically obsolete. This is because after the Japanese withdrawal of its recognition of the ROC in 1972 and the US withdrawal of recognition in 1979, all foreign oil companies have withdrawn from exploration activities in ROC zones north of Taiwan. The withdrawal of Japanese and American recognition effectively brought into question the ROC's sovereign legal authority to grant such concession zones. On the other hand, while the PRC claims Taiwan, including its surrounding seabed, as its territory, so far it has not interfered with the ROC's exploring activities there.

With respect to the overlapping concession blocks between the ROK and Japan, the issue has at least been shelved temporarily. On 1 January 1970, the ROK enacted the Submarine Mineral Resources

Figures 7.1:

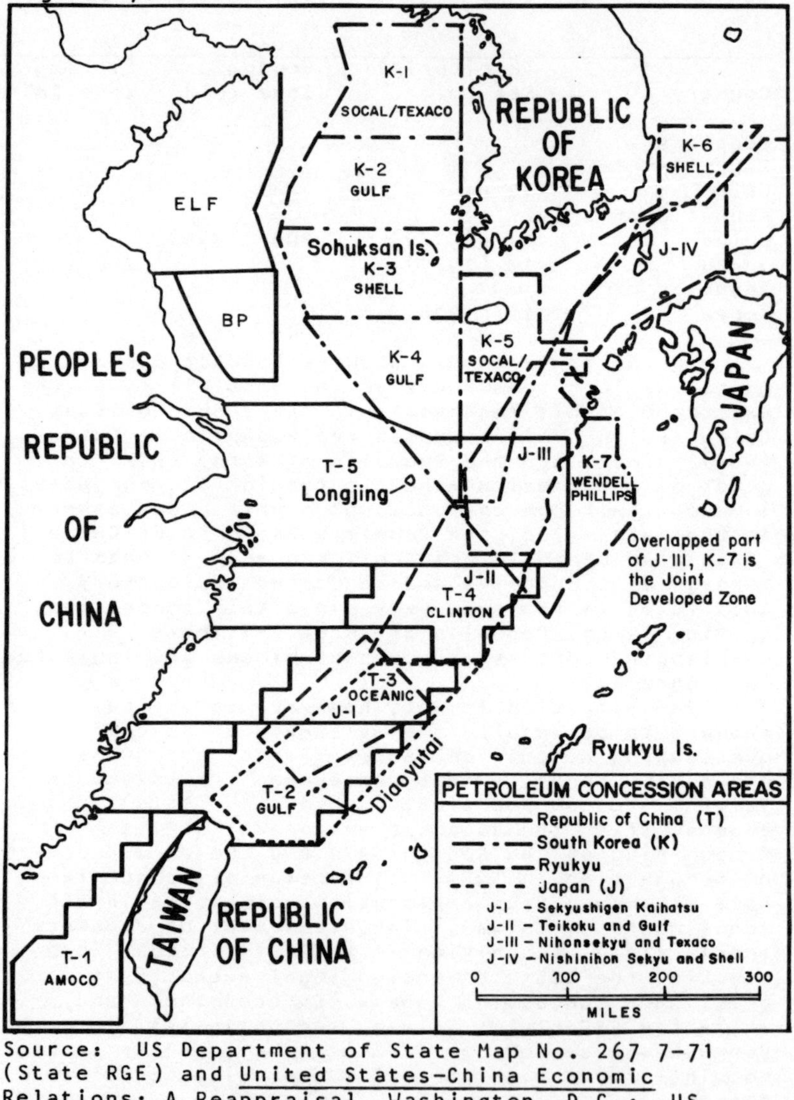

Source: US Department of State Map No. 267 7-71 (State RGE) and United States-China Economic Relations: A Reappraisal, Washington, D.C.: US Government Printing Office, 1982, p. 92. All island names and Joint Developed Zones were added by the author.

Development Law. Under this law, the ROK has designated seven different subzones and given concessions to several foreign oil companies for exploration. Subzone seven was immediately confronted with a similar claim by Japan. After long protracted negotiations, both the ROK and Japan concluded two agreements, the one for the continental shelf for the northern part of the ROK subzone seven and the other for the joint development zone (see Figure 7.1) in the southern part of subzone seven, where they could not agree on the delimitation line of the continental shelf, for 50 years.(6) While the PRC lodged protests in 1974, 1977 and 1980,(7) the PRC took no retaliatory action against Japan and the ROK.

The PRC has, since the late 1970s, engaged in extensive exploration activities in the East China Sea area. Several foreign oil companies, such as Elf, Total Chine, ARCO (Atlantic Richfield), Sante Fe Minerals, Japan National Oil Corp. (JNOC), and British Petroleum (BP), were granted exploration contracts by the PRC.(8) No country so far appears to protest the Chinese exploration activities in the East China Sea.

Despite the relatively quiet situation in oil exploration in the East China Sea, with the accelerated and increasing extensive exploration activities there, countries in the region in the foreseeable future must confront the issue of the delimitation of maritime boundaries. Before analysing this question, it is necessary to discuss the principles of international law concerning delimitation of maritime boundaries between countries of adjacent or opposite coasts. This part of the law was recently codified at the 1982 United Nations Convention on the Law of the Sea (hereinafter cited as the Law of the Sea Convention).(9)

While some major countries have so far refused to sign the Convention they are doing so solely on the ground of their dissatisfaction with the deep seabed mining arrangements of the Convention. They do not seem to challenge other parts of the Convention. For instance, in a statement on ocean policy accompanying the US proclamation on establishing an Exclusive Economic Zone issued on 10 March 1983,(10) President Ronald Reagan stated that the Convention 'contains provisions with respect to traditional uses of the oceans which generally confirm existing maritime law and practice and fairly balance the interests of all states ...';

that the United States is prepared to act in accordance with this balance of interests relating to traditional uses of the oceans which is reflected in the Convention; and that the United States will exercise its navigational and overflight rights on a worldwide basis 'in a manner that is consistent with the balance of interests reflected in the Convention ...'(11) Thus, a well-known authority on the law of the sea has noted:

> These two documents simply mean that the United States, though it did not sign the Convention, accepts its provisions relating to traditional uses of the sea (i.e., other than those relating to the novel problem of deep seabed mining) as customary international law binding on the United States.(12)

The Republic of China on Taiwan is a special case. It was unable to sign the Convention because of its exclusion from the Third United Nations Conference on the Law of the Sea (hereinafter cited as UNCLOS III) at the insistence of the People's Republic of China.(13) The ROC took, however, an attitude similar to that of the United States toward the Convention by accepting those parts of the Convention that codified customary international law.(14)

Apparently, the new Law of the Sea Convention, minus its provisions concerning the deep seabed mining regime, is generally acceptable to most countries. The next section will, therefore, discuss the maritime boundary delimitation provisions adopted by the UNCLOS III.

THE MARITIME BOUNDARY DELIMITATION PROBLEM AND THE 1982 UNITED NATIONS CONVENTION ON THE LAW OF THE SEA: RELEVANT PROVISIONS

Three articles of the Law of the Sea Convention deal with maritime boundary delimitation problems. Article 15 covers territorial seas; Article 74 treats exclusive economic zone; and Article 83 concerns the continental shelf between states with opposite or adjacent coasts. Article 121 relating to the regime of islands is also relevant to the delimitation problem. Among these articles, the adoption of Articles 15 and 121 was not controversial at UNCLOS III. In fact, the text of Article 15 is substantially the same as Article 12, paragraph 1 of the 1958 Convention on Territorial Sea and Contiguous Zone:(15)

> Where the coasts of two States are opposite or adjacent to each other, neither of the two States is entitled, failing agreement between them to the contrary, to extend its territorial sea beyond the median line every point of which is equidistant from the nearest points on the baselines from which the breadth of the territorial seas of each of the two States is measured. The above provision does not apply [The 1958 Convention provides: 'The provisions of this paragraph shall not apply ...'], however, where it is necessary by reason of historic title or other special circumstances to delimit the territorial seas of the two States, in a way which is at variance therewith.(16)

While Article 121 is new, there was little debate over the adoption of this article.(17) Article 121 provides:

> 1. An island is a naturally formed area of land, surrounded by water, which is above water on high tide.
>
> 2. Except as provided for in paragraph 3, the territorial sea, the contiguous zone, the exclusive economic zone and the continental shelf of an island are determined in accordance with the provisions of this Convention applicable to other land territory.
>
> 3. Rocks which cannot sustain human habitation or economic life of their own shall have no exclusive economic zone or continental shelf.(18)

Articles 74 and 83, however, were subject to lengthy debate at UNCLOS III. The Conference ultimately took the position that these articles' principles for delimitation of the continental shelf and exclusive economic zone (EEZ) should be the same. One group of countries had favored drawing the line equidistant between the two shorelines in question, although many of those countries contended that 'special circumstances' might justify another method; whereas, another group had emphasised 'equitable principles' and 'relevant circumstances'.(19) The Draft Convention on the Law of the Sea (Informal Text) issued by the President of the Conference on 22 September 1980 provides that the delimitation of maritime boundaries of the economic zone and the continental shelf between adjacent or opposite countries 'shall be effected by agreement in conformity with international law' and 'such an agreement shall be in accordance with equitable principles, employing the median or equidistant line, where appropriate, and taking account of all circumstances prevailing in the area concerned.'(20)

Among the countries that favored the 1980 draft arrangement were Canada, Costa Rica, Cyprus, Democratic Yemen, Denmark, the Dominican Republic, Ethiopia, Greece, Iceland, Italy, Japan, Malaysia, Nigeria, Norway, Oman, Portugal, the Republic of Korea, Sao Tome and Principe, Spain, Sweden, the USSR, the United Arab Emirates and the United Kingdom. New Zealand favored an earlier formula presented at the informal negotiation referring to equitable principles and citing the median line as one method to be employed in appropriate cases. Kuwait and Peru also endorsed the equidistant principle.(21)

Another group of States regarded the 1980 draft provision on delimitation as unacceptable. Among them were Algeria, Argentina, the People's Republic of China, Democratic Kampuchea, Ireland, Kenya, Libya, Mali, Morocco, Nicaragua, Poland, Romania, Senegal, Somalia, Suriname, Syria, Turkey, and Venezuela. They argued that delimitation should be based on agreement between the states concerned and the application of equitable principles, taking into account all circumstances, and without prejudicing the methods to be utilised. Some of them added that the text in the draft convention used terms such as 'relevant circumstances' which were open to misunderstanding and would not help to avoid disputes, and secondly that the text was at any rate legally invalid, since delimitation criteria already existed in international law. Also favoring an emphasis on equitable principles were Bangladesh, Dominica, the Ivory Coast, Mozambique, Vietnam and Zaire.(22)

Because of the deadlock over the question, the President of the Conference, Tommy T. K. Koh of Singapore, submitted a new compromise proposal at the Resumed Tenth Session in August 1981 which was finally accepted by the Conference(23) and became

Articles 74 and 83 of the Convention. Article 74 provides:

> The delimitation of the exclusive economic zone between States with opposite or adjacent coasts shall be effected by agreement on the basis of international law, as referred to in Article 38 of the Statute of the International Court of Justice, in order to achieve an equitable solution.(24)

Article 83 uses the same language as Article 74 to deal with the delimitation of 'continental shelves'.(25)

This compromise proposal was acceptable to the group in favor of subscribing to 'equitable principles' in resolving maritime boundary disputes because it omitted the reference to the equidistance or median rule in the text. According to this group, in the 1969 North Sea Continental Shelf cases,(26) the International Court of Justice (ICJ) referred to the equitable principle as the rule for delimitation. Thus, the reference to Article 38 of the Statute of the International Court of Justice appears to support this group's view because the Court's decision is at least a subsidiary means for determination of rules of law. On the other hand, the text only referred to the broad phrase 'equitable solution' and not to 'equitable principles', so that it was also acceptable to the group in favor of the equidistance or median rule.(27) The final text of these two articles relating to maritime boundary delimitation does not provide sufficiently clear guidelines for resolving the delimitation issue, as will be discussed later.

THE DELIMITATION OF THE TERRITORIAL SEA AND THE CONTINENTAL SHELF BETWEEN THE PEOPLE'S REPUBLIC OF CHINA, THE REPUBLIC OF KOREA, AND JAPAN

The PRC, the ROK and Japan have not yet declared an exclusive economic zone. Therefore, the delimitation of maritime boundaries between these countries relates only to the territorial sea and the continental shelf.

Territorial Sea and The Continental Shelf Between the ROK and Japan

There is no territorial sea delimitation question between the People's Republic of China and the Republic of Korea or Japan. The only place where a question involving delimiting the territorial sea might arise is in the Korea Strait because both the ROK and Japan have declared twelve-mile territorial seas, and the width of the Strait is between 16 to 26 miles.(28) However, both the ROK and Japan have excluded the application of their 12 miles territorial sea to the Korea Strait area.(29) Therefore, there is no need to delimit the territorial sea boundary between them. There has also been no protest to the ROK's straight baselines of the territorial sea, which measures from 3.14 to 60.30 miles.(30)

With respect to the delimitation of the continental shelf among the three countries, this issue between Japan and the ROK is partially resolved, and partially shelved for 50 years, as was explained earlier.(31) Therefore, only the shelf between the PRC and the ROK and that between the PRC and Japan are in need of delimitation. Before analysing the delimitation questions between them, it is necessary to discuss the applicable principles of international law on delimiting the continental shelf.

Principles of International Law Concerning Delimiting Continental Shelf between Adjacent or Opposite Countries

As stated in the earlier section, Article 83 of the 1982 Law of the Sea Convention only vaguely provides that the delimitation 'shall be effected by agreement on the basis of international law, as referred to in Article 38 of the Statute of the International Court of Justice, in order to achieve an equitable solution'. Thus, in actual delimitation, one is confronted with the crucial problem of how to determine the applicable rules of international law.

According to Article 38 of the Statute of International Court of Justice, there are five sources of international law: (1) Treaties; (2) Customs; (3) General principles of law recognised by civilised nations; (4) Judicial decisions; and (5) Writers' views. The first three sources are usually referred to as primary ones, while the last two are subsidiary. However, in finding applicable rules in resolving the issue of delimitation of the continental shelf between states of opposite or adjacent coasts, the third principle source is largely irrelevant. The 'general principles of law recognised by civilised countries' usually are interpreted to mean that international law can draw analogy from a domestic legal systems, which is a more developed system.(32) Because the continental shelf is a relatively new concept (while among the political subdivisions of a country there may also be a similar problem of delimitation), the domestic legal systems have not yet worked out satisfactory rules for possible use in international law, though some nations may face delimitation issues as between their political subdivisions. Ironically, some lawyers confronting domestic problems related to delimitation have even relied on international law practice in suggesting their resolution of the domestic legal context.(33) Nonetheless, Article 83 of the 1982 Convention is simply too general to be useful in most practical applications, with the exception that it establishes that the goal of delimitation is to achieve an 'equitable solution'. There are, however, a number of bilateral treaties on delimitation of the continental shelf between adjacent or opposite states which may be helpful in identifying a trend of practice in this area.(34) With respect to international custom, in order to ascertain the existence of applicable customary rules, one must resort to judicial decisions, arbitral awards and writers' views. Thus, these so-called subsidiary sources of international law are playing a dominant role, by default, in identifying applicable customary rules in the delimitation of the continental shelf between states of opposite or adjacent coasts.

It is generally agreed that there are two ICJ decisions and one arbitral award which provide some guidance in the delimitation of continental shelf problems. The first one is the *North Sea Continental Shelf* cases, decided by the ICJ in 1969.(35) In the *North Sea* cases, the Court laid down the following principles for delimiting the continental shelf between adjacent states:

> 1. [d]elimitation is to be effected by agreement in accordance with equitable principles, and taking account of all the relevant circumstances, in such a way as to leave as much as possible to each Party all those parts of the continental shelf that constitute a natural prolongation of its land territory into and under the sea, without encroachment on the natural prolongation of the land territory of the other;

2. [i]f, in the application of the preceding sub-paragraph, the delimitation leaves to the Parties areas that overlap, these are to be divided between them in agreed proportions or, failing agreement, equally, unless they decide on a regime of joint jurisdiction, user, or exploitation for the zones of overlap or any part of them;

[I]n the course of the negotiations, the factors to be taken into account are to include:

1. [t]he general configuration of the coasts of the Parties, as well as the presence of any special or unusual features;

2. [s]o far as known or readily ascertainable, the physical and geological structure, and natural resources, of the continental shelf areas involved;

3. [t]he element of a reasonable degree of proportionality, which a delimitation carried out in accordance with equitable principles ought to bring about between the extent of the continental shelf areas appertaining to the coastal State and the length of its coast measured in the general direction of the coastline, account being taken for this purpose of the effects, actual or prospective, of any other continental shelf delimitations between adjacent States in the same region.(36)

While the North Sea Continental Shelf case provides guidelines for delimiting the continental shelf between adjacent states, it is not clear whether the principles enunciated in this case are applicable to delimiting the continental shelf of states with opposite coasts. Moreover, the case does not discuss the question of islands in the delimitation issue. These questions were discussed in the 1977 Anglo-French Arbitral Award on the Delimitation of Continental Shelf.(37) Under Article 121, paragraph 3 of the 1982 Convention, only 'rocks which cannot sustain human habitation or economic life of their own' cannot serve as a basis for claiming an economic zone or continental shelf. In other words an island, as a matter of principle, can have an economic zone or continental shelf.

However, under certain circumstances, inequitable results will arise from giving full effect to an island in delimitation. In the Anglo-French Arbitral Award, the tribunal also addressed these issues.

In that case, because both France and the United Kingdom were parties to the 1958 Convention on Continental Shelf,(38) the Arbitral Tribunal considered Article 6 of the Convention applicable. On its face, that article seems to give preference to the median or equidistance rule. Paragraphs 1 and 2 provide that, in the case of opposite or adjacent coasts, the boundary of the continental shelf shall be determined by the agreement between the nations. In the absence of an agreement, and unless another line is justified by special circumstances, the boundary is the median or equidistance line. However, the Arbitral Tribunal considered that both 'the equidistance-special circumstances rule [stated by the Court in the North Sea Continental Shelf cases] have the same object--the determination of the boundary in accordance with equitable principles'. The Tribunal further observed that 'in the present case, whether discussing the application of Article 6 or the position under customary law, both Parties have had free recourse to pronouncements of the International Court of Justice regarding the rules of customary law applicable in the matter ...'(39) In other words, the Arbitral Tribunal confirmed the customary rules stated by the ICJ in the North Sea Continental Shelf cases as applicable to this case of delimiting continental shelf between states of opposite coasts.

In addition, unlike the North Sea Continental Shelf cases, the Arbitral Tribunal in the Anglo-French Arbitral Award was confronted with the problem of islands in delimitation. It took the position that if an island would cause a disproportionate effect in delimitation, then this would constitute a 'special circumstance' and thus the island should not be given full effect in delimitation in order to avoid an 'inequitable' result.(40) It also awarded a delimitation line between the two countries.

The third case concerning the delimitation of the continental shelf arose between Tunisia and Libya, and was decided by the International Court of Justice on 24 February 1982.(41) This decision further clarified certain principles relating to the delimitation of the continental shelf.(42) In contrast to the 1969 North Sea Continental Shelf case, which merely enunciated certain principles of delimitation and let the parties concerned negotiate the lines themselves, the ICJ determined a continental shelf boundary between the two countries as it had done in the 1977 Anglo-French Arbitral Award. With respect to the Tunisian Kerkennah Islands, the ICJ drew on the approach of the 1977 Arbitral Tribunal in not giving full effect of these islands in delimitation.(43)

Presumably, the above stated principles should be applied to the delimitation of continental shelf between the PRC and the ROK or Japan, as none of these governments or their writers have voiced objection to these principles.(44)

The Continental Shelf between the PRC and the ROK

The PRC's claim to the continental shelf in the Yellow Sea and the East China Sea is based on the natural prolongation principle,(45) though the PRC has not yet defined how far its claim would go.

The ROK has, as stated earlier, designated seven oil concessions, subzones, or blocks in the addendum to its Enforcement Decree of the Submarine Mineral Resources Development Law of 30 May 1970. Blocks K-1 to K-4 are in the Yellow Sea and East China Sea area. The outer limits of these blocks apparently demonstrate the Korean continental shelf claim here. The basis of the Korean claim is described by a Korean scholar as follows:

> [T]he manner with which the ROK has drawn her outward boundary of the continental shelf in the Yellow [Sea] and the part of the East China Sea, leads one to infer that the ROK adheres to the median line in that part of the continental shelf area. At the same time, the outward boundary of the ROK's continental shelf in the southeastern part of the East China Sea, which extends beyond the 200 nautical miles from her baseline of the territorial sea, demonstrates that the ROK relies on the doctrine of the natural prolongation of the land territory for her claim to the outer limit of the continental shelf in the East China [Sea]. Thus the ROK's claim to the outer limit of the continental shelf around her coast is based on combination of the two criteria, the median line and the natural prolongation theory. It should be noted in this connection that such claim of combined criteria for the entitlement to the outer limit of the

> continental shelf is not at variance with existing rules of maritime international law regarding the delimitation of the continental shelf.(46)

To justify the use of the median line in delimiting the continental shelf of the Yellow Sea by the ROK, this scholar stated:

> On the claim of the factor of proportionality of the relative lengths of the coastline for the PRC's continental shelf entitlement, it is doubtful that the PRC can successfully invoke this argument vis-a-vis the ROK. For the relative lengths of the coastlines between the ROK and the PRC in the Yellow Sea region is roughly equal, so that the PRC may not invoke the factor of proportionality of the relative lengths of the coastline vis-a-vis the ROK in the Yellow Sea region for the purpose of claiming a larger area of the continental shelf than the ROK.(47)

However, in addition to the proportionality of the length of the coasts issue, the ROK's claim on the continental shelf here is apparently based on giving full effect to Sasuksan Island, which lies about 62 miles off the southwest side of the Korean peninsula (see Figure 7.1). This is contrary to the view of the 1977 Anglo-French Arbitral Award and the 1982 Tunisia-Libya Continental Shelf ICJ Judgment.(48) In any future delimitation settlement, it is unlikely that the PRC would accept the ROK's position.

In the East China Sea area, the ROK's claim on continental shelf is significantly disproportionate to the length of its coast(49) and can hardly be justified on the natural prolongation principle because that part of the shelf is also the natural prolongation of the Chinese mainland. There thus appears to be no reason for the PRC to accept such a claim over the continental shelf by the ROK.(50)

The Continental Shelf between the PRC and Japan

The continental shelf in the East China Sea is the natural prolongation of the land territory of the Chinese mainland and Taiwan--not that of Japan. Under the natural prolongation principle, almost all of the shelf would go to China (the PRC and the ROC). Japan still asserts, however, a claim to the Diaoyutai Islets (in Chinese) or Senkaku Gunto (in

Japanese), which is contested by China. Both the PRC and the ROC consider the islets to be Chinese and under the administrative jurisdiction of Taiwan Province.(51) The Diaoyutai Islets consist of five uninhabited islets and three rocks in the East China Sea northeast of Taiwan. Diaoyu, the largest of the group is about 1.67 square miles; Huangwei is about 0.3861 square miles; and the remaining three islets, Nanxiao, Beixiao, and Chiwei, are each less than half a square mile. They are all situated at the edge of the southeast part of the East China Sea continental shelf extending from the Chinese mainland and Taiwan; they are separated from the continental shelf of Japan and the Ryukyu Islands by the Okinawa Trough, which is more than 3,280 feet in depth. The largest of the islets, Diaoyu, seems large enough to be able to claim a continental shelf or economic zone under Article 121 of the 1982 Law of the Sea Convention. Therefore, the ownership of these islets becomes very important in delimiting the maritime boundary in this area. Japan's ownership of these islets would provide it with a base to claim a continental shelf to the disadvantage of China (the PRC and the ROC). However, even if Japan did in fact own the islets, to what extent it could claim a continental shelf in the East China Sea remains in doubt. None of the three international cases discussed earlier(52) supports the view that these islets should be given an extensive continental shelf in light of their small size. The PRC naturally will not accept the position of giving these islets full effect in delimiting the continental shelf in the East China Sea. In this connection, a PRC scholar has commented that 'the attempt by any country to encroach upon the natural prolongation of another country's landed territory through the existence of one or two islands is erroneous.'(53)

THE QUESTION OF DELIMITING THE EXCLUSIVE ECONOMIC ZONE IN THE EAST CHINA SEA

Among the four East Asian countries, the Republic of China is the only one which has declared an exclusive economic zone.(54) However, there is always the possibility that any of the three other countries will declare an exclusive economic zone in the future. Therefore, it is also necessary to discuss the principles of international law relating to the delimitation of the exclusive economic zone first, and then analyse their possible application to the East China Sea area.

Principles of International Law Concerning Delimiting the Exclusive Economic Zone and Its Relation with the Continental Shelf

Article 74 of the 1982 Convention on the delimitation of exclusive economic zones is exactly the same as that of Article 83 on the continental shelf and, therefore, does not provide any concrete rule on delimitation issues.

Unlike the concept of the continental shelf, which is based on the geographical situation of the seabed, the Exclusive Economic Zone (EEZ) arbitrarily sets a limit of 200 miles from the baseline of a coastal state. This regime was originally advocated by certain Latin American states such as Chile, Peru or Ecuador which have almost no continental shelf. Indeed, one commentator has noted that in the early stages of the UNCLOS III, the trend was for the continental shelf regime to be absorbed within the 200-mile limit of the EEZ.(55) However, the broad-shelf countries, such as the United States, Australia, the Soviet Union, and Argentina, managed to reverse this trend. The 1982 Convention now allows a coastal state to extend its continental shelf beyond the 200-mile limit as far as 350 miles.(56) This parallel system of EEZ and continental shelf, however, creates a difficult problem with regard to delimitation between states of opposite coasts.

If one state's continental shelf extends beyond the median line, drawn with respect to the coasts of two opposite states, and the other state has declared an EEZ, there remains a question of whether that state still exercises sovereign rights in relation to natural resources situated in that part of the shelf under the other state's EEZ as provided in Article 77, paragraph 1, of the 1982 Law of the Sea Convention.(57) Since the regime of the continental shelf emerged earlier than that of the EEZ, and under both the 1958 Convention,(58) the 1982 Convention and writer's views,(59) 'the rights of the coastal State over the continental shelf do not depend on occupation, effective or notional, or on any express proclamation',(60) it is unlikely that a coastal state would give up its claim to its continental shelf beyond the median line of two states with opposite coasts even if the other state has declared an EEZ.

On the other hand, under Article 56, paragraph

1, of the 1982 Convention, a coastal state has 'sovereign rights for the purpose of exploring and exploiting, conserving and managing the natural resources, whether living or non-living, of the waters superjacent to the seabed and of the seabed and its subsoil ...' in the EEZ,(61) so it is unlikely that a state with an EEZ would allow an opposite state to claim the continental shelf under its EEZ.

One possible solution is to absorb the regime of the continental shelf within 200 miles into the EEZ. Thus, if the distance between two states with opposite coasts is less than 400 miles, then the EEZ should be delimited regardless of the continental shelf between them. Professor Shigeru Oda of Japan appears to favour this view.(62)

On the other hand, a state with a broad shelf vis-a-vis an opposite state with a narrow shelf is likely to oppose this view. Thus, a PRC scholar has considered Oda's view as 'erroneous'.(63) Under such circumstances, it is possible for that state not to declare an EEZ, but to base its claim exclusively on the doctrine of the continental shelf. Moreover, even if a state makes a declaration on an EEZ, it can still assert its rights on a continental shelf based on conventional and customary rules of international law. For instance, when the Republic of China made a declaration on its economic zone on 6 September 1979, it specifically pointed out:

> The sovereign rights enjoyed by the Republic of China over the continental shelf contiguous to its coast as recognised by the Convention on the Continental Shelf of 1958 and the general principles of international law shall not be prejudiced in any manner by the proclamation of the present exclusive economic zone or the establishment of such zones by any other state.(64)

Another solution is to have different maritime boundary lines for EEZ and the continental shelf. For instance, in the hearing on the Case Concerning the Continental Shelf Tunisia/Libya, held on 9 October 1981, Libya expressed the following view:

> Libya considers that, as between States with opposite or adjacent coasts, the delimitation of their respective continental shelf areas and of their economic zones ought not, in the majority of cases, to be different.

> Nevertheless, there may be factors relevant to fishing, such as established fishing practices, which have no relevance to shelf resources; and conversely, there may be factors relevant to shelf resources--such as geological features controlling the extent of a natural prolongation--of no relevance to fishing. _It therefore follows that the two boundaries need not necessarily coincide_.(65)

In actual cases of delimitation, a few states have agreed to have two different maritime boundary lines for different purposes. For instance, in the Treaty between Papua New Guinea and Australia concluded on 8 December 1978, the fisheries-jurisdiction line does not correspond to the seabed and subsoil boundary.(66)

Another problem relating to the delimitation of EEZs is the extent to which existing rules of international law, especially those relating to the delimitation of continental shelf, can _mutatis mutandis_ be applied to the delimitation of the EEZ. Since the EEZ concept disregards the seabed's geographical or geological situation, there seems to be a natural limit to drawing analogies from rules of continental shelf delimitation to apply to the EEZ case. On the other hand, there are also similarities that may justify such analogies. For instance, on the question of to what extent an island should be given effect in delimitation, drawing analogy from the continental shelf delimitation experience certainly may prove useful.

In the 1984 _Gulf of Maine Maritime Boundary Case_,(67) both the United States and Canada, as adjacent states, requested a Chamber of the ICJ to decide a single maritime boundary covering both the continental shelf and the superjacent fisheries zones. The ICJ Chamber noted that with respect to the applicable criteria and methods in delimitation, it must exclude criteria which, however equitable they may appear in themselves, are not suited to the delimitation of both of the two objects in respect of which the delimitation is requested--the continental shelf and the fishery zones.(68) Thus, it stated:

> ... [A] delimitation which has to apply at one and the same time to the continental shelf and to the superjacent water column can only be carried out by the application of a criterion, or combination of criteria, which does not give

> preferential treatment to one of these two objects to the detriment of the other, and at the same time is such as to be equally suitable to the division of either of them. In that regard ... preference will ... inevitably be given to criteria that, because of their more neutral character, are best suited for use in a multi-purpose delimitation.(69)

In view of these reasons, the Chamber turned to criteria derived from geography, concluding that it should favor the criterion whereby one should aim at an equal division of areas where the maritime projections of the coasts of the States between which delimitation is to be effectively covered and overlap. However, the Chamber also made the following provision:

> ... the adoption of this starting-point must be combined with the parallel and partial adoption of the appropriate auxiliary criteria insofar as it is apparent that this combination is necessitated by the <u>relevant circumstances</u> of the area concerned, and provided they are used only to the extent actually dictated by this necessity(70).

One of the relevant circumstances indicated by the Chamber is the proportionality of the length of the coastline in the delimitation area. Another relevant circumstance is the presence of islands. Like the court in the 1982 <u>Tunisia/Libya Continental Shelf</u> case, the Chamber gave a Canadian island only half effect in delimitation.(71)

<u>The Maritime Boundary between the ROC and Japan</u>

To what extent the above stated rules and proposed solutions can be applied to the delimitation of maritime boundary between the ROC and Japan is not clear, since both countries have yet to make known their position on this question. Moreover, the delimitation will be further complicated by the dispute over the title over the Diaoyutai Islets, as discussed earlier.(72) Japan certainly would like to use these islets to claim the continental shelf vis-a-vis Taiwan. On the other hand, if the ROC's sovereignty over the islets were established, it could use the islets to claim the EEZ vis-a-vis Ryukyu Islands of Japan.(73)

There is no continental shelf between the east coast of Taiwan and the southern tip of the Ryukyu

Islands (i.e. Irimote and Sakishina Islands), so the principles of delimitation of maritime boundaries enunciated by the ICJ Chamber in the 1984 Gulf of Maine Case can be applied here. The equidistance rule should be applied with adjustment based on the proportionality of the length of the coasts involved.

The Hypothetical Case of Delimiting the Exclusive Economic Zone between the PRC and Japan

The continental shelf in the East China Sea is the natural prolongation of the land territory of the Chinese mainland and not that of Japan. Therefore, under the concept of the continental shelf, Japan can hardly claim any of the continental shelf there. However, if Japan declares an EEZ, then it will make a claim to both the seabed and water column resources up to 200 miles from the baseline of its territorial sea under Articles 56 and 57 of the 1982 Law of the Sea Covention. This will give Japan a basis to claim some continental shelf in the East China Sea since the distance between Japan's Kyushu Island and Chinese mainland is roughly 400 miles.

Under those circumstances, it is questionable whether the PRC would agree to let Japan lay a claim on the East China Sea Continental Shelf. In this connection, a PRC writer commented:

> Whether there should be a single boundary for exclusive economic zone and the continental shelf should be decided in accordance with concrete situation. If the conditions [are appropriate] a single boundary may be demarcated. If not, then two boundaries should be respectively delimited. In case of complex situation, it seems proper to have superjacent water boundary as fishery boundary and the seabed boundary as the continental shelf boundary. Any country's attempt to encroach upon the natural prolongation of the land territory of another state through the concept of 200-mile economic zone is contrary to international law.(74)

The Hypothetical Case of Delimiting the Exclusive Economic Zone between the PRC and the ROK

The continental shelf in the Yellow Sea and the East China Sea is the natural prolongation of the land territory of the Korean Peninsula and the Chinese mainland. There appear to be no special circumstances, except the presence of certain islands, which would prompt either the PRC or the ROK to declare an EEZ to add to their respective claims. Even if the one or both of them declares an EEZ, the principles of delimitation stated by the ICJ Chamber in the Gulf of Maine case can be applied here to resolve the issue.

CONCLUSION

Among the four countries in the East China Sea, the maritime boundary between the ROK and the PRC would be the easiest one to delimit. This is because the geographical and seabed situation between the two is not complicated. Furthermore, the principles of international law governing such a delimitation are generally clear. However, the political relations between them make delimitation of their maritime boundary an unlikely event. The PRC does not recognise the ROK and has entered into official contact with the latter only in exceptional cases. The PRC has maintained cordial relations with the Democratic People's Republic of Korea and this has set a limit on its official contacts with the ROK.

Theoretically, Japan could declare an EEZ which would support a legal claim over the continental shelf of the East China Sea. But, in view of its close economic relations with the PRC, it is unlikely that Japan would attempt to do so in the foreseeable future. Any Japanese assertion of continental shelf claim vis-a-vis the PRC would jeopardise their mutually beneficial economic relations.

The maritime boundary between the PRC and the ROC will not be resolved formally because both consider mainland and Taiwan as a part of China and at present there is no urgency to resolve the maritime boundary between them. Both have exercised restraint with respect to each other's exploration and exploitation activities in the East China Sea.

Because Japan does not recognise the ROC, it is also unlikely that they will settle their maritime boundary issue in the near future. Neither side appears to be in any hurry to resolve this issue now.

NOTES

1. See Articles 1 and 2 of the 1958 Geneva Convention on Continental Shelf, United Nations Treaties Series (hereinafter UNTS), vol. 499,

p. 311ff. Article 2 grants to the coastal state 'sovereign rights' of an exclusive nature for the purpose of exploring and exploiting the natural resources of the shelf. Such rights 'are to pertain _ipso jure_ to it, and are not to depend on an effective or national occupation, or any formal claims by way of proclamation'. J.G. Starke, _An Introduction to International Law_, 8th edn (Butterworths, London, 1977), p. 241.

2. See Starke, _International Law_, pp. 252-3 and Part V--Exclusive Economic Zone (Articles 55 to 75) of the 1982 United Nations Convention on the Law of the Sea, UN Doc.A/CONF.62/122 (October 7, 1982). Complete text of the Convention is reprinted in _International Legal Materials_, vol. 21, no. 6 (November 1982), pp. 1261-1354 and in _The Law of the Sea_ (St. Martin's Press/The United nations, New York, 1983).

3. Information provided in a table prepared by the Office of the Geographer, U.S. Department of State, June 1984. The Republic of China's information is based on Hungdah Chiu, Rong-jye Chen and Tzu-wen Lee, 'Contemporary Practice and Judicial Decisions of the Republic of China Relating to International Law', in _Chinese Yearbook of International Law and Affairs_, vol. 1 (1981), pp. 151-2.

4. See K.O. Emery et al., 'Geological Structure and Some Water Characteristics of the East China Sea and the Yellow Sea', _Technical Bulletin, Technical Advisory Group Report_, vol. 2 (1969), pp. 39-40.

5. In February 1981 and April 1982 respectively, the PRC's Ministry of Geology drilled two exploratory wells, Longjing-I and Longjing-II in northern East China Sea, which are very close to the southwestern edge of the Republic of Korea's Block K-7. See Ying-jeou Ma, _Legal Problems of Seabed Boundary Delimitation in the East China Sea_, Baltimore - University of Maryland School of Law, Occasional Papers/Reprints Series in Contemporary Asian Studies. no. 3 - 1984 (62), pp. 51-2.

6. See Choung Il Chee, 'The Republic of Korea and the Law of the Sea', paper presented at _The International Conference on East Asia and the Law of the Sea_, co-sponsored by the Institute for Far Eastern Studies, Kyungnam University; the Law of the Sea Institute, University of Hawaii and the Environment and Policy Institute, The East-West Center, Seoul, Republic of Korea, July 3-6, 1984, p. 15. See also Ma, _Seabed Boundary Delimitation_,

pp. 58-9.

7. See Peking Review, Vol. 17, No. 5, 8 February 1974, p. 3; ibid., Vol. 20, No. 25, 17 June 1977, pp. 16-17. and Beijing Review, Vol. 23, no. 20, 19 May 1980, pp. 6-7.

8. See Teresa Ma, 'Foreigners too Would Like Some Offshoot Business', Far Eastern Economic Review, Vol. 121, No. 34, 25 August 1983, pp.61-3.

9. See The Law of the Sea.

10. Text in Int'l. Legal Materials, Vol. 22, no. 2 (March 1983), pp. 464-5 (Policy), 465 (Proclamation).

11. Ibid., p. 464.

12. Louis B. Sohn, 'Thoughts on Customary International Law', Dean Rusk Center for International and Comparative Law Newsletter, Vol. 1, no. 2 (January 1984), p. 2.

13. The ROC's seat at the United Nations was taken over by the PRC on October 26, 1971. From then on, the ROC has been unable to participate in any United Nations sponsored international conferences.

14. See ROC Foreign Minister's statement of 12 January 1983 before the Legislative Yuan, in Hungdah Chiu, Rong-jye Chen and Tzu-wen Lee, 'Contemporary Practice and Judicial Decisions of the Republic of China Relating to International Law, 1981-1983', Chinese Yearbook of International Law and Affairs, vol. 2 (1982), p. 248.

15. United States Treaties and other International Agreements, Vol. 15, (henceforward UST) 1606 ff.; Treaties and International Agreement Series (henceforward TIAS) 5639; 516 UNTS 205.

16. The Law of the Sea, pp. 5-6.

17. See Third United Nations Conference on the Law of the Sea, Official Records, vol. II (The United Nations, New York, 1975), pp. 278-89.

18. The Law of the Sea, p. 39.

19. See United Nations Press Release, SEA/399 (July 23, 1980), p. 16.

20. Article 74, paragraph 1 (economic zone) and Article 84, paragraph 1 (continental shelf) of the Draft Convention. UN Doc.A/CONF.62/WP.10/Rev.3, pp. 30, 34.

21. United Nations Press Release, SEA/425 (4 March 1981), p. 24.

22. Ibid.

23. Ibid., SEA/455 (28 August 1981), p. 1.

24. The Law of the Sea, p. 26.

25. Ibid., pp. 29-30.

26. 1969 International Court of Justice,

Reports of Judgments, Advisory Opinions and Orders henceforward I.C.J. Reports), p. 1.

27. Information supplied by a delegate who participated in the negotiations.

28. See Commander R.H. Kennedy, 'A Brief Geographical and Hydrographical Study of Straits which Constitute Routes for International Traffic', (UN Doc.A/CONF.13/6 and Add.1) in United Nations Conference on the Law of the Sea Official Records, Vol. 1: Preparatory Materials (The United Nations, New York, 1958), pp. 123-4.

29. Choung Il Chee, 'Korea and the Law of the Sea', p. 1.

30. Ibid., p. 2.

31. See supra note 6 and accompanying text.

32. See Max Srensen, Manual of Public International Law (St. Martin's Press, New York, 1968), p. 144.

33. See, e.g., Jonathan I. Charney, 'The Delimitation of Lateral Seaward Boundaries between States in a Domestic Context', American Journal of International Law, Vol. 75 (1981), pp. 28-68.

34. For a list of those agreements, see Ted L. McDorman et al., Maritime Boundary Delimitation (Lexington Books, Lexington, Mass., 1983), pp. 158-95.

35. 1969 I.C.J. Reports, p. 1.

36. Ibid., p. 53.

37. International Law Reports, Vol. 54, pp. 6-213.

38. 15 UST 471; TIAS 5578; 499 UNTS 311.

39. S75 of the Arbitral Award, in International Law Reports, Vol. 54, pp. 57-8.

40. See 244 and 245 of the Arbitral Award, in International Law Reports, Vol. 54, pp. 121-2.

41. 1982 I.C.J. Reports, p. 18.

42. See the discussion in Mark B. Feldman, 'The Tunisia-Libya Continental Shelf Case: Geographic Justice or Judicial Compromise?' American Journal of Internal Law, Vol. 77 (1983), pp. 219-38 and Nicholas P. Dunning's Introduction to this case in Elisabeth Mann Borgese and Norton Ginsburg, editors, Ocean Yearbook, Vol. 4 (University of Chicago Press, Chicago, 1983), pp. 515-20.

43. 128 of the Judgment, in 1982 I.C.J. Reports, pp. 88-9.

44. For PRC writers' views, see Wang Tieya and Wei Min, editors, Guoji fa (International Law), (The Law Press, Beijing, 1981), pp. 197-8 (making reference to the 1969 North Sea Cases and 1977 Anglo-French Arbitration Award); Shao Jin, 'The

Award of the U.K.-France Continental Shelf Boundary Arbitration and Principle of Equity', Zhongguo guoji fa niankan, 1982 (Chinese Yearbook of International Law 1982), (China Translation and Publishing Corporation, Beijing, 1982), pp. 239-57 and Lian Chuncheng, 'Principles for the Delimitation of Continental Shelf', ibid., Beijing, 1983, pp. 194, 200-1 (making reference to the 1969 North Sea Cases, 1977 Anglo-French Arbitration and the 1982 Tunisia-Libya Continental Shelf Case).

45. See Wang and Wei, International Law, p. 199. In the PRC's 7 May 1980 protest against the ROK-Japan Joint Development Zone in the East China Sea, it did not define the scope of the Chinese claim. It only said that signing the agreement by Japan 'with the South Korean authorities without consulting China and behind China's back is utterly illegal and null and void.' See 'China's Sovereignty Over East China Sea Continental Shelf', Beijing Review, Vol. 23, No. 20, 19 May 1980, pp. 6-7.

46. Choung Il Chee, 'Korea and the Law of Sea', p. 17.

47. Ibid., p. 21.

48. See notes 40 and 43 and accompanying text.

49. Choung Il Chee also acknowledged this in his article, 'Korea and the Law of the Sea', pp. 21-2.

50. A Chinese scholar has voiced his oppostion to the use of the equidistance rule in relation to delimitation of the continental shelf in East China Sea. He considers that the principle of natural prolongation should be applied in this area. Zhao Lihai, Haiyanfa di xin fazhan (new development in the law of the sea) (Beijing University Press, Beijing, 1984), p. 64.

51. For the ROC position on these islets, see Hungdah Chiu, 'A Study of the Tiaoyutai [Diaoyutai in Pinyin] Islets Problems', Chengchi law Review, vol. 6 (1972), pp. 241-70 (in Chinese). For the PRC position, see Jerome Alan Cohen and Hungdah Chiu, People's China and International Law, A Documentary Study (Princeton University Press, Princeton, N.J., 1974), vol. 1, pp. 346-53. For the Japanese position, see Special Issue on Senkaku, vol. 63 (Dec. 1972). For an analysis of this issue, see Tao Cheng, 'The Sino-Japanese Dispute Over the Tiao-yu-tai (Senkaku) Islands and the Law of Territorial Acquisition', Virginia Journal of International Law, vol. 14 (1974), pp. 221-66; Hungdah Chiu, 'Island Disputes in the Far East', Encyclopedia of Public International Law, vol. 6,

Regional Corporation, Organizations and Problems (Elsevier Science Publishers B.V., Amsterdam, 1983), pp. 233-6.

52. See notes 36 (proportionality of the length of the coastline and delimitation of continental shelf), 40 and 43 (effect of island on delimitation of continental shelf) and accompanying text of these notes.

53. Lian Chuncheng, 'Delimitation of Continental Shelf', p. 202.

54. See note 3 and accompanying text.

55. See D.P. O'Connell, The International Law of the Sea, vol. 1, I.A. Shearer (ed.) (Oxford University Press, London and New York, 1982), p. 579.

56. Article 76, paragraph 6 of the Convention, in The Law of the Sea, p. 27.

57. Ibid., p. 28.

58. Article 2, paragraph 3, note 38.

59. None of the writers appear to oppose Article 2, paragraph 3 of the 1958 Convention.

60. Article 77, paragraph 30 of the 1982 Convention, in The Law of the Sea, p. 28.

61. Ibid., p. 18.

62. Shigeru Oda, International law of the Resources of the Sea (Sifthoff and Noordhoff, Alphen aan den Rijhn, Germantown, Md., 1979), p. 93.

63. Lian Chungcheng, 'Delimitation of Continental Shelf', p. 206.

64. Cited from Hungdah Chiu, et.al., 'Contemporary Practice', 1981, p. 152.

65. Cited from 1982 I.C.J. Reports, p. 232.

66. See McDorman, et.al., Maritime Boundary Delimitation, pp. 194-5.

67. 1984 I.C.J. Reports, pp. 246-390.

68. Paragraph 192 in ibid., p. 326.

69. Paragraph 194 in ibid., p. 327.

70. Paragraph 197 in ibid., p. 328. Emphasis added by the author.

71. Paragraphs 218, 221, 222 in ibid., pp. 334-7.

72. See notes 51, 52 and 53 and accompanying text.

73. The Diaoyutai Islets are separated by the deep Okinawa Trough with the Ryukyu Islands and there is no continental shelf between them. Therefore, even if the ROC owns the islets, it cannot rely on the concept of continental shelf to claim the seabed in between and must rely on the concept of the EEZ which disregards the seabed situation.

74. Lian Chungcheng, 'Delimitation of Continental Shelf', p. 206.

Chapter Eight

CHINA AND THE DEVELOPMENT OF SOUTH CHINA SEA RESOURCES

Kim Woodard and Alice Davenport

INTRODUCTION

The South China Sea is an active area of both co-operation and competition in China's emerging relations with Southeast Asia. The importance of the South China Sea in the overall framework of China's regional policies arises from its strategic geographic position, seen from the multiple perspectives of defence and security, marine and hydrocarbon resource development, regional trade, and regional diplomacy. China's economic development programmes target the southern coastal areas of Guangdong Province contiguous to the South China Sea as a high-growth area. The reversion of Hong Kong to Chinese sovereignty in 1997 may affect the entire political and economic topography of the region.

The importance of the South China Sea is clear in the case of such nations as Vietnam or the Philippines, which lie on the sea and are dependent on its resources. But the South China Sea is also of major importance to other Asian countries like Japan, which rely on the international sea lanes of the area to bring in many of their raw materials and much of their energy supply. Besides these nations, the South China Sea is strategically important to the Soviet Union and the United States, which eye each other's movements from Cam Ranh Bay and from the Philippines.

This chapter will review the role of the South China Sea in China's regional policies and development programs. We believe that the People's Republic of China has a strong interest in stabilisation of the South China Sea region, and in the development of co-operative resource development and trade. In the longer term, China's interest in stabilty and co-operation will offset and soften public rhetoric which has asserted highly nationalist and one-sided jurisdictional claims to virtually the entire South China Sea areas as far south as the northern coasts of Indonesia.

MARINE RESOURCE DEVELOPMENT

China has a coastline of 18,000 kilometres and borders three seas (the Yellow Sea, the East China Sea and the South China Sea) with a total surface of 4.7 million square kilometres. China's marine resource technology is still relatively undeveloped, though it does have a capability in traditional marine resource areas such as fishing, salt-making, and coastal water transportation. However, China still lacks the trained personnel and equipment to exploit its mineral and other ocean resources on a wide scale.(1) In the 1960s China did make an effort to exploit its coastal and marine resources, but with little economic success. For example, China built dykes along the coast to extend farming areas. But this reduced fish harvests and the ensuing ecological imbalance contributed to the siltation of waterways.(2)

In May, 1983, sixty of China's leading marine specialists submitted a report to the State Planning Commission, pointing out the strategic and economic importance of China's program to exploit China's offshore resources.(3) Subsequent plans to develop Chinese coastal regions and exploit offshore resources include: providing services for oil and gas exploration, and assessing other sources for coastal energy supplying electricity to coastal areas, islands and navigation buoys; conducting research on estuary fishing and marine ecology; working with other organisations to improve coastal communications; strengthening marine laws and management of coastal areas, and the continental shelf; improving marine research capabilities and promoting sea water desalination.(4)

In 1984 China launched a national study of marine development and research. Under the State Council's research centre for technology and economy, and the State Bureau of Oceanography, the research focuses on developing fishing, salt-making, shipping, offshore oil and gas exploration, tidal energy, and deep sea mining. Results are expected to be published by the end of 1985.(5) At the closing ceremonies of a November, 1984 meeting of the Chinese Society of Oceanographhy, State Councillor Kang Shi'en called for increased co-operation with foreign countries in marine meteorology, marine communications and positioning, marine safety and rescue services, testing marine materials, diving, underwater engineering and seabed geological studies. Offshore petroleum exploration would remain a primary focus, but work would also begin on development of other offshore resources.(6)

In 1980 Chinese scientists began a survey of offshore resources along half of China's coastline, covering land areas up to 10 kilometres inland and waters as deep as 15 kilometres. The study is expected to be completed by the end of 1985. Specialists working on this study came from the fields of hydrology, meteorology, geology, morphology, soil science and biochemistry. By the end of 1983 about half of this survey had been completed.(7) At that time China had about 100 survey ships and had carried out general ocean surveys, fishing resource surveys, national coastal surveys, and submarine cable route surveys.(8)

China stepped up its marine survey efforts in 1984, when the State Oceanography Bureau sent out ships on 208 voyages, involving a total of 2,040 days and 134,625 nautical miles.(9) As part of this effort, China has set the 'Science No. 1' ship to survey mineral and oil resources in the East China Sea. The ship has facilities for research in seismology, satellite-guided navigation, gravity, magnet force, morphology and geochemistry. In 1982, it logged 30,000 nautical miles in 17 voyages throughout the East China Sea.(10)

Between April 1983 and July 1984, another ship (a Chinese Navy survey vessel) completed a survey of the Taiwan Straits. The ship travelled 72,966 nautical miles between Taishan Liedao to the north and Nanpeng Liedao to the south. The data it gathered 'filled in the last blank in New China's nautical chart-making.' (11)

In 1984 the Guangzhou-based South China Sea Institute of Oceanology completed a survey of the sea around the Nanshan Islands. The Institute, which is part of the Chinese Academy of Sciences, sent out the survey ship, Experiment III, with personnel including geologists, meteorologists, physicists, chemists, biologists, and hydrologists. The ship covered 4,000 nautical miles over the summer of 1984 and collected data from 49 separate points and covered the whole Nanshan area.

Following this, in 1985, Chinese scientsts concluded a survey of the central South China Sea area.(12)

Of the 9,000 kilometres surveyed so far, about half are included in a new coastal development program. This program will cover areas offshore Jiangsu, Qingdao, Wenzhou, and Shanghai as well as the Pearl River estuary.(13) Guangxi, Guangdong and Fujian have set up special survey teams to update coastal topographical information -- an area of research that has been neglected in the past.(14)

In the early 1980s, as oil exploration activities increased in the South China Sea, the Chinese set up a meteorological station in Guangzhou to improve weather forecasting and typhoon warnings. This is one part of China's overall efforts to improve its marine meterological science capabilities. Eight weather stations were set up along the coast in the 1950s, but very little had been done since. During the 1960s, Beijing emphasised agricultural weather prediction rather than marine weather studies, and during this period marine weather stations were transferred from the State Meteorological Administration to the jurisdiction of the Oceanographic Bureau. In the Oceanographic Bureau, marine meteorology languished until the 1983-84 emphasis on developing China's marine resources pushed the science to the foreground once again.(15)

Marine meteorology is not the only marine research which has suffered from organisational problems. Over the past thirty years, lack of unified management has also hindered the research efforts of Chinese marine resource scientists and has contributed to the overharvesting of fish and other sea resources. There have been recent calls to strengthen the State Ocean Bureau and to consolidate China's marine development work under this organisation.(16) This will be a formidable task, for over 70 Chinese departments are currently working on ocean resources. By 1984 China had about 25,000 people working in marine science and technology.(17) And in addition to such civilian efforts, the PLA Navy has also outlined plans to help develop marine resources as part of Deng Xiaoping's call for China's armed forces to become actively involved in the nation's economic modernisation.(18)

Reflecting the increased importance of China's coastal areas, and increased levels of offshore oil exploration activity, tough new regulations went into effect 1 April 1985 aimed at controlling marine pollution and waste dumping at sea.

PETROLEUM RESOURCE EXPLORATION

Although the South China Sea holds a rich potential in a wide variety of marine resources development, it is the area's petroleum resources which have attracted the most international attention in recent years. In 1978, China invited a number of foreign oil companies to assist with the geophysical exploration of the South China and Yellow Seas. The Chinese indicated that if the surveys showed promising oil deposits, they would be willing to co-operate with foreign oil companies in development efforts. During 1980 and 1981, forty-six companies spent over US $200 million to survey and assess the hydrocarbon potential of China's offshore areas. In the largest 'group shoot' in the history of the world oil industry, seismic surveys covered an area of the Chinese continental shelf equivalent to half the surface area of Texas.

Total Chine (France) was an early entrant into the South China Sea arena. Beginning in 1980, Total drilled 24 wildcat and delineation wells on a contract area covering about half of the northern Tonkin Gulf. Three small fields were discovered, but of these, only one (Weizhou 10-3) will be developed for commercial oil production. The field will begin test production from an Early Production System in 1987 with field output projected to peak at just 11,000-13,000 barrels per day.

Atlantic Richfield was the first American company to drill offshore China. Working the terms of a Production-Sharing Contract that subsequently became a model for the bidding process, ARCO has drilled eight exploratory wells on a large contract area south of Hainan Island. The result was the discovery of a very large natural gas field (Yacheng 13) that is thought to hold some 5-7 trillion cubic feet of gas reserves. Pending signature of a development agreement with the China National Offshore Oil Corporation (CNOOC), ARCO will develop the natural gas field with a single 40-well offshore platform costing US $500 million. The gas will then be shipped by pipeline to northern Hainan for use as feedstock in an ammonia-urea fertiliser plant and to the Hong Kong-Guangzhou corridor for use as an industrial fuel. The fertiliser plant and other gas distribution and utilisation facilities will be built by the Chinese under separate contracts with foreign companies other than ARCO.

Somewhat better prepared for the world of international oil after their experience with early entrants like Total and Araco, China opened the first round of competititve bidding in 1982 on 150,000 square kilometres of offshore oil exploration contract areas in the South China and Yellow Seas. Thirty-three of the forty-six companies active in the seismic surveys decided to submit bids. Concurrent with this round of bidding, China promulgated offshore petroleum regulations and a comprehensive corporate profits tax law. The newly-formed China National Offshore Oil Corporation (CNOOC) was given authority to negotiate oil exploration and development contracts with the foreign oil companies. Eighteen contracts were awarded to twenty-seven companies from nine different countries and by 1983, exploration of the South China Sea had begun in earnest.

Oil exploration in the South China Sea has not been without danger. The area is prone to seasonal typhoons, and on the might of 25 October 1983, the US drillship Glomar Java Sea (which was working on the Arco block) sank off the southern coast of Hainan in a typhoon. Eighty-one persons were killed in this accident -- half of them Chinese and half expatriate oil workers and advisors. Because the bodies proved hard to recover (many were trapped in the rig as it went down), there were early rumours that Vietnamese gunboats may have attacked the rig and that crewmen might be held in Vietnam. However, this incident was one case in which the Vietnamese showed a willingness to co-operate with both Chinese and Americans -- and, in fact, a number of Vietnamese vessels joined in the search for survivors. In investigating the incident, the US National Transportation Safety Board concluded that there was no evidence of explosions or ramming by another vessel and that the probable cause of the disaster was the flooding of the rig's standard wing tanks, through a fracture in the hull. The force of the storm was blamed for the structural damage.

Drilling results on first-round contract areas have been mixed at best. The Pearl River Basin area south of Hong Kong has been the biggest disappointment. Of 20 exploration wells drilled by the end of 1984, only four ranked as discoveries with commercial potential. Three fields have been discovered by Esso, Phillips, and the ACT (Agip-Chevron-Texaco) consortium. All three fields are thought to be in the small-to-medium reserves range. Largely because of the falling price of crude petroleum in the international market, no decision had been made at the time of writing to develop these discoveries.

The lack of large initial petroleum finds does not, in itself, prove that the South China Sea has little potential for oil production. As a comparison it took fifteen years to find major deposits in the North Sea. The international oil industry has not been unduly discouraged by the initial drilling results. But by 1985, in the middle of a slumping world oil market, foreign oil companies perceived the costs and risks of China's offshore development to be high. This perception coloured the industry reaction to the second Chinese invitation to bid on offshore areas.

For the second round of bidding, China offered 22 blocks, 16 of them in the South China Sea. By early July, 1985, 23 foreign companies organised into nine corsortia had bid on these blocks. Several second-round contracts were awarded by the end of the year (Huanan, Phillips, ACT). Given the drilling results on the first-round contract areas, the foreign oil companies were pressing CNOOC for contract concessions and lower operating costs during the negotiations. In order to encourage development of small fields, CNOOC dropped the 12.5 per cent royalty on output from fields producing less than 20,000 barrels per day. The 'x-factor' crude split terms have been allowed to slide in favour of the oil companies for small fields, raising the incentive for development of fields in the size range typical of early discoveries. If initial drilling is unsuccessful, exploratory drilling commitments may be 'rolled over' to new or expanded contract areas.(19) These concessions reflect objective supply and demand conditions in the world oil market and are a sign of increasing realism and flexibility on the Chinese side.

OFFSHORE SUPPORT AND COASTAL DEVELOPMENT

Even during the early exploration phase, the offshore oil projects have contributed substantially to coastal development, particulary along the southern coastline of Guangdong Province and Hainan Island. Four major supply bases have been established, including one in the Bohai Gulf, one at Shanghai on the Yellow Sea, and two on the south China coast (Shekou/Chiwan and Zhanjiang). These bases have contributed substantially to the coastal transportation and communications network.

Once the foreign oil workers and equipment began to arrive in the South China Sea, the Chinese were made sharply aware of the inadequacy of their offshore support capability. In the early 1980s the Chinese began to improve the offshore support capacity of the coastal area. For example, the Chinese have made efforts to improve offshore telecommunications in the South China Sea. In 1985, a Chinese company, the Huaying Nanhai Oil Telecommunications Service Company, placed a large order with a British firm for civil radio equipment. (Huaying is a joint venture between Cable and Wireless and China Nanhai Oil Corporation).(20) Also in 1985, a modern communications centre was completed in Zhanjiang. With a new receiving station, a transmitting station and a modern communications building, this facility substantially upgrades Zhanjiang's offshore communications capabilities.(21)

The offshore helicopter service sector provides a concrete example of the problems and promise of China's offshore support sector. With limited Chinese capability for offshore helicopter support, the number of western helicopters in the South China Sea increased as offshore oil exploration took off. Bell, Sikorsky and Aerospaciale helicopters fly out of Zhuhai and Shekou, with Chinese pilots flying the aircraft and supervision and support from western helicopter companies. The foreign helicopter companies supporting these efforts in offshore oil exploration share maintenance and fueling facilities at Zhuhai and pool weather information.(22) As of March, 1985, about 20 - 25 helicopters operated in the South China Seas area in support of offshore development efforts.(23)

In 1985 the Chinese also upgraded their offshore helicopter service capability when they instituted an airboard helicopter tracking system with base stations in Guangzhou, Zhuhai, and Zhanjiang. All helicopters operating in the South China Sea will be required to be equipped with special airbord telemetry units which interface with VFL/OMEGFA navigation systems and coding altimeters.(24)

This kind of improvement in regional air navigational capability, should decrease the chance of accidents such as the one which occured in 1984. On 1 November 1984, an S-76 helicopter chartered by Pennzoil crashed into the Gulf of Tonkin with two

Chinese and three expatriates aboard. The five persons had been flying from an offshore rig, the jackup Nanhai IV in block 22/36 of the Gulf. All five persons were killed.(25)

Two months after the crash, the US Federal Aviation Administration issued a report on its preliminary investigation. According to the report, a rotor had burst in two of the three turbine engines, and the pilot had shut down the remaining good engine for unknown reasons. The report also discovered a fatigue problem in the coupling which contributed to a turbine failure.(26) The investigation into the accident demonstrated Chinese willingness to co-operate with international investigative bodies. The investigation team consisted of the Civil Aviation Administration of China (CAAC), the US National Transportation Safety Board, and Sikorsky Aircraft, the helicopter manufacturer.(27)

Offshore exploration activities in the South China Sea have been supported out of two main base facilities -- Zhanjiang on the Gulf of Tonkin, and the Chiwan/Shekou area just north of Hong Kong near the Shenzhen Special Economic Zone. In addition, ARCO has provided some ancillary support out of the port of Sanya on the southern tip of Hainan Island.

Zhanjiang

The Zhanjiang supply base is located 400 kilometres southwest of Hong Kong on the eastern side of the Leizhou Peninsula. Zhanjiang itself is a former French colonial enclave with two small industrial towns, a naval base and a very large, and very ancient port. The Chinese have ambitious plans to turn Zhanjiang into a major petroleum industrial centre in the mid-1980s, but they still have a long way to go.

Although telecommunications facilities had improved somewhat by 1985, transportation links between Zhanjiang, Guangzhou and Hong Kong are still very poor, and many other support problems remain to be resolved. International oil company personnel who are used to the sometimes primitive working conditions in other areas of the world, have been particularly upset by Zhanjiang's facilities -- not so much because they are inadequate, as because the Chinese charge abnormally high rents and fees for the local services. In 1983, for example, a single telephone instrument (not the line) went for US $1,000. Office rents in Zhanjiang still rival those in Hong Kong.(28)

In March, 1985, Zhanjiang announced plans to build a new 'economic and technical development zone' in which advanced technology (including foreign technology) will be brought in to help develop a wide variety of new industries. These industries will include fisheries, household appliance manufacturing, biotechnology, and scientific and medical research. The main focus of the new development effort, however, will be to develop Zhanjiang's ports, upgrade its capability to manufacture and maintain vessels and to produce the parts and equipment necessary for offshore oil exploration and development.(29) Zhanjiang also has plans to build a major new oil refinery, which would include a catalytic cracking unit.(30)

Zhuhai

Another support base (still very much in the development stage) is the Zhuhai Special Economic Zone, located on the western bank of the Pearl River estuary, directly north of Macau. In 1985 Zhuhai awarded contracts to French and Hong Kong firms to develop a deep water port, an offshore supply base, and a commercial and residential building complex, The total cost of this development will be over US $40 million.(31) When completed these facilities will compete directly with the nearby Shekou/Chiwan complex on the Nantou Peninsula.

The Nantou Peninsula

To the northeast near Hong Kong, the Chinese are putting major effort into developing the Nantou Peninsula as an important offshore supply base. Shekou, on the western tip of the peninsula, is an established general cargo port. Because of space limitations, the use of Shekou as a supply base will eventually be integrated into newer and larger facilities at Chiwan, three kilometres further west, which was designed and constructed specifically to support offshore exploration and development activities.

Plans for the development of the Nantou Peninsula have been ambitious -- some say too ambitious, given the uncertainty of offshore oil development. For example, in March, 1984, China began developing the Nantou Petroleum Base, located inland from Shekou and Chiwan. By November of that year, over 30 million yuan (US $10 million) had been spent on the project. When completed, the base will include facilities such as 18 modern apartment buildings for Chinese and foreign professional workers; and an 18 storey service building, which will house a bar, a department store and a grocery.(32)

The Nantou Development Corporation is involved in other ambitious development efforts. In May 1985, an agreement was signed with Mutual Oil of America to co-operate in building four major projects -- an oil refinery, harbor facilities, a railroad, and an international information centre. Total cost for this project will likely be over US $450 million. When it is completed, Nantou hopes it can offer a wide range of attractive support services for offshore oil development efforts.(33)

Critics have charged that efforts like these are premature, and overly ambitious in terms of short-term market demand. Most foreign companies prefer to keep front end costs down during the exploration phase. Until the time major fields are discovered offshore, the Chinese may find little demand for their modern apartments and other facilities. Whatever the economic arguments for such investment, there is little doubt that these projects are a near-term stimulus to coastal development. Furthermore, the more China invests in the coastal areas along the South China Sea, the greater its stake in the continued stability and security of the region as a whole.

Hainan Island

To date, Hainan Island has not played a major support role for offshore oil activities, but as China has focused more attention on the South China Sea area, Hainan has come in for its share of development benefits. The island has long been one of China's most primitive areas. Until recently, it was largely inhabited by minority peoples and was often seen as a sort of unofficial banishment by those military or government officials who were assigned to the island. The combination of a sizable minority population and disgruntled Han Chinese residents has led to racial tensions in the past. The situation was further aggravated by a number of demobilised soldiers who were settled on the island and who competed with the local inhabitants for Hainan's resources.

Because of Hainan's strategic location, near Vietnam and major international shipping lanes, it is to China's advantage to foster a stable social, economic and political environment on the island. Beijing has made substantial efforts to improve infrastructure, communications, and shore facilities. Efforts are also being made to attract foreign and domestic Chinese investment to Hainan in such areas as mining, agriculture and food processing, construction, and tourism. Hainan is a special area in terms of investment and development.

Hainan will eventually also become a focal area for petroleum development. At present, ARCO runs transport helicopters out to its rigs from Sanya, where a small satellite supply base has been established. Assuming the the ARCO natural gas field is developed, a gas delivery pipeline and fertiliser plant will be built on Hainan, stimulating a massive input of foreign construction capital. Land oil exploration concessions have recently been offered in three sections of the northern coast of Hainan. One exploration contract with an Australian consortium has already been signed, and drilling will probably begin during 1986. Significant oil discoveries would add to the strategic and commercial importance of the island.

CHINA'S POLITICAL RELATIONS IN THE SOUTH CHINA SEA

Twenty years ago, China was totally isolated from the international community. Even ten years ago, in 1975, Mao Zedong was still in power and China continued to look inward, preoccupied by the aftermath of the Cultural Revolution. But after Deng Xiaoping and his supports ascended to power in the late 1970s China's international posture began to change. In trade relations, Beijing implemented an open door commercial policy, to increase its exports while acquiring modern techology and attracting foreign capital and expertise. On the political side, China became a much more visible actor in many international arenas ranging from support for Third World positions in the United Nations to security co-operation with the NATO countries. In the 1980s China has demonstrated increasing willingness to negotiate differences with its neighbors and has made attempts to lessen longstanding friction with regional neighbors such as South Korea, Malaysia and Indonesia. Most importantly, the PRC has evolved a strategic entente with the United States that has fundamentally altered political relations throughout the Western Pacific.

Despite the progress, there are many residual tensions between China and its regional neighbors. These tensions offset the movement toward stability and co-operative development of the marine and hydrocarbon resources of the South China Sea. The 'jurisdictional disputes' between China and its Southeast Asian neighbours regarding sovereignty over the South China Sea are usually seen as a principal cause of intra-regional rivalry and tension between China and its neighbours. In fact, if one observes the rise and fall of intensity in the jurisdictional disputes carefully, it soon becomes apparent that rhetoric over the jurisdictional disputes follows, rather than leading, tensions on other more pressing issues.

Taiwan

Before we look at China's relations with its neighbours in the South China Sea area, we should briefly mention the 'Taiwan question'. Taiwan is located at the northern edge of the South China Sea. Although Taiwan has made claims to the Spratley Islands, it has not been a major actor in the South China Sea area in recent years. Taipei's major effect on the politics of the South China Sea has been an indirect one. The Taiwan issue has remained a persistent sore point in U.S.-China relations and has had a limiting effect on security co-operation. Taiwan also competes politically and commercially with China in Hong Kong and in Southeast Asia. For example, Taiwan was able to keep the PRC out of the Asian Development Bank until very recently and has kept its seat in the ADB despite Chinese entry. Taiwan's economy is considerably more developed and trade oriented than China's, enabling the island to maintain a strong commercial presence even in countries in the region that have developed close political ties to the PRC. On the other hand, no government in the region takes seriously Taiwan's quixotic claims to legitimacy as the government of China.

China and Vietnam

China and Vietnam saw a steady deterioration of relations in the years after 1974. Up to this time Beijing supported Hanoi's efforts to reunify Vietnam by force and eject the United States from Indochina. During this period China and Vietnam were, in Mao's words, 'as close as lips and teeth'. In 1979 periodic military skirmishes on the Sino-Vietnamese border escalated into full-scale military conflict, as Chinese groups crossed over the border 'to teach Vietnam a lesson'. The PLA's undistinguished showing during the conflict was a serious loss of face for China, as Chinese divisions were forced to

face for China, as Chinese divisions were forced to withdraw with severe casualities -- estimates range from 10,000 to 20,000 dead.

Since 1979, relations have not been cordial between the two Communist neighbours, but escalation of border tensions seems to be triggered more by heightened Vietnamese military activities in Cambodia than by local incidents along the Sino-Vietnamese border itself. China has been the major source of financial aid and armaments for the Khmer Rouge, guerillas whom the Vietnamese overthrew in 1978 in order to install pro-Vietnam government in Phnom Penh.

One major problem facing the Chinese along its border region with Vietnam is the 280,000 Vietnamese refugees who have fled north into China. This number is second only to the number of Vietnamese refugees hosted by the United States. Although the United Nations has given US $3.9 million to help resettle the Vietnamese (and plans to give an additional US $12 million between 1986 and 1988) China says it has had to spend a substantial addtional sum to meet all the needs of these refugees. China has, in fact, reported to the United Nations High Commission on Refugees (UNHCR) that it will be very difficult for China to accept any more Vietnamese refugees because of the financial burden they impose on China.

Most of the refugees are of Chinese ethnic descent, and have been resettled primarily in southern and southeast coastal provinces-- Yunnan, Guangdong, Fujian, Jiangxi and Guangxi. In contrast to other countries in the region, China has offered the Vietnamese refugees permanent asylum. The UNHCR considers the resettlement program an overall success -- although there have been some problems while the Vietnamese, many of whom were formerly urban residents, try to adjust to life on the Chinese state-run farms where most now live. China has made some attempts to place refugees in appropriate work where possible. For example, about 11,000 Vietnamese fishermen have been resettled in Beihai on the Gulf of Tonkin and are working as trawlermen.(34)

From 1979 to 1984, during the winter dry season, hostilities escalated between Vietnamese and the Cambodian guerillas. And each year, China stepped up military pressure along the Sino-Vietnamese border, Hanoi's 'back door'. These border conflicts also serve the needs of Vietnam's ally, the Sovet Union, by drawing China's military

By 1985, China's military readiness along the Sino-Vietnamese border was far higher than in 1979, thanks to a Chinese build-up of infrastructure in the region. It has been difficult to verify exact events during these seasonal border hostilities -- since Chinese and Vietnamese versions have differed considerably, and because neither side has allowed independent observation in the mountainous border area. Both sides present each incident for maximum propaganda advantage, each side portraying the other as the aggressor.

The war of words may sometimes, in fact, have been fiercer than the actual border hostilities, for both sides have an interest in preventing an all-out border war. For example, China has spoken regularly of 'teaching Vietnam another lesson', but at the same time, Chinese military leaders have insisted that China will not jeopardise its domestic economic development by pursuing military 'adventures' with Vietnam.(35)

Even on the level of rhetoric along, however, China has developed a mixed message. In December, 1984 China began propaganda broadcasts to Vietnam from Guangxi. These broadcasts are intended to present China's people and policies in a favourable light while 'to establish in the minds of the Vietnamese people the image of socialist new China', and at the same time to put political pressure on Vietnam's rulers -- especially as regards the Vietnamese incursion into Cambodia.(36) But in the midst of the 1984-5 dry season hostilities, China took several opportunities to proffer an olive branch. China announced it would release 15 captured Vietnamese in time to reunite them with their families for the Lunar New Year. In another instance Chinese Foreign Minister Wu Xueqian sent a congratulatory message to the Vietnamese Foreign Minister on the thirtieth anniversary of the establishment of diplomatic relations between the two countries. Wu Xueqian's message said that the Chinese value friendly relations with Vietnam and would make every effort to re-establish good relations.(37)

Vietnam, for its part, has also delivered a mixed message. For example, Vietnam has kept up its bellicose rhetoric (accusing the Chinese of 'land grabbing operations' on its northern border in early 1985), but at the same time, is indicating a cautious interest in re-establishing diplomatic relations with China.(38)

One major reason for this confusing mixture of

friendship and hostility is that in spite of the war of words and the border clashes, China's indirect trade with Vietnam has continued to grow. Hong Kong government statistics indicate that unofficial trade between China and Vietnam (using Hong Kong as a middleman) reached US $32.05 million in 1984, almost twice the 1983 figure. Chinese goods sold to Vietnam consisted primarily of textile yarn and fabrics, while Vietnam supplied crude industrial goods and foodstuffs to China.(39) As close neighbours, China and Vietnam have much to offer each other as trading partners, and leaders in the two countries are allowing this to influence their relations to a greater and greater extent. In fact, the beginning of the 1985 monsoon season (and the concomitant decrease in military hostilities in Cambodia and along the Sino-Vietnamese border) saw the first private high-level meetings between Chinese and Vietnamese personnel since 1979,when Vietnam's ex-minister of foreign trade, Phan Anh, met with Chinese foreign trade chief, Li Qiang in May, 1985.(40) It is no coincidence that these initiatives have paralleled the relaxation of political relations between China and the Soviet Union, which have featured bilateral talks up to the level of Minister of Foreign Relations during 1985.

Jurisdictional Disputes in the South China Sea

As in the case of their border conflict, Chinese and Vietnamese attitudes towards offshore jurisdictional disputes have been marked by a mixture of overt hostility and apparent willingness to overlook differences in the near term. The early 1980s saw a number of offshore skirmishes between vessels from the two countries. For example, on 4 March 1982, immediately after the announcement of round one of bidding, the Chinese navy seized a Vietnamese fishing vessel which, it said had fired on three Chinese fishing boats.(41) The next year, on 11 October 1983, the Chinese Foreign Ministry lodged a protest with the Vietnese Embassy in Beijing, claiming that Vietnamese gunboats had intercepted and robbed two Chinese fishing vessels on the high seas of the Gulf of Tonkin, and had fired at two other Chinese fishing boats working off the Chinese coast. And in early 1985, Vietnam's official army newspaper reported that Chinese naval vessels has penetrated deep into Vietnamese territorial waters as part of a military build up along the Sino-Vietnamese border.(42)

Such hostilities in the South China Sea have

Such hostilities in the South China Sea have occurred against a backdrop of complicated jurisdictional disputes. As far back as 1974, the Chinese used force to establish their ascendency over the Paracel Islands. In September, 1973, the South Vietnamese government incorporated eleven of the thirty-three Spratley Islands into Phuoc Tuy Province. China responded in early 1974 with a relatively large combined, land, sea and air assault which swept the Vietnamese from the Paracel Islands. Even in the mid-1970s, though, regional stability in the South China Sea area was important to China, and once Beijing's control had been established over the Spratley, China took some pains to reassure its neighbours -- notably the members of the new-formed ASEAN -- that this would not affect China's relationship with them.(43)

China and Vietnam met in the late 1970s to try to resolve boundary disputes in the Tonkin Gulf and elsewhere, but both sides failed to reach an agreement.(44) In 1982 Hanoi issued a White Paper affirming Vietnam's claims to the Xisha Islands, Nansha Islands, and a large part of the Tonkin Gulf. This brought Vietnam into conflict with claims of Indonesia, the Philippines and China. Thailand and China both immediately re-affirmed their own claims, and China warned Vietnam against interfering with China's oil exploration in the Tonkin Gulf. Vietnam, for its part, issued a series of strong protests over joint Chinese-foreign drilling in the Gulf of Tonkin during the first round of bids in early 1983. According to the official Vietnam News Agency, China was 'encroaching on Vietnam's sovereignty' in granting foreign oil companies permission to explore for oil and gas in the Gulf of Tonkin. Furthermore, Vietnam warned that foreign oil exploration and development companies 'must bear all the consequences' of the alleged violation of Vietnam's sovereignty.(45) China responded to this by repeating its territorial claims to the Gulf of Tonkin, and rejecting Vietnam's 1982 White Paper claims.(46)

During this same period, in spite of its tough public position on sovereignty, Vietnam was assuring Thailand that it was willing to settle disputes through negotiation 'in conformity with international law and practice'. As was mentioned earlier the Vietnamese willingness to co-operate was demonstrated in practice when two Vietnamese naval vessels joined US and Chinese vessels in their efforts to locate the *Glomar Java Sea*, a drillship which capsized off of Hainan Island in October 1983.(47)

While demonstrating their willingness to co-operate with Vietnam in specific cases such as this, the Chinese have also used many forums to reiterate their claims to South China Sea Islands. For example, the head of the Chinese delegation to the 1984 world meteorological conference used that forum to criticise Vietnam's attempt to establish meteorological stations on islands in the South China Sea claimed by China -- including the long-contested Spratleys (Nansha) and the Paracels (Xisha).(48)

Vietnam and the USSR

Because of mounting economic problems, exacerbated by rapid population growth and economically draining military operations in neighbouring Cambodia, Vietnam has had to rely on all of Vietnam's fuel needs and much of Vietnam's fertiliser and heavy equipment. The total Soviet non-military aid package to Vietnam has been running over US $1 billion per year since 1980.(49) In addition, Moscow also provides substantial military aid to Hanoi. The U.S. Defense Department reported that in 1984 the Soviets supplied Hanoi with military equipment which included combat helicopters, fighter aircraft, and missile attack boats.(50)

In return for such assistance Moscow has gained a base for reconnaisance, a convenient anchorage for the Soviet Pacific fleet at Cam Ranh Bay (the deep water port built by the United States during its conflict with Vietnam). Hanoi is sensitive to accusation that this gives the Soviets a long-term base on Vietnamese soil. Possibly because of this, by late 1984, the Soviet presence in Cam Ranh Bay was still not a permanent one. Most Soviet assets were movable such as floating dry dock, refuel and repair facilities. The Soviets built their own, comparatively small, installations, and have not taken over the large components built by the U.S. in the early 1970s.(51)

China has been concerned about having a Soviet military presence near its southern border, and has regularly complained to the Vietnamese that Cam Ranh has become a Soviet military base for conventional weapons. In addition, in October 1984, China for the first time accused the Soviets of deploying nuclear weapons at Cam Ranh Bay.(52)

The Soviets' tacit support for Vietnamese incursion into Cambodia has also been extremely frustating for China, and on 17 April 1985 Deng Xiaoping appealed publicly for the Soviet Union to help persuade Vietnam to decrease its active military involvement in Cambodia. So important do the Chinese consider this, that Deng suggested for the first time that China would accept the presence of a Soviet naval base at Cam Ranh Bay if the Soviets could convince the Vietnamese to withdraw from Cambodia.(53)

The fluidity of Sino-Soviet relations was underscored when Soviet Foreign Minister Eduard Shevardnadze and China's Foreign Minister Wu Xueqian met on 26-27 September 1985 at the UN. This meeting was followed in December as Soviet Vice-Foreign Minister Mikhail Kapitsa visited Beijing for ten days to set an agenda for an exchange of delegations at the level of Foreign Minister in the first half of 1986. The Chinese have reassured the US that an easing of Sino-Soviet tensions would be contingent on resolution of outstanding differences over Vietnamese occupation of Cambodia, Soviet occupation of Afghanistan, and the withdrawal of forces from the Sino-Soviet border. The Soviets are unlikely to be responsive on any of these three fundamental issues. However, there is considerable room for improvement of relations on secondary issues, such as the Soviet naval presence in the South China Sea. Sino-Soviet trade relations are also improving, and Beijing has projected two-way trade at about US $3 billion per year by 1990.

Vietnam's Offshore Development

Vietnam began exploring its continental shelf in the early 1970s. Early exploration focused on the Mekong River estuary in the south. In 1973, the government of South Vietnam awarded exploration contracts to several US-based firms for drilling offshore the Mekong Delta. Of four initial wells, one (Mobil's Bach Ho discovery) tested at 2,500 barrels per day. When Saigon fell in 1975, the US oil companies were forced to abandon their exploration programmes in the area.

Three years later, in 1978, Vietnam signed contracts with Agip (Italy), Deminex (West Germany), and Bow Valley (Canada) to resume exploration off the Mekong Delta. The three companies developed a support base at Vung Tau, drilled 12 dry holes, and spent almost US $100 million. By 1980, however, all of them had run into contract negotiation obstacles and had pulled out of Vietnam.

Meanwhile, the Soviet Union entered into an

discovery (Bach Ho) jointly with the Vietnamese. A joint venture, Vietsovpetro, was set up in June 1981.(54) Most of Vietsovpetro's offshore efforts have been in the south, near Ho Chi Minh City (formerly Saigon), with the port city of Vung Tau as the base of exploration. In 1984 an estimated 700 Soviet technicians and dependents lived at Vung Tau, and by 1985, this number had increased to about 1,000.(55)

On 26 May 1984 after over three years of joint exploration, the Vietnamese and Soviets announced a bed of oil and gas had been discovered at an unidentified location at a depth of 3,000 metres.(56) In 1984 the Soviets and Vietnamese began a joint seismic survey of the Tonkin Gulf waters. In early 1985 Vietnam announced that it identified an estimated one billion tons in reserves, and that it would begin producing several million tons of oil by the end of 1985, with production increasing to 10 million tons per year (over 200,000 b/d) in three or four years. Production would be from an oil field 100 kilometres off Vung Tau (possibly the old Mobil Bach Ho discovery).(57) On 26 June 1985 the Vietsovpetro began drilling operations on the southern continental shelf. Crude oil from these fields will likely be shared by the Soviet Union and Vietnam.(58)

Vietnam has also looked to other countries as possible partners for developing its offshore oil resources. In 1984 Vietnam asked India for help in its offshore exploration activities and made arrangments to charter an offshore rig owned by the Indian Oil and Natural Gas Commission.(59) The next year, (1985), Vietnam began discussions with two Australian companies (CSR and BHP) regarding exploration offshore Vietnam.(60) In addition, Kaiyo Oil company (Japan) and Elf Aquitaine (France) have been negotiating to developing several offshore blocks with Petro-Vietnam. These blocks are located southeast of Ho Chi Minh City. Recently, Vietnam agreed to award an offshore block to Agip, Italy's State-owned oil company.(61)

There are both commercial and political obstacles to the participation of Western oil companies in exploration off the Vietnamese coast. Most of the companies talking to Vietnam already have exploration agreements with China. Beijing would without question object to the same companies having exploration contracts in areas of the Tonkin Gulf contested with Vietnam. The home governments for many of the same companies have outstanding differences with Vietnam and have urged these companies to move cautiously on new exploration contracts. Western participation in oil exploration in Vietnam will, therefore, move forward gradually as the overall climate of relations improves.

In addition to China and Vietnam, a number of other countries should be considered in any discussion of the development of the South China Sea. In recent years, most of these countries have seen increased levels of economic co-operation and trade with their powerful neighbour to the north -- even in the case of Singapore and Indonesia, which do not have formal diplomatic relations with China. These countries do not all lie along the South China Sea coast, but all are important regional actors whose relations with China (and with each other) affect the overall development climate for South China Sea activities.

Thailand

Thailand has had diplomatiac relations with China since 1975. Since this period, the volume of bilateral trade rose from US $23 million to US $330 million in 1984.(62) During most of this period, the balance of trade has been in China's favour, mostly because of the value of its oil sales to Thailand.(63) Vietnamese military actions in Cambodia, along the Thai border have thrown Beijing and Bangkok closer together during this period and military leaders of both countries have exchanged regular visits. China has given Thailand humanitarian assistance to help deal with Cambodian refugees who have poured over the border into Thailand. Recently, for example, China donated US $1 million to the Thai Red Cross Society for relief efforts.(64)

Burma

China has maintained diplomatic relations with Burma since 1950, and has encouraged trade in such items as textiles, light machinary and chemical products in return for Burmese rice, jade and timber.(65) In 1984 Sino-Burmese trade reached a value of nearly US $420 million. China has recently moved to further improve trade relations, for example, by replacing local regulations for trade across the Sino-Burmese border. China also scheduled a joint Burmese-Chinese border inspection in the latter part of 1985 to clarify boundaries.(66)

Malaysia

China's relations with Malaysia are basically cordial, though Malaysia is one of its larger neighbours and not entirely convinced that China will keep its hands off Malaysian internal affairs. About forty per cent of Malaysia's citizens are ethnic Chinese with family ties in China, and Malaysia has attempted to keep tight control over its citizens who wish to travel to China. More serious, however, is the Malaysian accusation that China has ties with the outlawed Communist Party of Malaysia. In addition, Malaysia suffered trade deficits with China from 1981-4 and there has been a certain amount of tension in Kuala Lumpur arising from this fact. However, both countries have made efforts to resolve the difficulties in their relationship. In July, 1985 the Malaysian government produced a comprehensive assessment of the Sino-Malaysian relationship. This report made a number of concrete suggestions for improving commercial and investment ties with China while retaining a vigilant posture on political and security issues.

China, too, wants to foster good relations with Malaysia. Chinese industry is interested in certain Malaysian products like rubber, and good relations are essential for the continued development of trade. China has demonstrated its willingness to invest in this trade relationship. China's first direct containership service between China and Southeast Asia, for example, was from Shanghai to Port Kelang, Malaysia.(67)

Philippines

China and the Philippines have had diplomatic relations since 1975. In 1984 China and the Philippines traded an estimated US $280.4 million in goods, with the Philippines running a trade deficit of about US $160 million.(68) Most of China's exports to the Philippines consisted of crude oil, for example, in 1984, China delivered 770,000 metric tons of crude oil to the Philippines. Philippine exports to China are mostly light industrial products, food and animal and vegetable oils.(69) In a 1985 trade protocol, China agreed to import other products -- including copper cathodes and phosphate fertilisers -- in order to help the Philippines offset its trade deficit with China. Under this protocol, China and the Philippines would increase their trade to US $500 million per year.(70)

The Philippines, like its neighbours China and

Vietnam, is very interested in developing its offshore resources. In 1985, the Philippines acquired a 500-ton, US $8.65-million research vessel. This was the Philippines' first geophysical survey ship and will be used to study and evaluate offshore structures and deposits.(71) The Philippines also maintains a small garrison in the Spratleys, along with Taiwan and Vietnam, and has never recognised Chinese claims to the area.

Singapore

Singapore and China do not have diplomatic relations, but economic ties have expanded considerably in the last few years. Trade reached US $1.4 billion in 1984, over 50 per cent higher than 1983.(72) Furthermore, from 1979 to 1984, Singapore citizens invested almost US $900 million in China.(73) Singapore refineries have processed Chinese crude oil for a number of years. The Singapore Petroleum Company, for example, began processing Shengli crude in 1980.(74) By 1985 contracts to process Chinese crudes had reached 100,000 barrels per day and had become a significant factor for Singapore's depressed refining industry. In 1985, Singapore and China set up a joint investment corporaton (the CIT-VIC Corporation) to establish joint ventures inside and outside of China.(75)

Both countries seem to want to improve their relations. For example, on its side the Singapore Immigration Office eased restrictions in February 1985 on Singaporeans travelling to China. Because of this, Singaporeans will no longer need to show a letter of invitation from relatives in China before receiving permission to travel.(76) But commercial ties will continue to move well ahead of political relations for the foreseeable future.

Indonesia

Like Singapore, Indonesia has no direct diplomatic relations with China. In 1967 Indonesia suspended diplomatic ties with China, claiming that China backed the Indonesia Communist Party during a 1965 abortive coup attempt. China has made overtures from time to time over the past 18 years, but has always been rebuffed by Indonesia. During this same period, however, China and Indonesia have carried an indirect bilateral trade through Singaporean and Hong Kong middlemen. Recent trade figures valued Indonesian exports to China at US $24 million, and Chinese exports to Indonesia at over US $200 million.(77)

Indonesia still has serious qualms about re-establishing diplomatic relations with China. Some Indonesians resent the economic influence of ethnic Chinese in Indonesia and on more than one occasion racial tensions have exploded into widespread violence. Indonesia has also recently gained a heightened visibility among non-aligned Third World nations and many observers believe that Jakarta wants a leadership role among this group.(78) For example, Indonesia has played an active role in seeking a regional solution to the Vietnamese occupation of Cambodia.

Indonesia's overall attitude to China is beset by contradictions. On the one hand, Jakarta sees Beijing's growing economic and political power as a threat to the stability of the region. On the other hand, it sees China as a promising market for non-oil exports like rubber, tea, coffee, and wood.(79) During a period when Indonesia's chief export, petroleum, faces a weak world market, Indonesia has been willing to encourage the resumption of direct trade with China, and has hinted at the possible future resumption of diplomatic ties if China agrees not to support Communist movements in the region.(80)

But China is a direct commercial threat as well as a potential customer. In addition to falling oil revenues Indonesia has also been hit with the problem of increased competition from China as an oil exporter. China produces 2.5 million barrels a day and is the largest Asian oil producer. A member of the Organisation of Petroleum Exporting Countries (OPEC), Indonesia produces just over one million barrels of oil per day. Chinese oil exports have increased to about 700,000 barrels of oil per day, more than Indonesia is permitted under its OPEC ceiling. China is not an OPEC member and is not subject to OPEC price or production guidelines. This places China in a more competitive position than Indonesia, and China has, in fact, been cutting into major Indonesian markets like the US and Japan.(81) In May, 1985, Indonesia's President Suharto complained publicly that Japan was not keeping its promise to buy at least 15 per cent of its total oil imports from Indonesia. In 1984 Japan only imported 13 per cent of its total from Indonesia. In 1985 this figure dropped to 12 per cent while the Chinese market share jumped to 18 per cent.(82) Japan, for its part, has maintained a tough bargaining stance, telling Indonesia that it must give better terms for crude sales to compete successfully against the similar, and less expensive, Daqing crude.

Overall, the economies of the Southeast Asia nations have been stable and prosperous in recent years. The economies of the Association of Southeast Asian Nations (ASEAN) have grown at an average of 7 per cent a year over the last decade, and this is about twice the global average, discounting for inflation.(83)

As their economies continue to develop, it is to the advantage of ASEAN nations to assist each other economically in order to ensure the continued stability of the region. For example, in 1985 ASEAN energy ministers meeting in Bangkok considered a proposal in which the Philippines, Singapore and Thailand would help buy oil from oil-producing countries (Brunei, Indonesia and Malaysia) if the oil export levels of the latter three countries fall below 80 per cent of normal levels.(84)

As a group, ASEAN members have been wary of their giant neighbour to the north -- seeing China as a promising market, especially for raw materials, while remaining suspicious of China's long term goals in the region. Some of this suspicion has been based on China's reported suport of Communist guerilla groups in Malaysia, Indonesia and Thailand. Possibly to allay such fears, and to contribute to the stabilisation of the region, China recently called off its support for Communist insurgents in Thailand.

Hong Kong and Macao

Leftovers from Europe's days of imperial glory, the colonies of Hong Kong and Macao sit on China's southern flank. Given China's rhetoric against imperialism and the evils of colonialism, it might be expected that Beijing would resent the presence of Great Britain (in Hong Kong) and Portugal (in Macoa) on what had been Chinese territory until the 1800s. China has, in fact, always refused to recognise either the New Territories Lease or the 'unequal treaties' of 1842 and 1860 which ceded Hong Kong Island and Kowloon to Britain. But as it moved into a less isolationist international posture in the late 1970s, Beijing demonstrated increased willingness to negotiate with both Britain and Portugal to find a satisfactory solution.

Of the two colonies, Macao has posed less of a problem. Macao has always been less economically important than Hong Kong and its recovery has seemed less important to Beijing. China and Portugal have enjoyed good relations since a coup in the mid-1970s installed a socialist government in Lisbon. Embarassed by the colonial baggage it had inherited the new socialist government reportedly offered to return Macao to China. The offer was politely refused at the time, and the Macao issue remained on the back burner until 1985, when China and Portugal announced that they would open talks on the eventual return of Macao to Chinese rule. It is likely that both sides were encouraged by the outcome of the 1984 Sino-British talks which outlined the procedure for returning Hong Kong to the Chinese. Given the recent smooth relations between Portugal and China, few observers see any major problems in any transfer of power.

In the case of Hong Kong, the economic stakes -- and the potential for disagreement -- are much higher. Hong Kong has become increasingly important as a conduit for Chinese trade. In 1984, for example, China imported US $1.4 billion worth of goods from Hong Kong. In the same year, Hong Kong's imports from China came to US $7.2 billion. Hong Kong is also heavily engaged in the re-export of goods to the international market. In 1984 this market amounted to US $3.6 billion.(85)

In September, 1984, British Ambassador Sir Richard Evans and Chinese Vice Foreign Minister Zhou Nan initialled a joint declaration which outlined the conditions of Hong Kong's return to China in 1997, and assured Hong Kong residents that their way of life would be 'basically unchanged' for 50 years. Most observers praised the joint declaration for its calm tone and its serious attempt to address troublesome issues in a mutually satisfactory manner. The declaration includes many provisions such as guarantees of human rights and the promise of no exchange controls which are aimed at reassuring Hong Kong's citizens.

The next step is to draft the basic legal framework under which Hong Kong will be governed. This may prove more difficult for the Chinese and British to agree upon, for it is here that the basic legal rights and obligations of Hong Kong's citizens will be ironed out.

It is unlikely, though, that negotiating problems will derail a generally good relationship between China and Great Britain in the period before 1997. It is to Beijing's advantage to encourage the colony's economic development and to increase China's trade with Hong Kong, since both Hong Kong's and China's economies will eventually become one. It is to London's advantage to hand over a thriving Hong Kong in 1997 -- both from the standpoint of international reputation, as well as for potential economic benefits which Britain might gain in the mean time from its strategically placed international port colony. Therefore, although many details still need to be discussed, 'the Hong Kong question' seems well on its way to a resolution which will satisfy Britain and China. Whether or not the outcome will be favourable to the citizens of Hong Kong remains to be seen. In any event, Hong Kong's strategic position in the South China Sea as an outpost of Western military and commercial power will shift dramatically in the next decade. China's strategic position in the South China Sea will be greatly strengthened by the acquisition of Hong Kong that of the West will be commensurately weakened.

STRATEGIC CONSIDERATIONS IN THE SOUTH CHINA SEA

China has the world's largest land army, the second largest navy and the third-largest air force, China's 1982 national census showed over 4 million people on active military duty, including rear echelons.

Deng Xiaoping, China's most influential leader in the period since Mao's death, has long spoken of the People's Liberation Army (PLA) as 'bloated' and has made control over the military one of his primary objectives. Political considerations as well as concern about overstaffing create this perception, for the PLA was one of the strongholds of support for Mao's policies during the Cultural Revolution, and even into the early 1980s there were reports of PLA resistance to Deng Xiaoping's economic reforms.(86)

Military modernisation came in a low fourth among the Four Modernizations economic reform programme instituted by Deng Xiaoping after Mao's death. From 1979 to 1984 the official military defense budget (about half of real expenditures on the military) declined from 22 billion yuan (US $14 billion) to 18 billion yuan (US $9 billion). This represents a decline of the military budget as part of the national budget from 17 per cent in 1979 to 13 per cent in 1984.(87) In the early 1980s military pay scales were frozen just at the time when economic reforms made it possible for peasants and factory workers to increase their earning dramatically.

The Central government plans a major re-organisation of the People's Liberation Army (PLA) in the period 1985-6. (The PLA also includes China's naval and air forces.) To take but one example, on 9 May, 1985, the Navy issued orders for streamlining and reorganising operations. To show its serious intent, the Navy sent the Commander of its East China Sea Fleet to 'carry out investigations' of the units at one naval base, and presumably to start the reorganisation process.(88) In another example, the Logistics Department of the PLA announced in June 1985 that it would reduce its total staff by 50 per cent. Many of the Logistics Department's existing barracks, warehouses, factories, and transport facilities will be transferred to civilian control.(89)

On a broader scale, in June, 1985 the PLA underwent a massive organisational shake-up, with the total number of military commands reduced from eleven to seven. Eight of the eleven original commanders were either retired or transferred to other, less influential positions. Linked with other efforts to streamline the PLA, including plans to reduce total military manpower from 4 million to 3 million and a drive to remove over-age officers, this reorganisation of the military commands will have far-reaching effects on China's whole military structure.

China seems quite serious about cutting the size of the PLA by one fourth, for the central government has pledged to spend 1 billion yuan (about $330 million) resettling and finding employment for 100,000 demobilised officers plus 400,000 demobilised soldiers. Special meetings were held at the provincial and municipal levels throughout China to prepare the localities to receive the demobilised forces in July 1985.(90)

Coastal Military Organisation

As one of China's major military regions, the Guangzhou Military Region did not lose from the June 1985 reorganisation of the military commands. The Guangzhou Military Region includes Shenzhen, Zhuhai and Shantou Special Economic Zones, the open coastal cities of Guangzhou, Zhanjiang and Beihai, and the Hainan Island Special Economic Zone. The reorganisation added several areas to this base.(91) Thus, the coastal areas of China along the South China Sea have been unified under a single military command that has significant strategic power in the area. The defence of Hong Kong may well be assigned to the Guangzhou Military Region after the reversion treaty takes effect.

There seems to have been substantial resistance within the PLA to opening up this region to foreign interests. Some of this may be ideological, but it may also have sprung from the fact that the economic reform programs in this region required that many PLA units give up, reduce, or share their land, installations or production facilities. This caused widespread resentment at the regimental level, and the Communist Party Committee of the Guangzhou Military Region found it necessary to call a special meeting to pressure the regimental leaders to co-operate with the economic reforms. As a result, the Renmin Ribao reported:

> In Shenzhen and Zhuhai alone, more than 300 military installations made available large tracts of land for facilitating and attracting foreign capital in operating factories and shops and in establishing tourist areas. Some defense islands near the mouth of the Pearl River removed their ban on the entry of guests and merchants and helped the locality establish nine joint enterprises with other nations ... At present, an absolute majority of the military hospitals, guest houses, dining halls, theaters, ball-playing grounds, and swimming areas have been opened to the local people.(92)

The PLA Navy has also been co-operating with local governments along the southern coast to open up certain scenic or historical naval areas to tourists. However, none of these areas are of great importance to China's coastal defence system.(93)

Modernisation of the Navy

Since 1970, in contrast to the other armed services, China's navy has experienced sustained growth. As China has increased its overseas trade and begun serious development of its offshore resources, its economic stake in coastal security has risen. Two top level leaders -- Defense Minister Zhang Aiping and former Assistant Chief of Staff, General Liu Huaqing -- have both been personally involved in the development of a naval modernisation programme designed to make China a major East Asian sea power by the year 2000. A naval modernisation programme designed to make China a major East Asian sea power by the year 2000. Much still needs to be done, however, and indications are that the PLA Navy will not reach full blue-water capability until the 1990s.(94)

New advisory groups have been established to assist the modernisation process, such as the Naval-Military Academic Research Commission, the Scientific and Technological Research Commission, and the Scientific, Cultural and Education Research Commission. Specific new naval modernisation efforts include: increasing levels of education and technical expertise among naval personnel; expanding operating bases; improving command, control, communications and intelligence; increasing use of satellites for reconnaissance, communication and navigation; developing new aerodynamic missile systems and advanced propulsion systems; and production of strategic submarines.(95)

The Chinese are believed to be constructing six nuclear-powered missile submarines. By the end of the decade this will enable China to deploy eighty-four 200-kiloton missiles at sea. Beijing is also building aircraft carriers. As many as five may be planned. These would be 20,000 ton carriers which could each carry as many as 25 helicopters, or 12 vertical/short take-off and landing (VSTOL) aircraft. China currently has no VSTOL aircraft, and thus would either have to purchase them or acquire the technology to build its own.(96)

Despite such efforts, the PLA navy continues to have major problem areas in its outdated radar and sonar capabilities and weaponry systems, unreliable nuclear propulsion systems, scarcity of naval aircraft with long range strike and surveillance capabilities, and antiquated, ineffective mine sweepers.(97)

Chinese wartime contingency planning includes five conventional warfare scenarios involving naval operations. Two of these scenarios involve China's southeastern flank. One deals with the increased Soviet activity in the South China Sea, and especially with the Soviet naval forces based in Vietnam. The other scenario centres on Taiwan and may conceivably involve the South China Sea area in a spill-over effect.(98)

Over the past few years, the PLA Navy has conducted periodic patrols and some large at-sea training exercises in the Gulf of Tonkin, South China Sea, and the Philippine region. China has also upgraded naval bases and facilities for its South China Sea Fleet, and has transferred some ships, submarines and aircraft from other areas into the South China Sea area. Sizable sea infantry forces have been deployed to Hainan Island and some of these units have participated in training activities in the Paracels (Xisha) and other islands.(99) Chinese squadrons have undertaken several sorties into the South China Sea and Philippine Sea. Activities include alongside refueling manoeuvers, and helicopter operations.(100)

Over the past years, the Soviet Union's Far Eastern forces have expanded considerably. The Soviets have built up their fleet of Bear and Badger aircraft, with a wide flight range which can take them throughout the sea lanes of Southeast Asia.(101) The Soviet Union has major naval units in five East Asian areas: The Bering Sea, the Sea of Japan, the Ryuku Island area, west of the Philippines, and the region stretching between Guam and Hawaii. This deployment pattern enables the Soviets to monitor US strategic submarine bases, Chinese sea manoeuvers, as well as general maritime movements from the Aleutian Islands to the Malacca Strait.(102)

The Soviet Pacific Fleet's highest priority is to monitor the movements of the US 7th Fleet. Soviet surveillance of the Japanese Islands and the Japanese Maritime Defense force are of next importance. However, in spite of their preoccupation with the US and Japan, the Soviets do not consider the Chinese Navy a negligible force, and Soviet naval air forces stationed in such places as Cam Ranh Bay in Vietnam also monitor Chinese naval movements. The Soviet facilities at Cam Ranh Bay are a mere 800 miles from the key US bases in the Phillipines.(103)

A Soviet naval squadron at Cam Ranh Bay and reconnaissance aircraft from the Soviet base at Danang carry out surveillance of the South China Coast. At the same time the Soviets are helping to modernise the Vietnamese Navy. For example, Moscow has given Vietnam four Petya Is, one ex-Barnegat frigate fitted with SS-N-2/Styx missiles, an Admirable Class Corvette, four SO1 PC's, a Shershen Class PTF, and eight OSA II Class PTG's.(104)

Concerned by the Soviet naval buildup in the Pacific region, the United States has recently been supportive of China's naval development. At the end of 1984 a Chinese delegation of naval specialists spent six weeks visiting the US. They agreed to buy sonar SX torpedoes, gas turbine engines, and a modern gatling gun designed to shoot down antiship missiles. The total value of the sales was estimated at several million US dollars. The Chinese indicated they would like to manufacture the torpedoes under a license, but would be willing to buy the rest of the equipment outright.(105) Taipei, not surprisingly, reacted negatively to the news of the proposed arms sales, saying its supporters will make every efforts to block the sale in the US Congress.

In January, 1985, General John W. Vessey, Jr., Chairman of the Joint Chiefs of Staff, visited China. He was the highhest ranking American officer to visit China since 1949. General Vessey's visit to China was more important for symbolic reasons than for its practical accomplishments. The trip was a public reminder to the Soviets that many current Soviet foreign policies are worrisome both to China and to the US and gives these two countries a common ground for military co-operation.(106) General Vessey's trip did see the beginning of arrangements for US 7th Fleet destroyers to visit Shanghai in the spring of 1985. This would have been the first US Navy port call to China since 1949. However, this port call was postponed when Beijing insisted that the US ships not carry nuclear arms. Washington in its turn, insisted on following its longstanding policy of not divulging whether or not US ships carry nuclear arms. This incident illustrates the difficulty of reaching and implementing strategic accords between China and the US for direct naval co-operation in the South China Sea.

CONCLUSIONS

The South China Sea region is an area of intense competition, both among littoral states and between the superpowers. This competition is expressed militarily, commercially, and in countervailing jurisdictional claims. At the heart of this competition there lies the perception that the South China Sea is a treasure-house of marine resources and a strategic maritime crossroads for Asia.

China's emergence into the international community and rapid economic development have projected Chinese power ever more directly into the South China Sea. Offshore petroleum exploration on the Chinese continental shelf has introduced more than a billion US dollars of direct foreign investment to the area of the South China Sea currently under Chinese control. The development of a coastal infrastructure for oil exploration, as well as rapidly increasing foreign trade have greatly stimulated coastal development in south China. Yet this commercial expansion has only just begun. The expansion of Chinese power in the South China Sea will culminate in the reversion of Hong Kong to Chinese sovereignty in 1997, at which point China will have become the dominant force in the area.

China's neighbours to the south have ample reason to regard this explosion of Chinese power in the South China Sea with a certain degree of apprehension. Exaggerated Chinese jurisdictional claims to the entire area of the South China Sea are hardly reassuring. China has a long and infamous history of support for Communist insurgencies in South East Asia and maintains covert contact with Communist parties in several countries in the region. In terms of its resource and population base, China is ten times the size of any country in the region. China has entered what will probably be a protracted period of rapid economic expansion with annual growth rates in the range of 10-12 per cent. Just as Asia has achieved new status as a high-growth region in the international system, so China is recapturing something of this ancient status as the 'central kingdom' in the region. Yet China is still governed by an authoritarian regime guided by a virulent ideological mixture of Marxism and nationalism. Even Japan is watching the reemergence of its giant neighbour with mixed feelings.

Yet there are also strong reasons to anticipate that China will adopt policies that favour greater stability in the South China Sea area. Despite rhetorical blasts reasserting its jurisdictional claims, China's record of enforcement of those claims has been modest. Chinese military force is present throughout the South China Sea, and yet has rarely been used. In every instance of direct military action in the past ten years -- the border dispute and incursion into Vietnam, the seizure of the Paracels, and gun boat incidents -- Vietnam has been the target. Political relations with Vietnam are improving, if only marginally. If this process continues, reinforced by the relaxation of tension with the Soviet Union, further hostilities will become less likely. As for China's other Southeast Asian neighbours, China has made every effort to put its best diplomatic foot forward and to convey an image of moderation.

It should also be remembered that China's own

investments in development of the resources of the South China Sea have increased sharply, providing Beijing with a powerful motivation for the preservation of peace and stability. The political and commercial cost of direct military assertion of China's jurisdictional claims would be astronomical and would centre on disruptions of commercial relations with the United States. Half of the oil companies operating offshore China are US-based. The rigs operating on Chinese contract areas, with their American crews, would be highly vulnerable to any overt hostilities in the South China Sea. The new and positive relationship between China and ASEAN would also be sacrificed. It is difficult to imagine an issue that would drive Beijing to incur these costs.

On the positive side of the ledger, there is every reason to believe that with the exception of Vietnam, China's overtures toward its Southeast Asian neighbours are genuine. China is developing politically as well as economically. Political evolution has typically followed economic growth in Asia -- in Thailand, Malaysia, Singapore, Taiwan, and South Korea as well as in China. China's point of origin and path of political evolution may be different than those of its immediate neighbours, but the destination may be quite similar. If so, then there is every reason to hope that China will join other countries around the rim of the South China Sea in forging a regional identity that is increasing stability and of benefit to the entire global community.

NOTES

1. China Daily (25 January 1984), p. 4.
2. China Daily (4 May 1985), p. 4.
3. Xinhua (8 May 1983), in Joint Publications Research Service (JPRS), (13 June 1983), p. 24.
4. Xinhua (4 February 1983) in Summary of World Broadcasts (SWB), (16 March 1983), p. A-1.
5. Xinhua (11 June 1984), in JPRS (13 July 1984), p. 1.
6. Xinhua (8 November 1984) in SWB, (21 November 1984), p. A-14.
7. Xinhua (15 October 1983) in JPRS (18 October 1983), p. K-18; Xinhua (12 December 1983), in JPRS (12 January 1984), p. 29; Xinhua (23 January 1984) in SWB (29 February 1984), p. A-1.
8. Zhongguo Xinwen She (13 September 1984) in

SWB (26 September 1984), p. A-1.

9. China Daily (9 February 1985), p. 3.

10. Xinhua (21 January 1983) in JPRS (21 January 1983), p. K-20.

11. Beijing Domestic Service (2 August 1984).

12. China Daily (CD) (5 September 1984), p. 5; CD (9 February 1985), p. 3; CD (8 January 1985), p. 1.

13. Xinhua (23 January 1984) in SWB (29 February 1984), p. A-1.

14. China Daily (4 May 1985), p. 4.

15. China Daily (31 January 1984), p. 3.

16. China Daily (25 January 1984), p. 4.

17. Zhongguo Xinwen She (13 Septmeber 1984) in SWB (26 September 1984), p. A-1.

18. China Daily (26 November 1984), p. 3.

19. 'Offshore Oil Draws 23 Foreign Tenders', China Daily (2 July 1985)

20. Pacific Defense Report (Australia), (March 1985).

21. China Economic News, (CEN), (3 June 1985), p. 10.

22. Aviation Week and Space Technology (4 February 1985), pp. 78-9.

23. Avionics News (March 1985).

24. Interavia Air-letter (Geneva) (11 February 1985).

25. Energy Asia (EA) (2 November 1985).

26. EA (25 January 1985).

27. Xinhua (12 April 1985) in JPRS (15 April 1985), p. B-1.

28. Newsweek (14 January 1985), p. 40; China Business Review (CBR), (May-June 1983), p. 23.

29. CEN (18 Mary 1985), p. 7.

30. South China Morning Post (8 January 1985), Bus. Supp., p. 1 in JPRS (9 January 1985), p. W-3

31. China Trade Report (Mary 1985), p. 3.

32. CEN (28 January 1985), p. 7.

33. Wall Street Journal (WSJ) (17 May 1985), p. 2.

34. China Daily (1 November 1984); New York Times (19 May 1985), p. 22; and Far Eastern Economic Review (FEER) (1 November 1985), p. 33.

35. New York Times (24 January 1985), p. 2.

36. 'Guangxi Radio Begins Broadcasts to Vietnam' (Broadcast) reported in JPRS (3 December 1985), p. E-2.

37. 'PRC Greets Vietnam on Relations Anniversary' (Broadcast) reported in JPRS (18 January 1985),p. E-3; Xinhua (29 December 1984) in JPRS (31 December 1984), p. E-1.

39. Business Times (Singapore) (7 March 1985).
40. Washington Post (2 May 1985), p. A-28.
41. The New York Times (12 Mary 1983), p. A-20.
42. FEER (7 February 1985).
43. Woodward, Kim, The International Energy Relations of China, Stanford University Press, 1980, p. 182.
44. Woodard, Kim and Alice A. Davenport, 'The Security Dimensions of China's Offshore Oil Development,' in Journal of Northeast Asian Studies, Vol. 1, No. 3, (September 1982), p. 6.
45. New York Times (14 February 1983), p. A-5.
46. 'SRV's Territorial Waters Claim Criticized,' Xinhua (18 February 1983) in JPRS (22 February 1983), p. E-1.
47. Petroleum News (January 1984), p. 92.
48. 'Vietnam's Plan to Establish Meteorological Stations in South China Sea Rebuffed,' Xinhua (17 November 1984) in JPRS (19 November 1984), p. A-2.
49. FEER (8 November 1984), p. 26.
50. FEER (6 September 1984).
51. FEER (8 November 1984), p. 26; FEER (6 September 1984), p. 41.
52. JPRS (25 October 1984), p. C-1.
53. Washington Post (18 April 1985), p. A-38.
54. Woodard and Davenport, p. 8.
55. Petroleum News (January 1984), p. 92; Energy Asia (19 April 1985).
56. Energy Asia, (1 June 1984).
57. Energy Asia (26 April 1985).
58. Energy Asia (19 April 1985); EA (12 July 1985).
59. Energy Asia (21 December 1985).
60. Energy Asia (19 April 1985).
61. Energy Asia (14 June 1985).; EA (5 July 1985).
62. China Daily (2 March 1985), p. 4.
63. Asian Wall Street Journal (13 March 1985), p. 3.
64. Asian Wall Street Journal (AWSJ) (13 March 1985), p. 3; Xinhua (12 March 1985) in JPRS (12 March 1985), p. E-4.
65. Xinhua (2 March 1985) in JPRS (4 March 1985), p. E-1.
66. Summary of World Broadcasts (3 April 1985), p. A-19; Xinhua (23 April 1985) in JPRS (25 April 1985), p. E-2.
67. Kuala Lumpur (29 March 1985) in SWB (10 April 1985), p. A-24; Journal of Commerce (30

January 1985), p. 24B; and FEER (4 July 1985), p. 2.

68. AWSJ (23 April 1985), p. 4.

69. China Trade News (April 1985).

70. AWSJ and CTN (see above).

71. Energy Asia, (22 March 1985).

72. Xinhua (16 May 1985) in JPRS (17 May 1985), p. E-2.

73. Business Times, Singapore, (6 February 1985).

74. Business Times, Singapore, (21 January 1985).

75. China Daily (9 April 1985).

76. Xinhua (10 February 1985) in JPRS (15 February 1985), p. E-7.

77. AWSJ (22 May 1985).

78. AWSJ (23 April 1985), p. 1.

79. AWSJ (22 May 1985), p. 3.

80. Zhongguo Xinwen She, (18 April 1985) in JPRS (18 April 1985), p. E-6; China Daily (17 May 1985), p. 1.

81. AWSJ (9 May 1985), p. 15.

82. Energy Asia (10 May 1985).

83. New York Times (18 April 1985), p. A-8.

84. Energy Asia (17 May 1985).

85. "Better Ties Aid Hong Kong-China Trade," AWSJ, (1-2 March 1985).

86. Washington Post (22 June 1985), p. A-8.

87. John F. Burns, '40 High Officers Retire in China in Army Share-Up', New York Times (11 December 1984), p. 2.

88. Zhongguo Xinwen She (11 May 1985) in JPRS (13 May 1985).

89. China Daily (25 June 1985).

90. China Daily (24 June 1985).

91. Wei Wen Po (12 June 1985) in JPRS (12 June 1985), p. W-2.

92. Renminribao (11 December 1984) in JPRS (27 February 1985), p. 111.

93. Xinhua (2 February 1985) in JPRS (4 February 1985), p. K-15.

94. Hahn, Bradley, 'China: Emnerging Sea Power', Proceedings, U.S. Naval Institute (March 1985), p. 107.

95. Hanh, p. 102.

96. Swanson, CBR, p. 28.

97. Swanson, CBR, p. 26.

98. Swanson, CBR, p. 28.

99. Hahn, p. 106.

100. Swanson, CBR, p. 27.

101. Washington Post (12 January 1985), p. A-1.

102. Hahn, p. 105.
103. Hahn, p. 105.
104. Swanson, CBR, p. 27.
105. Washington Post (12 January 1985), p. A-1; JPRS (15 January 1985), p. W-2.
106. New York Times (20 January 1985).

SELECT BIBLIOGRAPHY

The following bibliography of English language works relating to energy, security and economic development is not extensive; however, it selectively supplements the references which appear in the footnotes of the text.

Government and International Agency Publications

Japan External Trade Organisation, (JETRO), Publications Department China Newsletter, Tokyo.

Republic of Korea, Ministry of Energy and Resources, Korea's Energy Resources, Staff Briefing Paper 29-30, August, 1984.

Republic of Korea, Ministry of Energy and Resources, 1984 Yearbook of Statistics.

Taiwan, Republic of China, Department of Statistics, Ministry of Finance, Monthly Statistics of Exports and Imports.

Taiwan, Republic of China, Energy Committee, Ministry of Economic Affairs, Energy Balance in Taiwan, Republic of China.

UN, Department of International Economic and Social Affairs, 1982 Energy Statistics Yearbook, New York, 1984.

UN, Economic and Social Survey of Asia and the Pacific, Bangkok, 1983.

UN, The Law of the Sea, New York, 1983.

US, Central Intelligence Agency, Prospects for Soviet Oil Production, Washington, D.C., 1977.

US, Central Intelligence Agency, USSR Energy Atlas, Washington D.C., 1985.

US Congress. Committee on Energy and Natural Resources, Senate, Access to Oil--The US Relationship with Saudi Arabia and Iran, Washington, D.C., 1977.

__________ Geopolitics of Oil Parts 1 and 2, Washington, D.C., 1980.

__________ The Geopolitics of Oil: Staff Report, Washington, D.C., 1980.

US Congress, Committee on Foreign Relations, Senate, Taiwan, Washington, D.C., 1979.

US Congress. Committee on Science and Technology, House of Representatives, Background Readings on Science, Technology and Energy R and D in Japan and China, Washington, D.C., 1981.

US Congress. Joint Committee, China Under the Four Modernizations, Parts 1 and 2, Washington, D.C., 1982.

US Congress, Joint Economic Committee _Chinese Economy Post-Mao_. A Compendium of Papers, Vol. 1, Policy and Performance, Washington, D.C., 1978.

——— _The Soviet Economy in the 1980's_, Part 1, Washington, D.C., 1982.

US Congress. Subcommittee on International Trade, Finance and Security Economics, Joint Economic Committee, _Energy in Soviet Policy_, Washington, D.C., 1981.

US, Energy Information Administration _The Petroleum Resources of Indonesia, Malaysia, Brunei and Thailand_, Washington, D.C., 1984.

US, Joint Publications Research Service, _China Daily Report_.

World Bank, _China: Socialist Economic Development_, Vols. I-III, Washington, D.C., 1983.

Articles and Books

Barnett, A. Doak, _China's Economy in Global Perspective_ (The Brookings Institution, Washington, D.C., 1981).

Bornstein, Morris, 'Soviet Economic Growth', Seweryn Bialer, ed., _The Domestic Context of Soviet Foreign Policy_ (Westview Press, Boulder, 1981), pp. 227-56.

Buszyneski, Les, The Soviet Union and Southeast Asia Since the Fall of Saigon, _Asian Survey_, Vol. XXI, No. 5 (May 1981), pp. 536-50.

Campbell, Robert, _Soviet Energy Balances_, Rand Corporation, R-2257-DOE, Santa Monica, 1978.

Chang, Pao-min, 'Kampuchea in Chinese and Vietnamese Policies: The Root of the Conflict', _Studies in Comparative Communism_, Vol. 16, (Autumn, 1983), pp. 203-21.

Chang, Pao-min, 'The Sino-Vietnamese Territorial Dispute', _Asia Pacific Community_, No. 8, (Spring, 1980), pp. .130-65.

Chen, King C., ed., _China and the Three Worlds_, (M.E. Sharpe Inc., White Plains, 1979).

Chen, King C., ed., 'The Sino-Vietnamese War: Issues in Dispute', _Chinese Law and Government_, Vol. XVI, No. 1, (Spring, 1983), pp. 3-104.

Cheng, Y.S., 'Normalization of Sino-Japanese Relations: China's Bargaining Position Regarding the Taiwan Question', _Asia Quarterly_ (Brussels), No. 4, 1980, pp. 245-72.

Chiu, Hungdah, ed., China and the Taiwan Issue (Praeger Publishers, New York, 1979).

___________ and Leng, Shao-chuan, eds., Law in Chinese Foreign Policy: Communist China and Selected Problems of International Law (Oceana Publications, Dobbs Ferry, 1972).

___________ and Cohen, Jerome A., People's China and International Law: A Documentary Study (Princeton University Press, Princeton, 1974).

___________ and Park, Choon-ho, 'Legal Status of the Paracel and Spratly Islands', Ocean Development and International Law, Vol. 3, 1976.

Clough, Ralph, Island China (Harvard University Press, Cambridge Mass., 1978).

Conant, Melvin and Gold, Fern, The Geopolitics of Energy (Westview Press, Boulder, 1978).

Fisharaki, Fereidun and Brown, Harrison, et al., Critical Energy Issues in Asia and the Pacific: The Next Twenty Years (Westview Press, Boulder, 1982.

Frank, Jr., Charles R., Kwang, Suk Kim, and Westphal, Larry E., South Korea Columbia University Press, New York, 1975.

Galenson, Walter, ed., Economic Growth and Structural Change in Taiwan (Cornell University Press, Ithaca, 1979).

Gelman, Harry, The Soviet Far East Buildup and Soviet Risk-Taking Against China, Rand Corporation, R-2943-AF, (August 1982).

Griffith, William, 'Sino-Soviet Rapprochement?', Problems of Communism, Vol. 2, 1983, pp. 20-29.

Gumpel, Werner, 'Energy Policy of the Soviet Union', Hoover Institution Press, Special Project, Stanford, 1979.

Gustafson, Thane, 'Soviet Energy Policy: From Big Coal to Big Gas' in Bialer, Seweryn and Gustafson, Thane, eds., Russia at the Crossroads (Allen and Unwin, London, 1982), pp. 121-39.

Harding, Harry, 'Change and Continuity in Chinese Foreign Policy', Problems of Communism, Vol. 32, No. 2, (March/April 1983), pp. 1-19.

Harrison, Selig, China, Oil and Asia: Conflict Ahead? (Columbia University Press, New York, 1977).

Hasan, Parvez and Rao, D.C., Korea: Policy Issues for Long-Term Development (John Hopkins University Press, Baltimore, 1979).

Ho, Samuel P. S. and Huenemann, Ralph W. China's Open Door Policy. The Quest for Foreign Technology and Capital (University of British Columbia Press, Vancouver, 1984).

Ho, Samuel, P.S., 'South Korea and Taiwan: Development Prospects and Problems in the 1980s', Asian Survey, Vol. XXI, No. 12, (December 1982), pp. 1175-96.

Jensen, Robert C., et al., eds., Soviet Natural Resources in the World Economy University of Chicago Press, Chicago, 1983.

Kamiya, Fuji, and Weinstein, Franklin B., eds., The Security of Korea: US and Japanese Perspectives on the 1980's (Westview Press, Boulder, 1980).

Keith, Ronald C., 'China and the Pacific Rim', in Quo, F. Quei, ed., The Politics of the Pacific Rim: Perspectives on the 1980s (Simon Fraser University Publications, Burnaby, 1983).

__________ 'China's Modernization and the Policy of "Self-Reliance"', China Report, Vol. XIX, No. 2 (March/April 1983), pp. 19-34.

__________ 'The Origins and Strategic Implications of China's "Independent Foreign Policy"', International Journal, Winter, 1985-6.

Kim, Hong, N., 'Politics of Japan's Economic Aid to South Korea', Asia Pacific Community, No. 20 (Spring 1983), pp. 80-102.

Kimura, Hiroshi, 'Failure of Soviet Policies Toward Japan', Asia Pacific Community, No. 16 (Spring 1982), pp. 1-16. 'Japan-Soviet Relations: Framework, Developments, Prospects', Asian Survey, Vol. XX, No. 7 (July 1980), pp. 707-25.

Klinghoffer, Arthur, The Soviet Union and International Oil Politics (Columbia University Press, New York, 1977).

Leighton, Marian Kirsch, 'Perspectives on the Vietnam-Cambodia Border Conflict', Asian Survey, Vol. XVIII, No. 5, (May 1978), pp. 448-57.

Liang Chi-Yuan, Energy Demand Management Technical Assistance Project: Country Report of the Republic of China, Asian Development Bank, 1985.

__________ The Essence of Energy Crisis and Alternative Strategies, (translation), Economic Planning Council, Executive Yuan, Taipei, Taiwan, February, 1975.

__________ 'The Demand for Energy in Taiwan's Industry: An Application of Translog Production Function' (in Chinese), Taiwan Economic Forecasts, (The Institute of

Economics), Vol. 9, No. 2, (June 1978).
__________ 'Energy Policies of the ROC, ROK and Japan -- A Comparison', in Industry of Free China, (Taipei, September 1980).
__________ with Jorgenson, D. W., 'On Dynamic Energy-Economic Model of Taiwan, ROC Project Report of Energy Research and Development Fund', Energy Committee, Ministry of Economic Affairs, Taipei, Taiwan, ROC, May, 1985.
Martello, Joseph A., 'Some Aspects of the Chinese Petroleum Industry: Present and Prospective', China Report, Vol. 19, No. 3 (May/June 1983), pp. 23-37.
Mendl, Wolf, 'China's Challenge to Japan', The World Today, Vol. 35, No. 7 (July 1979), pp. 278-85.
__________ Issues in Japan's China Policy (MacMillan Press, London, 1978).
Morse, Ronald, ed., The Poliitics of Japan's Energy Strategy. Resources-Diplomacy-Security (Institute of East Asian Studies, University of California, Berkeley, 1981).
Nakauchi Kiyofumi, 'Problems of Delimitation in the East China Sea and the Sea of Japan', Ocean Development and International Law, Vol. 6, (Pacific Rim Issue, 1979), pp. 305-16.
Nemetz, P.N., Vertinsky, I., and Vertinsky, P., 'Japan's Energy Strategy at the Crossroads', Pacific Affairs', Vol. 57, No. 4, (Winter 1984-5), pp. 553-76.
North, Robert N., 'The Soviet Far East: New Centre of Attention in the USSR', Pacific Affiars, Vol. 51, No. 2 (Summer 1978), pp. 195-215.
Oshima, K., Suzuki, T., and Matsuno, T., 'Energy Issues and Policies in Japan', Annual Review of Energy, Vol. 7, 1982, pp. 87-108.
Pachauri, R. K., The Political Economy of Global Energy (The John Hopkins University Press, Baltimore and London, 1985).
Pakravan, Karim, Oil Supply Disruptions in the 1980s. An Economic Analysis (Hoover Institution Press, Stanford, 1984).
Park, Choon-ho, 'China and Maritime Jurisdiction: Some Boundary Issues', German Yearbook of International Law, Vol. 22, 1979, pp. 119-41.
__________ and Cohen, Jerome, Alan, 'The Politics of China's Oil Weapon', Foreign Policy, No. 20 (Fall 1975), pp. 28-40. 'The South China Sea Disputes: Who Owns the Islands and the Natural Resources?', Ocean Development and International Law, Vol. 5, 1978,pp. 27-59.
__________ Petroleum Economist, Special Report on

China, Offshore Oil Exhibition Guangzhou, (November, 1981).
Porter, Gareth, 'Hanoi's Strategic Perspective and the Sino-Vietnamese Conflict', Pacific Affairs, Vol. 57, No. 1 (Spring 1984), pp. 7-25.
Quo, F. Quei, 'Party Politics in Japan: the June, 1980 Election', Modern Asian Studies, Vol. 16, No. 2, 1982, pp. 251-76.
__________ ed., Politics of the Pacific Rim: Perspectives on the 1980s (Simon Fraser University Publications, 1982).
Simon, Shelden, 'China, Vietnam and ASEAN: the Politics of Polarization', Asian Survey, Vol. 19, No. 12 (December 1979), pp. 1037-52.
Smil, Vaclav, China's Energy: Achievements, Problems, Prospects (Praeger, New York, 1976).
__________ 'China's Energy Prospects', Pacific Affairs, Vol. 51, No. 2 (Summer 1978) pp. 230-44.
Snyder, Edwin, et al., The Taiwan Relations Act and the Defense of the Republic of China (Institute of International Studies, University of California, Berkelye, 1980).
Tow, William T., 'Sino-Japanese Security and Cooperation: Evolution and Prospects', Pacific Affairs Vol. 56, No. 1 (Spring 1983), pp. 51-83.
Tretiak, Daniel,'China's Vietnam War and its Consequences', China Quarterly, No. 80, (December 1979), pp. 740-67.
Tsurutani, Taketsugi, Japanese Policy and East Asian Security (Praeger, New York, 1981).
Valencia, Mark, ed., The South China Sea: Hydrocarbon Potential and Possibilities of Joint Development (Pergamon, Oxford, 1981).
van der Kroef, Justus M., 'ASEAN, Hanoi and the Kampuchean Conflict: Between "Kuantan" and a "Third Alternative"', Asian Survey, Vol. XXI, No. 5, (May 1981), pp. 515-35.
__________ Communism in Southeast Asia (California University Press, Berkeley, 1981).
__________ 'Hanoi and ASEAN: a New Confrontation in Southeast Asia?', Asia Quarterly, (Brussels), No. 4, 1976, pp. 245-69.
__________ 'The IndoChina Tangle: The Elements of Conflict and Compromise', Asian Survey, Vol. XX, No. 5 (May 1980), pp. 477-94.
__________ Kampuchea--The Endless Tug of War (University of Maryland, Baltimore, 1982).
Whiting, Allen, Siberian Development and East Asia: Threat or Promise? (Stanford University Press,

Stanford, 1981).

Woodard, Kim, 'China and Offshore Energy, Problems of Communism, Vol. 30, No. 6 (November/December 1981), pp. 32-45.

________ The International Energy Relations of China (Stanford University Press, Stanford, 1980).

________ and Alice Davenport, 'The Security Dimensions of China's Offshore Oil Development' Journal of Northeast Asian Studies, Vol. 1, No. 3, (September, 1982), pp. 3-26.

Woodside, Alexander, 'Nationalism and Poverty in the Breakdown of Sino-Vietnamese Relations', Pacific Affairs, Vol. 42, No. 3 (Fall 1979), pp. 381-409.

Wu, Yuan-li, Japan's Search for Oil. A Case Study on Economic Nationalism and International Security (Hoover Institution Press, Stanford, 1977).

Yergin, Daniel and Hillenbrand, Martin, eds., Global Insecurity (Houghton Mifflin Co., Boston, 1980).

York, Valerie,'Oil, the Middle East and Japan's Search for Security', International Affairs, Vol. 57, No. 3 (Summer 1981), pp. 428-48.

Zagoria, Donald, 'The Moscow-Beijing Detente', Foreign Affairs, Vol. 61, No. 4 (Spring 1982), pp. 853-73.

________ Soviet Policy in East Asia (Yale University Press, New Haven, 1983).

The Contributors

HUNGDAH CHIU, specialist in international law and Chinese foreign policy. Professor Chiu is the co-editor of Law in Chinese Foreign Policy: Communism in China and Selected Problems of International Law (1972) and co-author of People's China and International Law: A Documentary Survey (1974). He was formerly a Research Associate at the Harvard Law School and is presently Professor of Law, University of Maryland at Baltimore.

RONALD C. KEITH, specialist in China's development, domestic politics and international relations. His articles relating to these subjects have recently appeared in International Journal, China Report, Canadian Journal of Political Science, China Quarterly. Dr. Keith is an Associate Professor in the Department of Political Science, University of Calgary, Alberta, Canada.

CHI-YUAN LIANG, specialist in Taiwan's energy and economic development strategy. Professor Liang has authored several energy-related research reports for the Institute of Economics, and for the Asian Development Bank, he recently published The Demand Management Technical Assistance Project: Country Report of the Republic of China (1985). Formerly a visiting scholar at the Harvard-Yenching Institute, Dr. Liang is presently a Research Fellow of the Institute of Economics, Academia Sinica, Taipei.

F. QUEI QUO, specialist in Japanese domestic politics, trade and defence policies. Professor Quo is currently working on a Canadian SSHRC project relating to the pattern of Japanese regional trade in the Pacific. Professor Quo has edited two recent volumes, The Politics of the Pacific Rim (1982) and The Future of Taiwan (1985). He is Professor of Political Science at Simon Fraser University, Burnaby, British Columbia and currently Visiting Professor, Institute of Social Sciences, University of Tsukuba, Japan.

ALLAN RODGERS, specialist in the geography of regional development. Professor Rodgers has had five field periods in the USSR, and he is the author of two books and numerous articles including 'Commodity Flows, Resource Potential and Regional Economic Development: the Example of the Soviet Far East' in R. Jensen, et al. (eds.), Soviet Natural Resources in the World Economy, (1983). He is

Professor of Geography at the Pennsylvania State University.

THOMAS STERN, formerly Deputy Chief of Mission, US Embassy, Seoul, Korea and specialist for the US Department of State and the Agency for International Development. Among Mr. Stern's current affiliations, he is a consultant to the Korea Economic Institute of America and to the US Undersecretary for Security Assistance, Department of State.

JUSTUS VAN DER KROEF, specialist in Southeast Asian affairs. Professor van de Kroef is a prolific writer who has made many related contributions to journals such as Asian Survey. His recent monographs include Communism in Southeast Asia, (1981) and Kampuchea-The Endless Tug of War, (1982). He is Dana Professor and Chairman, Department of Political Science, University of Bridgeport, Connecticut.

KIM WOODARD AND ALICE DAVENPORT are with China Energy Ventures Inc., Washington D.C.. Dr. Woodard, a former Research Associate at the Resource Systems Institute of the East-West Center, Honolulu, is currently President of the above consulting agency. He authored The International Energy Relations of China (1980) and together with Alice Davenport co-authored the article, "The Security Dimensions of China's Offshore Oil Development", Journal of Northeast Asian Studies, Summer, 1982.

INDEX